# CHRIST AND LIFE

*In memory of my uncle*
*Reginald M. Harrington, O.P.*

Wilfrid J. Harrington O.P.

# CHRIST AND LIFE

FRANCISCAN HERALD PRESS
1434 West 51st Street . Chicago 60609

232.9'54

*Christ and Life* by Wilfrid J. Harrington O.P.,
Copyright © 1975 by Wilfrid J. Harrington O.P.
Published by Gill and Macmillan Ltd.,
Dublin, Ireland
and Franciscan Herald Press,
Chicago, Illinois U.S.A. 1975.

Library of Congress Cataloging in Publication Data
Harrington, Wilfrid J.
    Christ and life.
    Bibliography: p.
    1. Jesus Christ — Teachings. 2. Christian life —
Catholic authors. I. Title.
BS2415.H28        232.9'54        75-12510
ISBN 0-8199-0571-2

Nihil Obstat
    Benedict Hegarty O.P.
    Redmond Fitzmaurice O.P.

Imprimi Potest
    Flannan Hynes O.P.
    Provincial
            1 April 1975

Printed in Great Britain

# Contents

# PREFACE

THE New Testament was written within a christian community and for a christian community. This is true not alone of the Pauline letters but of all the writings, including the gospels. The christian community, the Church, at a local level, was a fact of christian life right from the beginning. And yet, the New Testament remains firmly Christocentric. For the community is built up around Christ, it exists because of him, it lives with his life. I believe that here is where the emphasis ought to lie. I write because of my concern that the emphasis seems to lie elsewhere today.

What I really seek to suggest is that we should strive to get our priorities right. I feel that we have tended, or do tend, to get too concerned about matters that are not unimportant, but which, in a christian context, should keep their secondary place. Accordingly, the first part of this book looks at the person of Christ and to his message, with particular attention to his distinctive word of Good News for the *poor*. Then we turn to an emerging Christology in the Synoptics, Paul and John. In the second part it is shown that existentialist categories can help our understanding of biblical thought, so concerned is it with life and the quality of life. Freedom is a mark of christian living— at least it emphatically is in Paul's view. And prayer is a christian need. Yet, first and last, the decisive factor we need to face, squarely and honestly, is the place of *Christ* in a christian Church.

W.J.H.

6

# INTRODUCTION

# The Church—or Christ?

T H E 'institutional Church'! What is this entity that causes distaste, even revulsion, in many quarters? For, one cannot deny, or ignore, the fact that people do react, and reject. Admittedly, there may be some naïvety here. Some people seem to resent structure as such and seem to desire a 'Church' that would be without form. But, as a society of men and women, a human grouping, the Church must have structure and must have 'institutions'. This is simply a sociological axiom. More often, it would seem, what is criticised or rejected is *this* institution. Such an attitude is more reasonable and the situation, therefore, more serious. It is all the more serious because the unfavourable reaction comes, in the main, from within the institution itself.

Here, as in other areas of Roman Catholic practice and theology, in these post-Vatican II days, too many of pre-Vatican II views and practices are still with us; views and practices, that is to say, which we ought to have outgrown. We have mentioned naïvety, and it would be naïve indeed to seem to suggest that all that pre-dates that magical watershed must be abandoned. What one has in mind is attitudes that have truly been made obsolete by Vatican II theology and its authentic development. One thinks of the Church seen as the hierarchical Church or the teaching Church: an entity over against the laity, the passive, obedient mass. Or, again, there was the moral theology which set so much emphasis on meticulous observance of commands and prohibitions, and which made so much of personal morality and not nearly so much of social con-

7

cern. And closely allied to this was an individualist spirituality—with emphasis on 'saving one's soul'—and a preoccupation with 'merit'.

Now, one has no wish to 'knock' all that was right and good in former attitudes. What matters is that even the right and the good must be set and seen in a new perspective. Because the Church is a human society, there is a hierarchy, there are leaders; but their authority ought to be inspired by a spirit of *diakonia*. There is a teaching office in the Church, but it is always the humble servant of the Word of God. Those who hold office in the Church are not an élite, nor do they stand over against 'the rest': they are part of the whole people of God, serving the interest and the welfare of the whole people. Because there is right and there is wrong, there is place for moral directive and for law; but directives and laws can never become absolute and must be valued and used as the tools they are. Law must guide, and not hamper or frustrate, and directives are meant to challenge the responsibility and the good conscience of the Christian and to operate in an atmosphere of free decision. Always the basic commandment uncomfortably reminds the Christian that he is his brother's keeper. His relation to God, despite the fervour of his observance, is suspect if it does not find issue in concern for others (cf. 1 *John*). And we do not lay up *merit* for ourselves. We are only poor servants who, hopefully, do our duty (cf. *Luke* 17:10). There will be recompense—because the Lord is good—but surely no merit.[1]

Now, it is true that we have moved to a better understanding of the Church, to more concern for ecclesial values. That is good—so far as it goes. For one feels that, in the process, the most important factor of all may have been largely lost to sight. We are still preoccupied with Church structure—though no longer, as before, passively taking the existing structure for granted. Now we want to change: to make episcopal collegiality—the joint responsibility of the bishops, precisely as a group or 'college', for the whole Church—a reality, to extend the principle of subsidiarity (the sharing of authority) into all areas of Church life, to give the laity their proper place and role. With the interest in community, the liturgy has taken on a a fresh significance. And there is new emphasis on the social duties and responsibilities of Christians.

Again, all this is to be welcomed. If structures are necessary, that is not to say that the structures of our day, whether they be traditional, or refurbished, or even newly forged, are the best, or that they are even helpful at all. We should be open enough to envisage a radical change of structure, not as a possibility, nor even as a probability, but as something inevitable. We need to be alive to the fact that the Church's danger and temptation is its own self-edification rather than God's—a placing ecclesiology over Christology, dogmatics over the divine love.[2] We ought to realise by now that the liturgy is going to remain flexible, that it will become more so. And we have become aware that we Christians are very much in and of *this* world, that we have no right to opt out of it or waive our concern for it.

All this is to be welcomed, except that we have become preoccupied with this emphasis and these concerns; all this is welcomed, but one must fear because of the missing factor. What has become of Christ in all this preoccupation of ours? Modified and varied Church structures, flexible liturgy, real concern for our fellowmen, a bold stand against injustice—what do all these mean, in *Christian* terms, if he is not the inspiration of them? What is the Church, if he is not a reality in the lives of Christians? We have become preoccupied with our ecclesiology. We must learn to place the emphasis firmly where the New Testament places it: on Christology.

9

We need, not only to remind ourselves, but to learn as a living reality, that Christianity is, exists, because of Christ, and for no other reason at all. We need to take the realism of Paul and John with the utmost seriousness. For them, christian life is a new creation, a new birth. I am a Christian because Christ lives in me, because his life quickens me; I am a Christian because I am a branch of him, the true Vine, livened by the living sap of him. I am not a Christian *primarily* because I have been initiated into this society of his disciples, because I worship around the table of the Lord, because I seek to love my neighbour as he has commanded. I am a Christian in and through fellowship with him. Everything else follows on that. But it must necessarily follow on it. Through him I have fellowship with the Father. He is the bond who binds Christians together into the one Body. Christian life, because it is Christ-life, must be incarnational; it is lived in and through community.

This is surely the message of the New Testament. The gospels, all of them, are written that we may believe, and go on believing, that the man Jesus of Nazareth is the Messiah of Jewish hope—more, that he is the Son of God. They are written that, through faith, we may have life in him. Paul's gospel is the good news of salvation by faith alone: openness to the salvation offered by God in Jesus Christ, and commitment to him. And Paul came to realise that, though it must seem folly and scandal, the christian message is always Christ, a crucified Christ. The author of Hebrews can find no more effective way of calling back his readers from the brink of apostasy than by holding up before them Christ, the living high priest. The Apocalypse of John was written to encourage Christians faced with persecution; it was meant to assure them that Jesus had indeed overcome the world. But it insists that *christian* victories can be won in one way only, the way in which he won his victory: through suffering and death. The Pastorals, already reaching beyond the apostolic age with their concern for orthodox doctrine and their interest in incipient ecclesiastical office, are still quite sure that there is one Mediator only between God and men: the man Christ Jesus (1 *Tim.* 2 :5). In brief, the first letter of John puts the New Testament view, the christian view, with simple and chilling clarity: 'God gave us eternal life, and this life is in his Son. He who has the Son has life; he who has not the Son has not life' (1 *John* 5 :11f.).

We thank God for Vatican II and its blast of fresh air that has swept away so many cobwebs. But that great miracle of the Spirit will not have achieved what it was meant to achieve if christian life does not become a Christ-life. One feels more and more that one of the most important texts of the Council is in the programmatic second article of *Perfectae Caritatis*, on religious life. It reminds religious that they are, first and foremost, Christians, and then gives, as the fundamental norm of religious life, what is, in fact, the fundamental norm of christian life: 'the following of Christ as proposed by the Gospel'. Christian life is the following of Christ—a truism for one who knows and heeds the New Testament, but a truth that needed to be stressed, even for religious, in our day. Two things are at stake here: it must be the Christ of the gospel (the New Testament), for in the New Testament alone can we be sure of finding the true image of Jesus. Nor is it any kind of following, but the following of him as the gospel knows it.

Thus, the need for Christology is pressing. The Church, the 'institutional Church', no matter how we update it, will still repel many, or will seem irrelevant to many, unless it is seen to be animated by the life of Jesus. Our eucharistic liturgy will seem an empty ritual in its more traditional dress, or pathetic gimmicry if we strive to make it 'contemporary', unless he is seen in the midst of it. Our

Church-sponsored charitable organisations will seem no more than the reaction of decent men and women to human misery unless he is seen to be the motivation of our concern. Jesus, and he alone, sets his followers apart. He sets them apart precisely as his followers—this Son of Man who came not to be served but to serve. They are marked as his followers by the quality of their life—a shared life. The hall-mark of christian service is love. They are his followers in community and live the Christ-life through community. Dissatisfaction with the 'institutional' Church is particularly acute and particularly well-founded just here: It is not, even at the local level, notably expressive of true community.

We are disciples of the risen Lord; but he remains the Incarnate One. We are disciples of the Word-made-flesh, of one who, Son of God, is become like us in all things. Yet, we must see that 'reverence' can become one of the most perverse factors in religion! Jesus addressed his father as *Abba*, in the most intimate, informal manner, and taught his disciples to do the same. Our God is the father of the prodigal son; he is the father of our Lord Jesus Christ, the God who so loved the world of sinful men that he gave his only Son. And we have put him back into the Olympic obscurity of omnipotence and transcendence. Jesus has given us his body and blood as our food and drink because we have need of this sustenance—and we came up with the absurdity of the extreme eucharistic fast. God came to us, in human form, he humbled himself, taking the form of a slave—and we have reacted by looking only to the divinity of the One who became man for us. Thus, he has become, tautologously, 'our divine Lord' (we had lost the significance of *Kyrios*, the early Church's term for expressing its faith in the divinity of Christ). But the New Testament shows us a *man*, limited as we. He shared our lot of suffering and death. He knew sorrow and fear. He was faced with real decision and real choice. He prayed to the Father. His life was lived in faith—commitment to the Father. No neat *a priori* Christology can prevail over the New Testament Christologies of God-made-*Man*.

Why do we seem to be afraid of the God-Man of the New Testament, the only real Incarnate One? We Christians need to take seriously—need to learn, perhaps—that we can know and find God only in Jesus. Not for us the god of the philosophers; not for us the God of Abraham. For us he can only be the Father of our Lord Jesus Christ. For us, Jesus, and he alone, reflects the glory of God and bears the very stamp of his nature. To us God has spoken by a Son, the son who has become like us in all things (*Heb.* 1:2f.; 2:17; 4:15). And we speak to men of this Son and in the power of this Son, or not at all—as Christians.

## CHAPTER I

# Jesus and His Message

'A N D you shall call his name Jesus, for he shall save his people . . .' (*Matt.* 1 :21). So familiar to us are the words from the Christmas story and (we like to think) so familiar is the Person whose name bears the meaning of 'Saviour'. Most of us know him because we have been taught 'about' him from childhood; and what we did not learn there, or did not think to investigate further, we have come to know through the yet deeper knowledge of 'I believe'. And then, many of us feel that Jesus is familiar to us because we have experienced in a unique, personal way his having called us his own friends (*John* 15 :15). But really, who *is* this Jesus? Who is this Jesus, not only as God's Son, but as the man who lived in our history? To use his own words, 'Who do you say that I am?' (*Mark* 8 :29). Is there some way in which our knowing him through faith and personal encounter can join hands with the factual know-ledge about the Jesus of history which can be delved out of the New Testament?

### The Life of Jesus

Around the turn of the century there was a wave of concern to get back to the 'Jesus of history', to uncover what really happened in the life of the Man from Nazareth. But soon Rudolf Bultmann was to claim that such a quest was futile because the gospels were products of the *faith* of the early Church and hence did not necessarily record the facts concerning Jesus. They were the creation of the community which arose after his death, and hence we

14

today could never know for sure the historical Jesus. Radical as this approach may seem, Bultmann has made many valuable contributions to understanding the gospels. He was intensely concerned to bring the religious value of the New Testament home to men: though he discounted a knowledge of the 'Jesus of history' as being essential for the christian faith, we cannot but admire his insistence on personal response to the presence of God in Jesus, and his reliance upon pure faith, rather than 'knowledge', in meeting Jesus as a living challenge.

However, more recently, many of the disciples of Bultmann have taken a stand independent of their master. Recognising the importance of knowing about Jesus as well as believing in him, though still considering that anything like a complete record of his life was impossible of discovery, they began a new 'quest of the historical Jesus' as essential to New Testament preaching.[1] Their concern was not to show that the 'kerygma'—or apostolic preaching—is 'true', since it is in a realm of faith beyond proof. Rather they have set out to show that this kerygmatic portrait is faithful to the historical Jesus. At the same time there have always been not a few scholars who, as a result of the most careful scriptural analyses, have taken Jesus seriously—have taken him 'at his word' as he asked. It is among these that we find the present-day authors of two remarkable studies which epitomise the healthy reaction to the more sceptical evaluation of the Jesus of history: Joachim Jeremias and C. H. Dodd.[2] The combination in these men of precise scholarship as theologians and devoted faith as Christians has revealed the trustworthiness of the traditions concerning Jesus. These latest works of theirs adequately serve our purpose in this chapter and we are, in the main, content to follow their lead.

Both works begin with a consideration of the reliability of the documents and records underlying the gospel story,

15

the Semitic and Palestinian backgrounds to the tradition; and both works conclude with the Easter event and its significance. Jeremias has chosen to intertwine events in Jesus' life together with his person and message throughout the whole book. Dodd, by contrast, has concentrated on the person of Jesus in his opening chapters and has placed the story of his life in three sections at the end. But, the result for the reader in each case is a deepened awareness of how interrelated are the events, words and works in the life of Jesus with the person he is. There is indeed a unique creative genius behind Christianity. Rather than any community or member of it, this creator is Jesus himself.

Wherever one turns there is this fact: the documents in the New Testament are about a person whose role in history has been remembered, about an event which is still close at hand rather than being some remote episode in the past. And the body of sayings in the gospels, even making allowances for limiting factors in the formation of the gospels, remains so coherent and consistently distinctive that they must represent the thought of a single, unique teacher. One may confidently assert that the traditions about Jesus in these records are far more trustworthy than New Testament scholars have often assumed. A study of the language and style of Jesus shows how clearly his personal characteristics stand out in the sayings; in their simplicity, their closeness to life, through masterful, short description, and their evident Semitic usage, they point back to the person of Jesus. In these sayings we meet with an imaginative apprehension of the wonder and beauty of nature, and we are in touch with a mind of a poetic and imaginative cast. These factors must be borne in mind in interpreting the teaching of Jesus.

It might be as well at this point to remark on the historical value of the gospels. They are documents at once historical and religious; and there need not be a division between 'fact' and 'interpretation'. Indeed, interpretation is necessary if an occurrence, what happens, is to have meaning and any impact at all. And the interest and meaning which an event bore for those who were conscious of it as event and felt its impact, becomes part of the event, becomes historical in its turn. The evangelists presented the 'facts' with the intention of bringing out the meaning which the events had for those who encountered them.[3] They set out to voice the faith of the early Church; the nucleus of that faith was that the crucified Jesus has risen from the dead. 'Clearly, *something* had changed these men. They said it was a meeting with Jesus' (Dodd).

*The Beginning.* Jesus did not appear unheralded; one had come to prepare his way. Jesus has much in common with the Baptist whom he recognised as the intermediary between the old age and the new; yet there is a fundamental difference between them. John proclaimed judgment, Jesus the kingly reign of God; John stood within the framework of expectation, Jesus claimed to bring fulfilment; John belongs in the realm of law; with Jesus the gospel begins. Still, the starting point for an account of the message of Jesus is in his encounter with the Baptist: the call which Jesus experienced when he was baptised by John. Jesus is conscious of being authorised to communicate God's revelation because God has made himself known to him as Father; his *Abba* as a form of address to God expresses the ultimate mystery of the mission of Jesus. The Baptism was a symbolic scene summarising the purpose of Jesus' life and work: he undertook his mission as Messiah, Son of God and Servant of Yahweh, in the power of the Spirit. It was the acceptance of his vocation.

Jesus' first public appearance was preceded, too, by quite a different event: his rejection of the temptation of a political messiahship. The episode is intimately connected with his mission—a life-work which included not only the Father's commission, but also the Son's own acceptance of it in his victory over temptation. For, the Jesus who confronts us is not one who has been tested but one who has emerged victorious from his testing. The Temptation may be seen, too, as a drama recalling Israel's having been 'tempted' or 'tested' in the wilderness. In the person of the Messiah, Israel is again put to the test; but whereas historical Israel had failed, he stands firm. At any rate, we may already discern, at the very beginning of his mission, the strength behind Jesus' whole mission, the driving force and source of energy for what seemed—and was—humanly impossible. This strength can be found in Jesus' statement, not as 'theology' but as his own spontaneous and personal confidence: 'No one knows the Son but the Father, and no one knows the Father but the Son' (*Matt.* 11:27; *Luke* 10:22). That is, though Jesus experienced increasing loneliness and lack of understanding, there was One who really did know him. Strengthened by this certainty, he could go forward with inflexible resolution even unto death in the service of his mission: 'I am not alone because the Father is with me' (*John* 16:32).

*The Ministry.* The Baptism was the moment at which Jesus accepted his vocation. According to the general run of the gospel narratives Jesus, during the first part of his ministry, was engaged in three main types of activity: 1. He was engaged upon a broad appeal to the public. His aim was to make people aware of the presence of God as an urgent reality and to invite their appropriate response. 2. He set himself to minister to human need by healing the sick in body and mind, by awakening faith in those who had lost hope, and he sought to lead people into a new life under the inspiration of a personal attachment to himself. And by thus going about doing good, he gave concrete form to his message of ultimate salvation. 3. While his outward vocation took the form of a teacher of religion and morals, his whole outlook and orientation differentiated him from rabbinic Judaism. He challenged the people to rethink their ideas and hopes, only to be branded as a blasphemer. He censured his contemporaries for casting aside God's warnings. Thus, in his mission, controversy bulks largely—an activity forced upon him.

*The Passion.* In the faith of the Church, the passion is not the end, but the goal and the crown of the earthly activity of Jesus. Yet, we still have to ask whether Jesus himself gave his own death a place in his preaching. The synoptic gospels agree in giving three predictions of his passion by Jesus (*Mark* 8:31; 9:31; 10:33f.); as they stand, those predictions have been formulated *ex eventu* and, furthermore, are better designated as variations of *the* passion prediction.[4] The earliest form of it is in the saying found in Mark 9:31—'God will [soon] deliver up the man to men'. However, the evidence that Jesus did treat of his future suffering is not to be sought only in a few key texts. It is unfortunate that scholars, in investigating whether or not Jesus had announced his sufferings beforehand, have concentrated almost exclusively on the so-called passion predictions, and have ignored the variegated and more important material elsewhere in the synoptic gospels. When all the evidence is taken into account (and the eucharistic words are the most important allusion to Jesus' suffering) it is no longer possible to deny that Jesus expected and announced his suffering and death. The evidence also shows that Jesus had found the answer to the necessity of his death in Scripture, primarily in Isaiah 53. And it is not at all surprising that the instances of Jesus' interpretation of his sufferings are limited; he had spoken of this only to his disciples and only during the last period of his ministry.

*The Resurrection.*     The early Church saw the resurrection as the divine confirmation of Jesus' mission. Because the disciples did not experience it as an 'event' in history but rather as belonging to the last age (it is an eschatological rather than a historical reality), Christ's rising from the dead is presented as a resurrection to *doxa* (glory) rather than as a return to earthly life.[5] Through believing, the early community really experienced the dawning of God's new world, and this in turn gave birth to the Church. We have noted that history in the New Testament is an expansion of the meaning which the *facts* held for the Church's faith, which centred upon the resurrection. It thus follows that the facts remembered about this event are recorded in the gospels as understood on the further side of resurrection. Rather than a falsification this is simply in keeping with the whole mystery implied by the resurrection : only symbol and imagery, not literal prose, could tell this story. Something had happened to these men which they could describe only by saying that they had 'seen the Lord'. This phrase did not refer to some general christian experience but rather to a particular series of occurrences confined to a limited period. Such occurrences, on the threshold of ordinary human experience, just would not submit to customary precision of detail. 'The original witnesses were *dead sure* that they had met with Jesus, and there was no more to be said about it' (Dodd).

### The Person of Jesus

Let us look, briefly, at this Person—as the disciples met him then and as we meet him now. Firstly, Jesus is conscious of himself as the bringer of salvation; hence, his testimony to himself is part of the good news which he

20

preached. This is why the emphatic *egō* ('I') permeates the entire tradition of his sayings. However, the character of Jesus is discerned not only in these sayings but in his every action. Marking an incursion of the new Kingdom into old social standards, there are his loving understanding of 'the poor' and his new attitude towards women and children. He accepted women as disciples because he expected all his disciples to control their desires; he brought children closer than adults to God. He shows, too, a marked reverence for daily life. For him, no circumstance of daily life is too trivial to serve as a window into the realm of ultimate values, while the most profound truth can find an illustration in common experience. Thus, the Jesus who speaks the parables is aware of those principles of human action and processes of nature which fall within a universal order established by the Creator : the assumption is that life is like that, from the lowest level to the heights. As an individual person himself, Jesus' whole ethical approach is concerned with the dignity and responsibility of each human before God. He taught 'with authority', with an authority which respected the freedom of the person. It was an authority resting not on any official status or prestige, but on some indefinable quality in Jesus.

It is the unanimous testimony of all four gospels that Jesus spoke of himself as 'Son of Man'; this is the only title used by Jesus of himself whose authenticity is to be taken seriously.[6] Though it can be shown that the majority of the fifty-one Son of Man sayings in the gospels carry the title as a later addition, a notable residue of sayings held the title from the start. Indeed, the fact that the employment of the title was extended in the gospel tradition is quite remarkable when we recall that, even at the time of Paul, the Greek-speaking Church avoided the (enigmatic) title, Son of Man. Significantly, while the instances of it increase, the usage is still limited to the sayings of Jesus. The only possible explanation is that the title was so rooted in the sayings of Jesus right from the beginning that it had become sacrosanct. In the sayings, Jesus spoke of the Son of Man in the third person, thereby making a distinction between himself and the Son of Man. (This is a clear indication that the designation dates from before Easter; for the community Jesus simply was the Son of Man.) It is impossible that he should have had in mind a future saving figure who was to be distinguished from himself; the distinction he makes is between his present, and his future state of exaltation. While not yet, before the resurrection, the Son of Man, he will be exalted to be the Son of Man. The title already suggests the true nature of Jesus, his transcendence.

## The Message of Jesus

Though Jesus was conscious of being a prophet and bearer of the Spirit, he did not simply take his place in the sequence of the Old Testament messengers of God. In the conviction of the synagogue, the prophetic sequence had been broken off and the spirit had been quenched. Now, with the Baptist and Jesus, the long-quenched spirit had returned; the new presence of the Spirit was a sign of the dawn of salvation and the time of grace. God was turning again towards his people, and Jesus was to be his last messenger; God was speaking his final word. But Jesus comes, into a world enslaved by Satan, not only to exercise mercy, but above all to join battle with evil. Jesus comes with a proclamation and the central theme of his message is the kingly reign of God. The *basileia* is always and everywhere understood in eschatological terms; it denotes the time of salvation. The really new element in Jesus' preaching of this kingdom is that *here and now* its consummation is dawning. And the heart of Jesus' message can be found in a promise, the first beatitude: 'Blessed are the *poor*!'.

In promising to these, the poor and the heavy-laden, the reign of God, Jesus was making his most radical reversal of the standards of the time which held that all those who were disreputable or ignorant (such as precisely Jesus' own followers) were barred from access to salvation. Yes, an extraordinary new message was this—that salvation was destined only for 'beggars' and 'sinners'.

Jesus censured his contemporaries for the carelessness with which they cast God's warnings aside. There are three groups of people whom he particularly sought to shake into alertness: the priests, the scribes, and the Pharisees. The pious men of the day stand in the gravest danger because theirs is 'the piety that separates from God' (Jeremias). Pharisaic Judaism had a markedly vivid consciousness of sin and yet, paradoxically, sin had been made innocuous by casuistry and by the idea of merit. The casuistry of the scribes blinded them to seeing sin as a rebellion against God, and their notion of merit cancelled out their sense of sin. In such a self-assured piety they thought too well of themselves and rejected their need for love; they saw God's gift of salvation as an earned right. They became self-assured, self-righteous, and without love.

*Repentance.* Jesus uttered a call to repentance and gave the assurance of forgiveness. Repentance is for Jesus less *metanoia* (conversion) than an unconditional trust in the Father; it is learning to say *Abba* again like a child.[7] And because it brings a child's freedom from care through trust in being cared for, repentance is *joy*. Jesus' call to repentance reached beyond individuals to a whole people of God which had lost its way and was in a state of spiritual crisis upon whose outcome depended their future in the world. Jesus' mercy is especially expressed in the forgiveness of sins. Although this is promised explicitly in only two passages of the gospels, the subject of forgiveness is present in much the imagery of Jesus' words as well as in his actions. The divine forgiveness which the new community of his followers has experienced, is the motive for their own unlimited capacity to forgive one another. Indeed, he laid down this one essential presupposition for the prayer of his disciples: forgiveness—one's readiness to forgive, one's request of forgiveness where one has committed an offence.

The parable of the Unmerciful Servant (*Matt.* 18:23–35) is rooted in many other sayings of Jesus which express the same message—for example, the petition for forgiveness in the Lord's Prayer (*Matt.* 6:12), where Jesus teaches us to ask for pardon as we ourselves are ready to forgive. One who has received God's forgiveness should be himself forgiving. However, the motives for showing mercy cannot be in any abstract or distant God, but in this God who is present in the person of Jesus. Jesus' entire life demonstrates the mercy which he brings out in the parable: he took flesh upon himself, he suffered with man, he invited sinners to table-fellowship and promised them forgiveness, and he died for them—and for all of us. This parable is far more than a communication of an abstract truth, more than the teaching of a sage; it marks the presence here and now of the hour of divine compassion, the beginning of divine salvation. And it is to be noted that human forgiveness is neither the cause, nor the condition, nor the measure of God's forgiveness of men: 'I forgave you all this debt . . . and should not you have had mercy on your fellow servant, *as I had mercy on you*?' (*Matt.* 18:33f.).

*The Community.* Jesus sought to gather together a community of salvation. Though the word *ekklēsia* occurs only in Matthew 16:18 and 18:17, yet in a wealth of pictures Jesus constantly spoke of the new people of God whom he was gathering. His favourite, among the great variety of images, is that of the comparison of the community of salvation with the eschatological family of God, a family that finds its communion in table-fellowship, in anticipation of the Messianic Feast. The new people of God stood in contrast to other 'remnant' groups—Pharisaic and Essene groups, even the disciples of the Baptist—because of one decisive element : a keen awareness of the boundlessness of God's grace. They were sure of this through poignant personal experience : the disciples, formally installed as the new people of God at the Last Supper, so soon deserted their Master. How, then, could the Church get on its feet at all? The early Christians answered that, though the 'little flock' had melted away and though they had nothing to show for all the works they had done, yet Jesus' *forgiveness* re-created them, and they emerged as the new Israel. They knew that, as the first members of his Church, they owed their position to the 'magnanimity of their ill-used Master' (Dodd). For, the new people of God, re-created by Jesus' forgiveness, was founded really when a new community became embodied in the disciples and hence emerged from the old people of God which had lost its way. And, quite apart from its meaning their reinstalment after failure in their hour of trial, we can grasp what the resurrection really meant to these men : now they were truly new—new men in a new world, confident, courageous, and enterprising, the leaders of a movement which was progressing with impact. What caused this tremendous sense of being 're-created'? It happened because the return of Jesus after the crucifixion meant the 'recovery of a treasured personal relationship which had seemed dead forever' (Dodd).

## Following Jesus

The proclamation of Jesus always leads to a personal appeal, a call to faith. His message is a summons to accept

25

the offer of salvation and to trust in his word and in God's grace. Discipleship involves the following of a real person. Indeed, discipleship begins, really, through attachment to a definite figure known to our senses and partaking of our humanity. What can be 'seen' through friendship with the man Jesus can inspire what must remain 'unseen' through faith in the Son of God. The demands of Jesus upon his disciples are so absolute that rather than pretending to comprise a complete moral code they simply lay claim to the disciple's entire life. While Jesus did set himself up to minister to human need by healing the sick in body or in mind, his deeper healing lay in the faith he awoke in those without hope and the new life into which he led people through personal attachment to himself.

*Disciples.* With rare exceptions, the New Testament reserves the title *mathētēs*, 'disciple', for one who has recognised Jesus as his Master. Jesus calls 'whom he wills' (*Mark* 3:13), even 'sinful men' (*Luke* 5:8) and the tax-collector Matthew (*Matt.* 9:9). To the sovereign call of Jesus there corresponds the answer of those called. They leave all, father, net, and desk and follow Jesus immediately. In the synoptic tradition the relationship between Jesus and his disciples is quite distinctive—it is a close personal relationship, and mutually so. The decisive factor is the person of Jesus himself. To become a disciple of Jesus it is not necessary to be an exceptional person. What counts is not intellectual or moral aptitude but a call in which Jesus takes the initiative (*Mark* 1:17–20; *John* 1:38–50) while always behind him is the Father who 'gives' his disciples to Jesus (*John* 6:29; 10:29; 17:6, 12). Jesus issues the invitation, 'Follow me', and in the gospel the verb 'to follow' means the following of Jesus, attachment to his person (e.g. *Matt.* 8:19). It was the mighty, immediate impression of Jesus on Peter and his companions, reinforced by a personal word of Jesus, that brought them into his following and made them his disciples (cf. *Mark* 1 : 16– 20; *Matt* 4 : 18–22). To follow Jesus is to model one's conduct on him, to listen to his word (*Mark* 8 : 34f.; 10 : 21, 42–45; *John* 12 : 26). No one can be a true disciple of Christ—no matter how he may protest that he is one— unless he is obedient to the Lord (*Luke* 6 : 46), for only so will he bear fruit (*John* 15 : 8). And since the way of Jesus, his own obedience, led to the cross, so the entry into discipleship results in the obligation to suffer. Jesus had left his disciples under no illusion on that score.

He had told them : 'If any man would come after me, let him deny himself and take up his cross daily and follow me' (*Luke* 9 : 22). Three conditions are listed : denying oneself, that is, not being preoccupied with oneself and one's personal interests, but having in mind only him whole disciple one would be; taking up one's cross daily by patiently bearing trials and so dying to the world (cf. 1 *Cor.* 15 : 31)—the 'daily' taking up of one's cross indicates a spiritual interpretation (by Luke) of a saying of Jesus which originally pointed to martyrdom (cf. *Mark* 8 : 34). These first conditions prepare the way for the third : the following of Jesus by the acceptance of his way of life. Luke has explained (in 9 : 24f., on the losing and saving of one's life) what the renunciation demanded of a disciple of Jesus entails. The obstacle to self-denial (a necessary condition for following Jesus) is the attraction of the world; in other words, one must choose between Jesus and the world. Nor can there be any turning back. 'Another said, "I will follow you, Lord; but first let me say farewell to those at home." Jesus said to him, "No man who puts his hand to the plough and looks back is fit for the kingdom of God." ' (*Luke* 9 : 61f.). Like Elisha (1 *Kings* 19 : 19–21) this man wants to return to take leave of his people; Jesus is more demanding than Elijah. His reply is in proverbial form. The man who is suitable for the proclaiming of the kingdom is one who gives himself to it without reserve like a ploughman who must give his whole attention to ploughing a straight furrow. The sayings teach, in forthright language, that sacrifice and total self-commitment are demanded of the disciples of Jesus.

Jesus' comment on the parable of the Unprofitable Servant (*Luke* 17 : 10) draws out the moral of the parable (17 : 7–9). It is a parable which would have shocked Jesus' hearers—not through use of the term *doulos* ('slave') but through the manner in which this servanthood is to be lived before God. The picture he has painted is starkly clear. A slave has no claim on his master—for either wages or thanks—regardless of how much he may have done for his master. His service is simply taken for granted. The application of the parable (v.10) strikes at the roots of the ethic of contemporary Judaism, a system dominated by the notion of merit. In the Jewish religious consciousness God 'owed' man salvation in view of the just man's fidelity to the Law. But Jesus sets man in *direct* relationship to God, that is, without the Law intervening. He established man as a *doulos* over against God, standing in obedience to the personal and acknowledged sovereignty of God. There is no doubt that the parable is part of Jesus' criticism of the theology of his contemporaries: he pronounces a radically negative verdict on the idea of reward. What he does acknowledge is something very different: the reality of the divine recompense, God's sheer goodness.

*Precepts of Men.* The fact is that discipleship, being a child of God, transforms a man's whole life, affecting his relationship not only to God but also to man. The disciple of Christ stands under the new 'law' of Christ. If Jesus shows an independence in regard to the Law, the written Torah, his attitude is not antinomian; he is not concerned with destroying the Law but with fulfilling it, bringing it to its full eschatological measure. His attitude towards the oral Torah, the *Halakah*, is quite different: he totally rejected it. *Mark* 7:6–8 gives the reason for his rejection of it.

A precise incident lies behind this dispute with the Pharisees and scribes: they had observed that the disciples of Jesus did not respect the ritual washing of hands before meals. In their eyes, this constituted a transgression of the 'tradition of the elders', the *Halakah*—the oral law. It was a body of unwritten traditions based on decisions handed down by successive generations of leading rabbis. These traditions were transmitted orally in the rabbinical schools and were not fixed by writing until the second century of our era, in the Mishnah.[8] They claimed to interpret and complete the Mosaic Law, and were considered equally authoritative and binding (cf. *Gal.* 1:14; *Col.* 2:8, 22). At the time of Jesus these precepts were so numerous (613 different precepts in all) that observance of the Law had become an impossible burden (cf. *Matt.* 23:4, 13; *Luke* 11:46, 52; *Acts* 15:10). Only the specialists, the scribes, who spent their life 'searching the scriptures' (cf. *John* 5:39) could hope to know them all, let alone observe them, while the 'people of the land', ordinary folk, were in inevitable ignorance (*John* 7:49).

In Mark 7:1-8 Jesus does not confine himself to the precise point of ritual purifications but turns the debate on a wider issue: the relative worth of oral law and Mosaic Law. He cites Isaiah 29:13 against the Pharisees, drawing a parallel between the 'precepts of men' of which Isaiah spoke and the 'tradition of men' on which the Pharisees count. Implicitly, he accuses them of putting their traditions on the same level as, and even above, the Word of God. Jesus rejects the *Halakah* because it is entirely the work of men and because it can and does conflict with the

Law of God. The oral law had put casuistry above love. He instances the manner in which a son might avoid all obligations to his parents by fictitiously dedicating to the Temple the money that should go to their support; this was the overturning of the precept of the Decalogue: 'Honour your father and your mother'. By their traditions, the Pharisees had 'made void the word of God'.

The deepest reason why Jesus rejected the 'tradition of the elders' is because a more efficacious economy has been inaugurated. The theology underlying the Marcan passage can be expressed in terms very like those of Hebrews 10: 1–10. In Mark 7:6–13 Jesus pronounced the tradition of the elders obsolete; then, in 7:14–23, he declares all foods clean, so bringing to an end all the distinctions of Judaism between clean and unclean. Like the author of Hebrews, Jesus shows that legal discrimination between 'clean' and 'unclean' is incapable of purifying the heart of man, and can only be a provisional expedient. But if Jesus can now pronounce the disposition obsolete, it is for one reason: because the definitive order has brought the provisional order to an end. Jesus' abolition of the Jewish traditions manifests, to whoever can understand, that a new order has come. And, in a christian context, any return to attitudes which he had set aside, and branded as a making void of God's Word, is infidelity to him and a betrayal of his precious gift of freedom.

*Neglected Words.* It is not only a matter of his criticism of the spirit and practice of pharisaism. Jesus made some new and strikingly radical demands. There is, for instance, his attitude towards swearing (*Matt.* 5:33–37). In the new kingdom which he ushered in there is no place for oaths because there can be no place for dishonesty or untruthfulness. It is not only a stand against certain Jewish casuistic practices according to which a man swore by the name of

God without explicitly mentioning it; Jesus rejects oaths altogether: 'I say to you, do not swear at all (*mē omosoi holōs*) (5:34), for oaths are but a concession to an imperfect older order.' Then, there is Jesus' prohibition of violence: 'Do not resist any one who is evil. But if anyone strikes you on the right cheek, turn to him the other also' (5:39). He declared that evil, even violence, should not be opposed by violence. G. B. Caird's comment on Apocalypse 13:9f. opens up the perspective of Jesus' demand: 'When one man wrongs another, the other may retaliate, bear a grudge, or take the injury out on a third person. Whichever he does, there are now two evils where before there was one; and a chain reaction is started, like the spreading of a contagion. Only if the victim absorbs the wrong and so puts it out of currency, can it be prevented from going any further.'[9] Are such demands unrealistic in our imperfect state? We seem to have judged them so—without seriously taking the trouble to find out whether they might really work.

Jesus acknowledges (*Mark* 9:35) that there is greatness in discipleship: the dignity, the greatness of service. And this is so because the loving service of the least member of the community is service of Jesus and of the Father. But Jesus solemnly asserts (10:42-45) that, in the community of his disciples, there is no place for ambition. His Church is a human society: there is need of authority, there must be leaders. But those who lead will *serve* their brethren and the spirit of authority is *diakonia*. Surely, Jesus has intended the paradox and asks for it to be taken seriously. There is the shining light of his own example: he served God's purpose, the salvation of men, by laying down his life in the service of men. There really can be no justification at all for styles and trappings and patterns of authority inspired by the powers and princes of the world. Centuries of tradition cannot weigh against the stark words of the Lord.

*It shall not be so among you*—we have no right to urge the burden of history against a demand as clear as that. Sooner or later we must find the courage to admit, not only in word but in deed, that we have not hearkened to this word of the Lord.

*The Father.* More important than anything else in the life of this new people is the new relationship to God. God is Father, the disciples are his children; it is significant that Jesus spoke of 'your Father' only to his disciples, never to outsiders. The Son alone can make the Father known. Luke tells us that Jesus, who had witnessed the power of God at work through his disciples (*Luke* 10:17–20), 'rejoiced in the Holy Spirit' and then declared:

> I thank, thee, Father, Lord of heaven and earth, that thou hast hidden these things from the wise and understanding and revealed them to babes . . . All things have been delivered to me by my Father; and no one knows who the Son is except the Father, or who the Father is except the Son and any one to whom the Son chooses to reveal him (10:21f.; *Matt.* 11:25–27).

The saying, so reminiscent of John, clearly expresses the unique relationship of Father and Son. The 'wise' are the leaders of Israel; the 'babes' are the simple folk—the disciples who hear and do. The secret which the Father has confided to the humble is the mutual knowledge of Father and Son, revealed to those disciples whom the Son chooses. The prologues to two other New Testament writings tell us why the Son alone can reveal the Father. John declares: 'No one has ever seen God; it is God the only Son, ever at the Father's side, who has revealed him' (*John* 1:18). And the author of Hebrews informs us that God, who had spoken variously through the prophets, has uttered his final word, by a Son who 'reflects the glory of

God and bears the very stamp of his nature' (*Heb.* 1:3). The inevitable conclusion, of immense practicality for the christian life, is that we cannot find God except in and through Jesus. This he has expressly declared: 'I am the way, and the truth, and the life; no one comes to the Father but by me' (*John* 14:6). Our Father is, at all times, the Father of our Lord Jesus Christ.

Children talk with their Father—Jesus taught a new way of praying. He himself talked to his Father as naturally, as intimately, and with the same sense of confidence and security as a child talks to its father. He urged his disciples to do the same. He withdrew prayer from the liturgical sphere of the sacral, where it had tended to be confined, and put it in the centre of everyday life. In Jesus' eyes being a child of God brings the certainty of a share in future salvation, grants everyday security, and gives the courage to submit to what is unpredictable in the divine will. In particular, the disciple, the child of God, will see suffering in a new light. The Reign of God comes through suffering and tribulation—and only thus. Proving one's discipleship means staying by Jesus in his trials. No longer does the disciple ask 'why' God sends suffering, but 'for what'. 'Above all, when one is a child of God, the eternally unfathomable riddle of evil is left in God's hands . . . Nothing happens without God. Jesus believes that unconditionally. Stronger than all questions, riddles, and anxieties is the one word *Abba*. The Father knows' (Jeremias). One could add nothing to the strength to be found in that insight—except the childlikeness to believe in it.

We have paused awhile to look at a Person, an event, 'that has never dropped out of the memory of the oldest surviving society in the western world' (Dodd). But, let us more than merely 'remember'. Let us 'believe and come to know' (cf. *John* 6 : 69) how fully this person, this Jesus, is present to us. Let us experience anew what the disciples experienced after the Resurrection. *God* has come to be *with man*! Our fresh light upon this reality is to look anew at Jesus of Nazareth and at his message. Knowing this Man and his Word, we shall feel in our hearts that he does indeed fit the name Emmanuel—God-with-us, as well as Jesus—Saviour. 'If a man loves me, he will keep my word, and my Father will love him, and we will come and make our home with him' (*John* 14 : 23).

# CHAPTER II

# Good News for the Poor

'THE Spirit of the Lord is upon me, because he has anointed me to preach good news to the poor . . .' (*Luke* 4:18f.; cf. *Is.* 61:1-3). Astounding proclamation! These are the words with which (according to Luke) Jesus really opened his public ministry. He stands before the people in the Nazareth synagogue, reads the portion of Scripture in which the prophet knows himself to be Spirit-anointed for his task, and describes this mission of preaching to the poor, healing the blind, releasing the captives. He then declares, quietly but solemnly, that these words in the Scriptures of old were being fulfilled in the very hearing of his people. They were being fulfilled in himself—yes, astounding declaration. And we, hearing these words in the light of christian faith, think at first of the glorious Messiah arrived at last with all of God's Spirit upon him to do wondrous deeds—healing, freeing, and preaching the good news.

But do we really grasp the import of this proclamation? Do we not tend to look only at the verbal forms and the marvellous manifestations of power which they imply? Such an understanding is incomplete; we must look even more to the recipients of these deeds and see the stark contrast they create. For, who are they? The captives, the blind, the oppressed—all those who are weakest and most abjectly powerless? Who are these who are the ones to receive the 'good news'? They are the *poor*!

And so, 'because he has anointed me to bring glad tidings to the poor' provides the 'why' for this chapter.

We wish to define the message of Jesus as being precisely that 'consolation of Israel' which Simeon, as representing all the 'poor' of his people, had long awaited (*Luke* 2:25). We shall do this by drawing on two authors (one we have already met) who have made this theme central to their recent studies on the New Testament.[1] Jacques Dupont develops his thesis in a detailed analysis of the first three beatitudes common to Matthew and Luke (*Matt.* 5:3–6; *Luke* 6:20f.)—the poor, the hungry, and those who weep (the fourth common beatitude, concerning the 'persecuted', he treats on its own as delivering a different message). He shows how Jesus' mission not only announces the kingdom but actually reveals it—precisely through his attitude and actions on behalf of all types of 'poor'. He shows how the beatitudes are not so much a portrayal of what man should be as of what God is—the God who does not seek to dominate but to save, and to save in the first place, quite gratuitously, the most unfortunate of men, those on whom the consequences of sin weigh most heavily. Joachim Jeremias traces the theme throughout the whole gospel, with special emphasis on the parables. He shows how, when Jesus indicates the different 'signs of the time of salvation' to the Baptist's disciples, his main stress lies on the final sign : *ptōchoi euangelizontai*—'the poor have the good news preached to them'.

## Defining 'The Poor'

The idea (the reality) of a dire need for God's comfort runs throughout the Old Testament and embraces many classes of people—it is only fitting that they should enter into the definition of the term 'poor' as used by Jesus. The background is found in that particular Old Testament usage which lists different types of afflicted persons under certain descriptions and images—all of which can be seen concentrated in the term 'poor'. Thus, the first three beati-

36

tudes should be taken together as envisaging the same type of people: the 'poor', the 'hungry' and the 'mourning' in the New Testament should be compared with similar lists in the Old Testament mentioning the contrite, the sojourner, the broken-hearted, the blind, the deaf, the lame, and so on. These beatitudes, then, extend to all classes of *miserables*. The beatitudes concerning the poor and the mourners refer directly to Isaiah 61 : 1f., while that concerning the hungry echoes other promises of consolation associated with that oracle. Moreover, Isaiah 61 : 1–3 must in turn be related to other Old Testament texts in order to grasp what Jesus really meant in describing his mission as one of 'preaching good news to the poor'.

Similarly, the preaching of good news to the poor of Matthew 11 : 5 (par. *Luke* 7 : 22) should be related to the bringing of good news to the afflicted of Isaiah 61 : 1–3. One explains the term 'poor' by the parallel expressions in the Isaian passage: the broken-hearted, the captives, those who are bound, those who are of faint spirit. The 'poor' are the oppressed in the general sense given to *ani* or *anaw* elsewhere in prophetic literature: all those who cannot defend themselves and are so hopelessly helpless that they know they are thrown on God's help alone. Not the Old Testament only, but the New Testament itself provides the context for Jesus' use of the name 'poor'. 'The poor' are not mentioned alone; they are connected with the blind, the lame, the lepers, the deaf, the dead, with the prisoners and oppressed, with the sick (*Matt.* 11 : 5; *Luke* 4 : 18; 7 : 22; 14 : 21). In his parables and sayings, Jesus broadens the circle of the poor through a whole range of imagery and designations: the last, the lost, the heavily-burdened, the labouring, the little ones . . . and even the harlots and publicans and sinners! Yes, imagine that of all the desolate and derelict people for whom God shows special care in that they are 'the poor', it is the 'sinners', those who have supposedly rebelled against him, that he most cherishes! We can speak of a real 'privilege' of sinners, who have an advantage in their very sinfulness, in their very spiritual distress. Their privilege consists not in their being 'repentants' who 'reform', but in their absolute *need* for Jesus lest they be wholly lost. To bring them—the first-fruits of the poor—salvation, has Jesus been especially sent.

The familiar gospel designations of Jesus' followers must be seen in a twofold perspective. On the one hand, they are terms of derision coined by Jesus' opponents. In Judaism the stigma 'sinner' was attached not only to those who failed, morally, to keep the Law, but also to those of despised trades which were thought to lead to immorality and dishonesty. To this must be added the designation of Jesus' followers as the 'little ones' (*Mark* 9:42; *Matt.* 10:42; *Luke* 14:21), the 'least' (*Matt.* 25:40, 45), and the 'babes' or 'simple ones' (*Matt.* 11:25; *Luke* 10:21). In the mouth of his opponents, these terms derided Jesus' disciples as backward, uneducated, and hence irreligious; they were the 'people of the land', or common folk, who were considered 'accursed' because they 'did not know the law' (*John* 7:49). They were held in contempt as men 'whose *religious* ignorance and *moral* behaviour stood in the way of their access to salvation, according to the convictions of the time' (Jeremias). For, in Judaism, the supreme religious duty was to avoid 'sinners' because God's help was only given to the righteous, and the sinner might receive his merciful help only when he had repented and become 'righteous'.

The situation is well illustrated by the parable of the Pharisee and the Tax Collector (*Luke* 18:9–14).[2] From the first the parable maintains a dramatic contrast. The two men who, at the same time, pray in the Temple, represent the two extreme strata of Jewish society: the Pharisee, taking his stand on meticulous observance of the Law, is the embodiment of Jewish faith and morality; the tax collector, by his office marked off as one who does not observe the Law, scarcely merits the name of Jew. The Pharisee comes boldly into the presence of God. He is not a hypocrite, for everything he says is true; what is wrong with his prayer is not what he says but what he does not say. He is quite convinced that he stands right with God and he feels no need to ask for forgiveness. The tax collector does not come boldly into the Temple but, conscious of his sins, stands at a distance from the Holy Place. But he does come into God's presence (hoping against hope) and his attitude—downcast eyes and the beating of his breast—proclaim his feelings. Like the Pharisee, he is thinking of himself; but what he contemplates is his sin and misery, and he feels no temptation to compare himself with other men. His prayer is very simple, a cry from the heart, a cry for pardon.

The Pharisees who had listened to the parable so far would perhaps have expected to be told that God did grant pardon to the tax collector, in virtue of the righteousness of the other. They were quite unprepared for the verdict of Jesus: the tax collector was justified—his sins were forgiven. He had asked for pardon and his prayer was heard; he had won the divine favour. The Pharisee was not justified: his sins were not forgiven because he had not asked for pardon. His error, his blindness, was that he did not see himself for what he was; in his own eyes he was assuredly righteous.

The three sayings which concern the privilege of children (*Mark* 10:14, 15; *Matt.* 11:25f.) evoke, by contrast, this concept of 'righteousness'. A common trait in the passages referring to the 'little ones' is that Jesus' contemporaries would see such persons as of little account, for to have any status it was necessary to have had instruction in the Law in order to be worthily prepared for the privilege of the Kingdom. But lo, the 'poor', these 'children', and this inferior part of society led by the sinners themselves, become *the* chosen ones! Here is the reverse side of the double perspective. For, 'when you love someone, you love him *as he is*' Péguy has written. And those whom the opponents of Jesus named 'poor' with contempt, he himself named with love. The poor, the sick, the sinners, the simple and humble ones are for him all those who labour and are burdened, all those in need of refreshing rest. Yes, an extraordinary new message was this—that salvation is destined for 'beggers' and 'sinners': Here lies the gentle power behind Jesus' proclamation, the heart of his message: through him it is precisely these people who have the hope of salvation. It is precisely because they are 'the poor' that the Kingdom is theirs.

Let us try to pinpoint what Jesus meant by the term *ptōchoi*. The 'poor' are not merely those with few possessions; nor are they those whose poverty is 'spiritual'. In the biblical context, the 'poor' are all the 'little people' who are incapable of defending themselves or caring for themselves and hence, by their very dependent need and sorry state are God's protected ones. The designation *ptōchoi* is not an idealisation: the poor really do need help, the hungry really have no hope of nourishment, the mourning are visibly sorrowful. They truly are in need of compassion. The 'poor' to whom Jesus announced the good news of himself and whom he declared 'blessed' are not men whom he is proposing as an example of virtue, but rather persons who are literally 'down and out'. It may be suffering in the heart—but it is real suffering. It may be a poverty, a lack, felt in the soul—but it is real poverty. The paradoxical antithesis of the beatitudes must be taken seriously. 'The Kingdom of God, supreme honour and glory, belongs to destined for 'beggars' and 'sinners': Here lies the gentle The marvellous consolation of the world to come is

ERRATUM: Second last line should read, 'despised men, to the weak who cannot defend themselves.'

promised not to those who flee the reality of this world and take refuge in dreams, but to men who suffer, who weep, and who sorrow' (Dupont).

## The Stumbling Block

But before we go further to look at the marvellous implications of 'good news for the poor', we must pause over that which halted many would-be followers of Jesus in his own time : *the* stumbling-block, the *skandalon*. And this is the incredible paradox that this 'good news' was—is— precisely for the *poor*! Yes, the great 'stumbling block' that the Father's love was directed even to despised and lost children! Here is the reason why the Good News was a slap in the face and received with indignation: Jesus did not come to call the 'righteous' about whom the whole of Pharisaic Judaism revolved. He did not base man's relationship to God on moral conduct; and thus he seemed to dissolve all the ethics which the Pharisees had constructed. He actually declared 'sinners', the very sinners they were to avoid, closer to God than they! The Good News itself was the offence.

For this news was good precisely because it was for the poor. Jesus' final sign of the time of salvation (*Matt.* 11 :5) —the poor have the good news preached to them—is followed at once by his saying, 'and blessed is he who is not scandalised in me' (11 :6). At first sight, such a saying would appear to be out of context. But, when we understand the reaction of scribes and Pharisees to this aspect of Jesus' proclamation, it is very much in place. This stumbling block is revealed also in the first beatitude when the poor are called blessed because 'theirs is the kingdom' : the emphasis is on the 'theirs' (or 'yours' in Luke's version). In Semitic style, Jesus is saying that the kingdom belongs to the poor . . . *alone*! This was such an extraordinary proclamation that surely in the first beatitude we must be standing upon the very bed-rock of tradition and hearing the *ipsissima vox* of Jesus—his very words.

There, in a nutshell, is the heart of Jesus' message and the heart of the 'offence'. It is a paradox which the exegete must take seriously without attempting to make the beatitudes into pious exhortations, denying the real, existential conditions of the people they envisage. The paradoxical note is intentional: it is exactly the unhappy whom Jesus calls happy! The 'little ones' should not be interpreted as childhood idealised or the 'poor' as noble simplicity of heart. These are real persons for whom God is determined to show his special compassion and care because of their littleness and distress, not in spite of it. He is determined to make them the first beneficiaries of the Kingdom—by sending his beloved Son to inaugurate that reign through preaching good news and through revealing in his own person that glad tidings are for the *poor*.

### Jesus' Proclamation

Having looked at both the term 'poor' and its effect upon Jesus' contemporaries, we are now ready to see more clearly the position of this theme in the whole proclamation. Jesus' emphasis upon 'good news for the poor' was intimately associated with the sense of his own mission. It was that which made it uniquely his. The exegesis of the first three beatitudes has an historical corollary in that they are the application or actualisation of his message: 'the Kingdom of God is at hand'. They correspond to a definite situation in Jesus' ministry: the first phase before all the opposition and controversy was aroused. As such, they witness to his earliest preaching. The passages about the 'little children' and the 'simple' also have similar applications for Jesus' mission: in thanking the Father for revealing his 'secret' to little ones, he also confesses his own mission as doing the same. His tenderness towards children indicates the privileges they are to enjoy in the Kingdom, and entrance into the Kingdom depends on child-like response to his own person and message. God's love for the poor is fully realised, made manifestly concrete, at just that moment in history which coincides with the mission of Jesus. In this ministry God makes his supreme effort on behalf of sinners.

Indeed, this proclamation of 'good news for the poor' is unparalleled at the time of Jesus. The message that God's love reaches to sinners (and sinners only) represents the great pre-Easter 'scandal' (the post-Easter offence being the Cross) and cannot have been derived from Judaism or the early Church. The very action of Jesus demonstrated that the poor and the sinners had been accepted by God, for his ministry is a time of grace, pardon and mercy on their behalf. Having identified his mission, as we have seen, with that of the message of good news in Isaiah 61, his ministry sets the stage for events which must follow immediately; as such, it is the font of new joy for all the *malheureux*, the unfortunate, the unhappy. Moreover, in order to perceive the meaning of Jesus' ministry, they must have first grasped that their own sufferings were ending.

Those parables which deal with the reprieve of sinners are Jesus' answer to the offence taken by the Pharisees to the gospel. The parables are a vindication of the good news for three reasons : because in them the sinners are shown to be sick men (only the sick need a doctor) and grateful men (only those burdened with debts can know the meaning of remission); because they reveal the true nature of God as the loving, merciful Father he is; and because they show the 'sinners' as closer to God than the 'righteous'. The parables of Mercy (*Luke* 15) reveal God's compassion towards sinners—not however, as a timeless, general truth, but as realised in the Incarnation. The lost sheep is dearer to this Shepherd, this Jesus, precisely because it is lost! The parable demonstrates that the words and actions of Jesus are inseparable: he is not a teacher of morals delivering principles of conduct to men; rather, his very attitude towards, and daily life with, the poor are the model for our own behaviour. He has already fulfilled perfectly the words of counsel later given to his followers: 'Little children, let us not love in word or speech, but in deed and in truth' (1 *John* 3:18).

'I came not to call the righteous, but sinners' (*Matt.* 9:13). This declaration is not only a scandal to the 'righteous' —it is hope for sinners. The poor are thereby promised that God will intervene and that his doing so involves the remission of debts (as illustrated by the parables of the Two Debtors, the Unmerciful Servant, and the Prodigal Son). Though Jesus promises only seldom a 'forgiveness of sins' in as many words, the subject of forgiveness and God's mercy is ever present in the rich picture language of his parables and sayings. The 'little ones' and the 'poor' are indeed privileged, but the privilege is not to be found in their own dispositions of heart, or in their poverty, but solely in the heart of God—his *eudokia,* his gratuitous benevolence. Jesus is not promising the poor and the humble a 'reward' for their way of life, but a participation in the favour which God grants to what is little, weak, and despised.

Perhaps Jeremias' greatest contribution to the understanding of the good news for the poor lies in his specifying this as Jesus' table-fellowship with sinners. This is the supreme form in which Jesus proclaimed forgiveness. He freely accepted invitations to dine with them (*Mark* 2:15f.; *Luke* 15:2). He was taunted because he excluded no one from these meals (*Matt.* 11:19; *Luke* 7:34). In the Near East, to share a meal meant to share in peace, trust, brotherhood, and life itself. Moreover, since table-fellowship meant fellowship before God, in that all who broke bread together partook in the blessing upon that bread when it was yet unbroken, Jesus' meals have a deeper significance than expressing merely social generosity. They express his own mission and anticipate the eschatological meal of God himself—the salvation of the 'end time'. 'The inclusion of sinners in the community of salvation, achieved in table-fellowship, is the most meaningful expression of the redeeming love of God' (Jeremias).

We may appreciate more fully the significance of Jesus' table-fellowship with sinners when we reflect on the deep-rooted Jewish animosity to such fellowship. This is most dramatically evident as an acute problem *within* the primitive christian community. The so-called 'James-clause' of Acts 15:20f. and 28f. was meant to facilitate the participation of converts from Pharisaic Judaism in common meals with their Gentile brethren. The famous clash between Paul and Peter at Antioch hinged precisely on this issue (*Gal.* 2:11–14). In Jewish eyes, Gentiles were, automatically, 'sinners' ('we ourselves who are Jews by birth and not Gentile sinners', *Gal.* 2:15) and table-fellowship with them was out of the question—but so it was, too, with any other category of 'sinner'. The real problem of Jewish Christians surely underlines the shock of scribe and Pharisee at Jesus' deliberate flouting of what was something far more serious than a social convention. Here, too, he was striking at the heart of their ethic, their whole elaborate system of 'righteousness'.

But there is another side to it. If Jesus' opponents saw at once the significance of his conduct, so, too, did the 'sinners'. They, also, were Jews, and they understood what he was about. They had been classed by the theologians of their religion as 'sinners', beyond redemption. They were despised by the 'righteous' as accursed ones, outside the Law. They had come to accept that verdict and were people without hope. But now, Jesus had come into their

45

lives—and they were no longer hopeless. He did not come mouthing fine words, he did not summon them to his presence. No, he went to them, he sought them out, he held table-fellowship with them. His actions spoke louder than his words as he showed them, in his very presence among them, the loving mercy of God, the heart of a Father. He himself, and not any words of his, was the sermon that won them.

Dupont's special contribution is his understanding of the Kingdom of the poor in terms of the nature of its King and their God. In the ancient Near East it was expected of kings that they be protectors of the poor, the unfortunate, and the weak—not because these people were more meritorious citizens, but because it was an attribute of the royal function to assure equal rights to all subjects. Thus the privilege of the poor is not founded on their own poverty, but on the ideal of the king. More basically, this concept was applied to Yahweh, who was expected to exercise not a retributive justice in which he vindicated the rights of the poor, but a royal justice in which he could not but protect outcasts precisely because of his position and attributes. Their privilege was found not in themselves but in the way God wished to exercise his rule. It is this presupposition which underlies the beatitudes and makes it advantageous to present oneself to God as a 'poor man' with no other source of help. 'Here is no idealising of poverty; rather, here is a theology of the justice of God, a theology of hope which is concerned with the eschatological kingdom of God' (Dupont). The beatitudes invite the poor and the unfortunate to rejoice in God's goodness which will be bestowed upon them abundantly once his kingdom has been established—for God himself as king will care for them and make them the object of his royal solicitude. And, God did establish this living kingdom through his Son who taught, we recall, that it is open only to those who

46

can call this highest King *Abba*—'Father'—like a little, trustful child.

## The Good News: Salvation

The message of Jesus is precisely that 'consolation of Israel' which Simeon, as representing all the 'poor' of his people, had long awaited (*Luke* 2 : 25). But, how did he know it had come, and why did he pray for God to allow him to depart his life in peace? Because . . . 'my eyes have seen your *salvation*' (2 : 29–32)—yes, because he had held in his arms the One whose name and whose mission meant 'saviour'. If the good news is good because it is for the *poor*, it is also good because the entire content of the glad tidings is their salvation. Here is the fulfilment of all the prophecies of old, giving to the poor the invaluable, inviolate riches of a 'treasure in heaven' . . . on earth. This good news is *the* gift of the dawning time of salvation, and its import lies in its being given not 'some day' in an indefinite future, but *now* in Jesus' ministry. Jesus ends the sermon at Nazareth, in which he had quoted Isaiah 61 : 1f., by declaring : 'Today this scripture has been fulfilled in your hearing' (*Luke* 4 : 21). The proclamation of the beatitudes presupposes that the moment has arrived when their promises will be accomplished. The poor are called to rejoice because God is on the verge of inaugurating his Kingdom for *them*—even though it must always include the eschatological perspective of a time of waiting.

And so, as the angels had sung to the shepherds, the glad tidings or good news should be just that : glad and good (*Luke* 2 : 8–11). It should be an occasion of great joy for all peoples (for who is not among 'the poor'?) in that the Saviour with his message of consolation has arrived. If, as the parables portray, God exults over the returning sinner, that sinner exults in God's welcoming him so lovingly. God's goodness, surpassing all understanding, means gladness for the poor. Far from being barred from access to salvation, as the religious conviction of the time held, the poor are the very first to be 'saved', to be invited to the Marriage Supper of the Lamb.

We have noted that the key-text, Isaiah 61 : 1–3, is a list of the beneficiaries of salvation. Among them we find the 'broken-hearted', those who have lost courage to live. The manner in which Yahweh, through his prophet, is to 'bind them up' perhaps best expressed all that is done for all types of 'poor' when the good news is preached to them. Here then, in this and related passages of Isaiah, we have the implicit background for the beatitudes, we have the key to understanding why the poor are called 'blessed'. For the Kingdom given to them corresponds to the 'reign of Yahweh' of which the prophet announces glad tidings.

But, who is it that makes the words of the oracle explicit, who is it that assumes for himself the role of Yahweh's mediation through a prophet? It is, of course, Jesus. 'The Spirit of the Lord is upon *me* to preach good news to the poor'—to heal the blind and deliver the oppressed and proclaim release to captives, and perform all the other untold blessings associated with Jesus' ministry of love then and now. Significantly, Jesus concludes with the words describing the present 'acceptable year of the Lord' and omits the clause about God's 'vengeance' with which the Isaian text ends. And it is noteworthy that in the companion text to this episode in the Nazareth synagogue, that of Matthew 11 :5f. (par. *Luke* 7 :22f.) referring to the 'signs of salvation', Jesus there too passes over reference to eschatological vengeance on the Gentiles, even though it was a theme included in all the Isaian texts underlying the New Testament passage.

Finally, let us turn once again to those signs of salvation which Jesus announces to the disciples of John the Baptist —and to all of us (*Luke* 7 :22, 23):

> Go and tell John what you have seen and heard:
> The blind receive their sight, the lame walk, lepers are
> cleansed, and the deaf hear, the dead are raised up, the
> poor have the good news preached to them.

All show one thing: that here is indeed an 'acceptable time, a day of salvation' (2 *Cor.* 6:2), the time of God's grace and favour. And, as we have seen at the beginning, it is the final note which sounds the clearest, giving the key to all the rest and drawing them back to the prophetic context: 'the good news is preached to the poor'. But we perceive that this list contains age-old images for the 'time of salvation', six examples associated with the perfect fulfilment of God's Kingdom. We perceive that this saying is actually Jesus' eschatological cry of joy. 'Now help is extended to those in the depths of despair; now those who were as good as dead are raised to life . . . The water of life flows, the time of the curse is at an end, paradise is opened. Even now, the consummation of the world is dawning' (Jeremias). Yes! all because 'the poor have the good news preached to them'!

But still there is that verse which follows after all those 'signs': 'And blessed is he who takes no offence at me—who is not scandalised by me.' Yes, there is still the stumbling-block, the paradox, that it *is* the poor—that 'God has chosen the weak instead of the strong, and things that are not instead of the things that are' (1 *Cor.* 1:27f.). Well might this be the supreme beatitude: Blessed are they who believe!

# CHAPTER III

# The Lord

IF Jesus had made an impact on his disciples during their
time with him, this was as nothing compared with the
transformation wrought in them through his presence as
Risen Lord. His resurrection had made all the difference.
Now, and not until now, did they truly begin to understand who and what he really was. Now they began to
grasp the significance of his person, his life and his teaching. Now Christology was born.

It is not our purpose to discern the origin of or to trace
the growth of christological thought. It will be enough to
look to the Synoptists, to Paul and to John. But we can
point to a development. We do find in Mark—and in
Matthew and Luke outside of their infancy gospels—a
two-stage Christology. This involves the casting of the
titles and the understanding of the risen Christ back to
Jesus of Nazareth in the gospel account of his ministry and
passion. In other words, the synoptic gospels reflect the
evangelists' understanding that the Lord Jesus Christ was
Lord too throughout his ministry. Both Paul and John,
each in his own way, pushed the titles and the understanding back to a third stage, that of pre-existence, thus produc-
ing a threefold christological pattern of pre-existence,
incarnation and exaltation. But Matthew and Luke, who
do not refer to Jesus' pre-existence, have a three-stage
Christology of their own. Their third stage is found in
their infancy gospels where understanding of Jesus as
Messiah, Saviour, Lord, Son of David and so on, is pushed
back to the infancy period. It represents a stage in the

developing understanding of him who is the Christian Lord: he is Lord not only in and through the resurrection, not only during his ministry, but also from the beginning of his earthly existence. The final step was the one to pre-existence and incarnation.[1]

Christology cannot remain abstract but must be concerned with the events and meaning of Jesus' life. The fact of the *incarnation* is fundamental. In becoming man, Jesus proclaimed that he came as one who serves—and this is the basic christian ethic. The same ethic is marked by Jesus' realistic attitude towards the world and its conditions because he, too, has been made man in our midst. Yet, the incarnation must necessarily be a veiling as well as a revealing of the light. John views the incarnation as both revelation and stumbling-block—the world can either believe and enter into its fullness, or not believe and be merely 'the world' in a negative sense. And the incarnation is not a 'dogma' but the very core of salvation.

The incarnation involves the poignant fact of paradox or 'scandal', this mystery of Jesus as both God and man. The Johannine Word-made-flesh is the 'offence'; the revealer comes as a man who cannot *prove* to the world his claim to be Son of God. The offence must be overcome by accepting Jesus in faith. The bold grandeur of the Son of Man is that, while he is still the afflicted one identified with everyman, the earthly person with 'nowhere to lay his head' and about to suffer, he is also the same Son of Man to be seated at God's right hand. The paradox of the incarnate Christ, the life-giver, is that he must tread the earthly road of distress to conquer that distress, he must assume human life to deliver humanity, and he must suffer in order to be raised from suffering into glory. The man Jesus is decisively important for Paul's theology; the emphatic message of John is that God in Christ has set men free from the domination of the world of sin and death. Finally, the enduring 'scandal' of Christianity is that the total 'otherness' which alone can save man is *God* as he has revealed himself historically in the *man* Jesus.

Emphasis on the cross must occur throughout New Testament theology, simply because it is at the heart of the New Testament. Though sin and anguish and death are still in the world, the problem of 'guilt' *has* been solved by the cross; the sinner finds gracious forgiveness. Paul understood his ministry, through his own personal, humanly painful experiences, and, for him, preaching meant 'the word of the cross'. By experiencing the dying of Christ, the apostle communicates Christ's *life* to the community through the effects of his preaching. The cross is not the end, and there is a similar necessary emphasis on the resurrection—understood not as a return to earthly life but as a resurrection to *doxa* (glory). The resurrection may be seen as a new revelation in the history of God's word; it is 'God's interpretation of the cross'. Resurrection-ascension means the final victory over evil, and the joyful meeting of the early Christians to break bread together was the strongest evidence for the certainty of the resurrection.

There is the special fruit of the resurrection-ascension : Jesus' sending of the Holy Spirit. In John, the Spirit comes to complete Christ's presence rather than to supply for his absence. Jesus promised the Spirit because he had much to say that his disciples could not yet have comprehended (cf. *John* 16 : 12); to confess that Jesus has come in the flesh is to receive the Spirit of truth. For Paul the presence of salvation is manifest in the fact that the risen Christ is present, through his Spirit, in his community, and rules the life of the Christian.

The New Testament theologians—the Synoptists, Paul, John, and the others—all build their more or less impressive Christologies on essentially this message : that God's salvation is found in Jesus of Nazareth, the carpenter and

teacher whom God had made Messiah. This was the Easter
faith which overcame the scandal of the cross and held
out hope to the early Church that God's mercy would
overcome even the final 'No' of the world. For New
Testament eschatology concerns itself with the fact that
he who comes is not only victor and saviour but also the
person familiar from the gospel record of his earthly life
of humility and suffering.

One does not venture to outline, in a single chapter,
the christological wealth of the New Testament. It will
suffice to look at some specific contributions of the evangelists and of Paul, and so to catch a glimpse of their
portrait of Christ.[2]

## I. MARK

In Mark's gospel, Jesus appears as the Son of God and
as a Man among men. If the introductory verse tells us
that his gospel will be a testimony to 'Jesus Christ, the Son
of God', it testifies to this by revealing the humanity of
Jesus. In a world where hearts were hardened and where
the cares of society as a whole left little time for the needs
of individual persons, here was a human being—Jesus—
who came and cared. Jesus was a Man who himself knew
pain and sorrow, the pain of being rejected by his own
people in Nazareth and of their persistent disbelief (6:6).
When he sought to go apart in prayer to a lonely place
and his disciples searched him out with the remark that
everyone was searching for him (1:37), he must himself
have felt lonely on realising that the people looked only
for signs and wonders. The more abiding works, and the
sufferings in store for him, were so far from understood or
completed. While in the simplicity of its early traditions
and of its author's own style, Mark's gospel is the one which
perhaps most reveals the humanity of Jesus, his purpose
in writing the gospel was to reveal Jesus as the Son of

God. Mark is the evangelist who most explicitly brings out Jesus' human limitations in his saying that not even the Son knows the hour of the End (13:32). But Mark is also he who tells us that, when Jesus' own end had come upon the cross, all the world was to recognise him in the exclamation of the Roman centurion: 'Surely this man was the Son of God' (15:39).

## Son of Man

*The Mysterious Son of Man.* The idea of the mystery associated with Jesus as Son of man is characteristic of Mark's theological outlook and is introduced into his gospel by recurrent words and themes. Like the other synoptics, his gospel contains Jesus' proclamation of the Kingdom. However, Mark reserves this proclamation to Jesus alone. It is his view that the Kingdom which Jesus announces, the gospel which he proclaims, is not a body of doctrinal teaching, but a mystery or secret which Jesus himself embodies and reveals only to his disciples. This is intimately connected with Mark's theory of the parables (4:10–12)—indeed, the very term *parabolē* for Mark suggests a secret, hidden 'dark saying' which can be understood only through a special divine enlightenment. The 'secret' that the Kingdom was already present in the person of Jesus was hidden from 'those outside'; therefore he necessarily used an enigmatic form of teaching for them.[3] But although this 'secret' had been revealed to his closest disciples and he is seen in Mark to be constantly instructing them 'privately', yet even they were incapable of understanding the mystery of his person. This occasions other characteristic Marcan expressions concerning lack of understanding and hardening of hearts—all contributing to the enigmatic, mysterious quality of this Jesus. Only at the first prediction of his passion does Jesus at last 'speak the word plainly' (8:32). Thus we glimpse that the mystery

54

of his messiahship is bound up with his passion and death.

*The Teaching Son of Man.* In Mark's gospel the age of salvation foretold in the Old Testament has become in Jesus the time of the *kerygma* or proclamation. This *kerygma* is both a call to repentance and a proclamation of the good news. It begins with John the Baptist (1 : 4, 7) and is taken up by Jesus (1 : 14f., 38f.). The disciples continued this proclamation, and it forms part of the Church's universal mission (13 : 10, 14 : 9). But, as distinct from this proclamation of repentance and of the Good News in general, it is Jesus alone who proclaims God's Kingdom. His entire mission is a revelation of his own place in this Kingdom, a revealing which takes place through 'teaching'. Mark predicates this function only of Jesus (except in 6 : 30, the return of the disciples from their mission, which seems a later addition, and in 7 : 7 which is a quotation of Isaiah 29 : 13).

In Mark, Jesus' exorcisms and other manifestations of power are inseparable from his 'teaching'. Less of Jesus' actual doctrine is recorded in Mark than in the other synoptics; yet here his teaching activity is more closely associated with his self-revelation. His teaching causes amazement because of his assurance and impressiveness : 'They were astonished at his teaching, for he taught them as one who had authority, and not as the scribes' (1 : 22). He speaks with prophetic authority, in a manner very different from the traditionalism of the scribes. The audience he teaches is specified : except for the teaching contained in the controversies, the parable of the Sower (4 : 1–9), and the saying of 7 : 14–16 on defilement, all Jesus' words are addressed to his immediate followers. He instructs the people only in the beginning, then turns to concentrate on the disciples. Exactly *what* he teaches is only revealed in the second half of the gospel : on his

passion and resurrection (8:31; 9:31), on divorce and in-
dissoluble marriage (10:1–12), on David's son (12:35), on
caution against the scribes and Pharisees (12:38). For the
rest, Jesus teaches only the 'secret of the Kingdom'—and
only in the veiled way of parables (4:10–12, 33f.).

## The Suffering Son of Man. Mark's Theologia Crucis
### 1 Who is Christ? (*Mark* 8:27–33)

Throughout the first half of the gospel (1:1–8:30)
the question of Jesus' identity is repeatedly raised and
meets with various answers. Some, the religious leaders,
reject the evidence of his works and of his teaching;
others are impressed and are prepared to acknowledge
him as a prophet or as an Elijah-like figure (6:14f.).
The chosen disciples react with fear and wonder, but fail
to understand him. Only the evil spirits acknowledge Jesus
for what he is. But after this we come to the point where
the disciples do, at last, proclaim him as Messiah. The
passage is the hinge of Mark's work, at once the climax of
the first part, the secret of the Messiah (the identity of
Jesus) and the transition to the second part, the mystery of
the Son of Man (his destiny of death and resurrection).
The second half of the gospel (8:31–16:8) provides the
answer to the question raised in the first half: 'Who is
Jesus?' But this answer is not understood by the disciples
who cannot grasp his suffering messiahship. We may look
to that central passage (8:27–33) to find the purpose of
Mark's gospel.

It is noteworthy that, in the first half of the gospel, the
disciples, despite their privileged position, have shown
themselves to be less perceptive than the 'crowds'. The
Caesarea Philippi episode marks a turning-point. This is
not to say that there is an improvement: Peter may acknowledge Jesus as Messiah (8:29), but he immediately
shows that he cannot accept the idea of a suffering Messiah

(8 : 32). The change is one from imperceptivity to misconception. Before, the disciples had failed to recognise Jesus as Messiah; now, they misunderstand the nature of his messiahship. We must appreciate the importance of the Caesarea Philippi episode in Mark's theology.

It is evident that 8 : 29 stands out in high relief.

And he asked them, 'But who do you say that I am?' Peter answered him, 'You are the Christ'.

Here Jesus is formally acknowledged as the Messiah of Jewish expectation, and as the Christ of christian worship —for this narrative is concerned with Christology. In the evangelist's eyes, the unique significance of Peter's confession rests upon the fact that here, for the *first* time, the disciples speak with Jesus about what he is in their estimation. Jesus takes the initiative and asks the disciples about the opinions of 'men'—'those outside' (4 : 11)—and learns that they would regard him not as messianic figure but, at most, as a forerunner of the Messiah. It is very clear that not only was his teaching full of riddles for them but that they had missed, too, the import of his works. Peter, however, has at last begun to see: '*You* are the Messiah.' The sequel will show that this is but the first stage of his enlightenment : it is the risen Lord who will open his eyes fully. Again, the disciples are bidden to keep silence but now, for the first time, the prohibition is related to Jesus' own person. Mark, indeed, looks beyond Peter and the disciples to the christian community that was his concern and bids his Christians take care that they really understand who their Christ is.

The central importance of Peter's confession in Mark's editorial structure is indicated by the brusque change of tone and of orientation after Peter has acknowledged the Messiahship of Jesus. In the actual structure of the gospel the prediction of the passion (8 : 31–32a) is Jesus' response to the confession of Peter, and the evangelist sees an intimate link between this first prediction and Peter's confession. The following section of the gospel (8:31–11:10) is dominated by the prophecies of the passion (8:31; 9:12; 9:31; 10:33f.); and the violent protestation of Peter in 8:32 ('And Peter took him, and began to rebuke him') shows clearly that this is a new and unexpected teaching. 'And he said this plainly' (8:32a)—it is indeed a turning-point in the self-revelation of Jesus: until now he has said nothing explicitly about his messiahship. If he still charges his disciples not to reveal his messianic identity ('And he charged them to tell no one about him', v. 30)—because their understanding of him is still so imperfect—he now speaks to them quite plainly of his destiny of suffering and death.

'And Peter took him, and began to rebuke him' (v. 32b). The idea of a suffering Messiah was entirely foreign to Peter; despite his confession he had not grasped the essential meaning of discipleship. In his surprise and his upset at the unexpected prospect he dares to 'rebuke' Jesus—something that no other disciple had ever done. In his turn Jesus rebuked Peter: 'Get behind me, Satan!' (*hypage opisō mou, Satana*)—the words recall Matthew 4:10, 'Begone, Satan' (*hypage, Satana*). The temptation in the wilderness (*Matt.* 4: 1–11; *Luke* 4:1–13) aimed at getting Jesus himself to conform to the popularly accepted messianic role, to become a political messiah; it was an attempt to undermine his full acceptance of the will of God; here Peter plays Satan's role. Peter's acknowledgment of Jesus as Messiah had set him and the disciples apart from 'men' (v. 27), but now Peter is rebuked for thinking as men think. Peter, and all like him, who stand 'on the side of men', stand opposed to God's saving purpose and align themselves with Satan.

Thus, we find that the passage is concerned not primarily

with the historical situation of the ministry of Jesus, but with the historical situation of the Church for which Mark is writing. The reply to Jesus' first question refers to opinions available in the Palestinian situation of the ministry (v. 28); in the reply to the second question, the title 'Christ' has christian overtones, and the prediction of the passion is cast in the language of the early Church (vv. 29, 31). Peter's reaction and the sharp correction of it (vv. 32f.) have much to do with an understanding of Christology. Historically, Jesus and Peter engage in dialogue. At a deeper level, 'Jesus' is the Lord addressing his Church and 'Peter' represents fallible believers who confess correctly, but then interpret their confession incorrectly. Similarly, the 'multitude' (v. 34) is the people of God for whom the general teaching (8:34–9:1) is meant. Thus, a story about Jesus and his disciples has a further purpose in terms of the risen Lord and his Church.

Here, then, more obviously than elsewhere, Mark is writing for his community. Here, above all, he is concerned with Christology. The confession of Peter is the facile profession of too many of Mark's contemporaries: 'You are the Christ'. Everything depends on what they mean by that profession and its influence on their lives. They cannot have a risen Lord without a suffering Messiah; they cannot be disciples without walking his road of suffering. Mark's admonition here is quite like that of Paul: 'When we cry "Abba! Father!" it is the Spirit himself bearing witness with our spirit that we are children of God, and if children, then heirs, heirs of God and fellow workers with Christ, *provided we suffer with him* in order that we may be glorified with him' (*Rom.* 8:15–17).

2   The Way of the Son of Man (*Mark* 8:31–11:10).

This, the first unit of Part II of his gospel, is the unit in which Mark's *theologia crucis*, his central theological

59

preoccupation, is most evident. We can discern in it a precise pattern, signposted by four announcements of the fate of the Son of man (8:31–32a; 9:9, 12–13; 9:30–31; 10:32–34). The first illustrates the pattern. A passion prediction (8:31–32a) is followed by the theme of the incomprehension of the disciples (8:32b–33). Then, Jesus stresses the demands of discipleship—Mark makes the point that discipleship involves following the Crucified One, that it is an *imitatio Christi* (8:34–9:1). The passage closes with a scene depicting Jesus as Messiah, invested with messianic authority (9:3–8—the Transfiguration).

The passage on the demands of discipleship (8:34–9:1) asserts, unequivocally, that the disciples of this Son of man must necessarily walk in his path: 'If any man would come after me, let him deny himself and take up his cross and follow me' (v. 34). Only one who is willing to be called as a disciple and truly answers the call really understands Jesus. The loyal disciple cannot be preoccupied with his personal interests but will be faithful unto death in a sustained fidelity to Jesus. 'For whoever would save his life will lose it; and whoever loses his life for my sake and the gospel's will save it' (v. 35). The way of discipleship is not easy and one may well be tempted to shrink from what it entails. But to seek thus to evade the risk and save one's life is to suffer the loss of one's true self. Only one who is prepared and willing to risk all for Jesus and his gospel will attain to authentic selfhood. 'For what does it profit a man, to gain the whole world and forfeit his life? For what can a man give in return for his life' (36f.). If man's life is so much more precious than anything else in creation, if no man can put a price on it, how much more precious is the eternal life that is won by the faithful disciple?

'For whoever is ashamed of me and of my words in this adulterous and sinful generation, of him will the Son of

60

man be ashamed, when he comes in the glory of his Father with the holy angels' (38). A warning sounds for the one who will not follow, who draws back and is ashamed of the Way, who seeks to save his life. Christ, too, will be ashamed of such a one, will disown him, when he returns in glory at the end of time. 'And he said to them, "Truly, I say to you, there are some standing here who will not taste death before they see the kingdom of God come with power"' (9:1). And his return will not be long delayed—in this generation, God's reign will be manifest in power.

Mark undoubtedly looks beyond the ministry of Jesus. Like the author of the Book of Revelation, his concern is for a persecuted community of his own day. He reminds those Christians that as disciples of a rejected and crucified Messiah they should not be surprised that they, too, are called upon to suffer. The cross has turned the values of this world upside down—it is indeed 'scandal' and 'foolishness' (1 Cor. 1:23). They must be steadfast in face of persecution. They must not be ashamed of Jesus' way of humiliation and suffering and death, if they do not want the glorious Son of man to be ashamed of them at his coming. And they have his comforting assurance. 'Surely, I am coming soon' (Rev. 22:20).

3  The Messianic Secret

Throughout this gospel, Jesus is at pains to hide his messiahship. The devils know him and cry out: 'You are the Son of God'—and he commands them to be silent (Mark 1:25, 34; 3:11f.). Silence is enjoined after notable miracles. For instance, after he had raised the daughter of Jairus, he turned to those who were present 'and he strictly charged them that no one should know this' (5:43; cf. 1:44; 7:36; 8:26). Again, when at Caesarea Philippi Peter had recognised his messiahship, and later when Jesus was transfigured before Peter and James and John, he admonished them to tell nobody until he had risen from the dead (8 : 30; 9 : 9). From time to time he withdrew from the crowd on secret journeys (7 : 27; 9 : 30). He gave his disciples private instructions (e.g. 4 : 10f., 33f.).

Strictly speaking, the secrecy motif, at least in the direct form of the imposition of silence, is found only in the first part of the gospel. The related motif of the incomprehension of the disciples, on the other hand, spans both parts of the gospel and is integral to both sections. Thus the motifs, though related, are distinct. The disciples' lack of understanding prevails to the end and is even more prominent in the second part than in the first. The insistence on secrecy can lessen and disappear in the second part as it becomes clearer and clearer in what direction the path of Jesus lies.

The *identity* of Jesus and the *nature* of his messiahship —these are the themes of the first and second part of the gospel respectively, and they are the stuff of the messianic secret. 'Those outside' (4 : 11), 'they' (4 : 33f.), 'men' (8 : 27) are those who are hard-hearted and who will not understand or accept the person of Jesus, his messiahship : they represent Israel who rejected his message and himself. They do not grasp the inner meaning of his parables—God has not revealed it to them because they are not receptive. Compare Romans 9–11. 'Israel failed to obtain what it sought. The elect obtained it, but the rest were hardened' (*Rom.* 11 : 7). In regard to his miracles they did not 'see signs' (cf. *John* 6 : 26) : they did not perceive the true significance of his works. The imposition of silence after the miracles makes that point : the bystanders have not understood, therefore they are to keep silent (cf. *Mark* 1 : 44; 5 : 43; 7 : 36; 8 : 26).

Twice (8 : 30 and 9 : 9) silence is enjoined on the disciples, but each time the situation is different. In the first case (8 : 30) they have perceived and acknowledged his

messiahship. In the other case (9:9) they are given the
limit of that silence: 'until the Son of man should have
risen from the dead'. However, the resurrection marks not
only the limit of the secret: it lies at the centre of their
failure to understand—'So they kept the matter to themselves, questioning what the rising from the dead meant'
(9:10). Until they had recognised Jesus as Messiah they
had nothing to reveal. But they are not yet ready to
preach him: they must learn what his suffering, death,
and resurrection mean before they can give a true picture
of him. The imposition of secrecy on the disciples is not
permanent. Indeed, it will be their duty to proclaim not
only the messianic identity of Jesus but also the nature of
his messiahship—but this will be beyond the cross and
resurrection. Half-way through the gospel they discover
the answer to the question, 'Who is Jesus?' (8:29). And
the gospel closes with the message that will open their eyes
to the full reality of his person: 'Go, tell his disciples and
Peter that he is going before you into Galilee; there you
will see him as he told you, (16:7). And, all the while
Mark is writing out of a community and for a community.
The messianic secret is concerned with Christology. It is
another way of insisting that one cannot have Christianity
without the cross. 'Was it not *necessary* that the Christ
should suffer these things and enter into his glory?' (*Luke*
24:26).

### Son of God

*The Son of God.* In Matthew, Jesus is primarily the
Messiah who fulfils all the promises and hopes of Israel.
In Mark, this aspect is present: Jesus' healing activity is
a sign that he is the Messiah; Peter's confession suggests
that at a given moment Jesus' disciples did recognise him
as the Messiah; and Jesus himself testified to his messianic
identity before the Sanhedrin (14:62). However, Mark has

developed another aspect of Jesus' personhood which has more relevance to his Gentile readers: the dignity and personhood of Jesus is expressed in the name 'Son of God'. The actual title sprang not from Jesus, but from the community; however it is true to Jesus' evident consciousness of his unique relationship to the Father. The Marcan Son of God is a divine being who appears in human form, and if deity is concealed behind a fully human life, it is visible for those who have eyes to see in the personality, teaching and deeds of Jesus. Such is the character of the Marcan Christology, though the evangelist would not have expressed it with such precision.

The title 'Son of God' may occur seldom in the narrative, but where it does occur, it is at a crucial point: in the heading (1:1), in the mouth of evil spirits whose compulsive testimony is all the more weighty (3:11; 5:7), at Jesus' trial (14:61f.), and in the centurion's acclamation beneath the cross (15:39). The divine sonship is proclaimed by a 'voice from heaven' on two occasions (1:11; 9:7). However, the message that Jesus is the Son of God goes beyond the use of the title.

When Jesus claimed that he had the power to forgive sins (2:5) and that he was lord of the sabbath (2:28), when he commanded the sea (4:39–41) and raised the dead (5:41–42), the Jews would have seen such claims as tantamount to divine prerogatives. For an audience unfamiliar with Jewish thought, Mark underlines the commanding air in Jesus' very bearing, thus filling out what is implied in the title 'Son of God'. His teaching has incontestable authority: 'What is this? A new teaching with authority behind it! He commands even the unclean spirits, and they obey him!' (1:27). He seems to control evil spirits effortlessly, as in the story of the Gerasene demoniac (5:1-20). His preparations for the Last Supper indicate his calm foreknowledge and his ability to direct events (14:13–15). His walking on the sea demonstrates his majestic power over the elements (6:45–52).

Jesus' power of command, in Mark, is seen especially in the idea of a 'conflict of spirits'. This is a powerful notion because his contemporaries were familiar with the idea that evil spirits were an ever-present menace and a cause of illness and disruption. The conflict becomes clear even in the introductory passage where Jesus, first anointed by God's Spirit at his baptism, is then led by the same Spirit to wrestle with Satan (1:9–13). The whole of Jesus' ministry is anticipated in this struggle between the Spirit-anointed Messiah and Satan; they are truly locked in a life-death combat. The issue cannot be in doubt: the Son of God emerged victorious from this trial of strength (1:13), and from the final desperate assault (15:39; 16:6).

*The Healing Son of God.* It is unanimous New Testament evidence that Jesus did work miracles and, especially, healed many sick. Mark has a particular insistence on Jesus' miracles. However, he never recounts them for their own sake but rather to show that they are in the service of Jesus' preaching. Nor does Mark attribute every sickness to the influence of Satan, for he seems to distinguish between sickness and possession. The opposition contained in the theme of 'conflict of spirits' becomes strikingly visible in the exorcism stories, where the violence of evil spirits is quelled by Jesus' rebuke. Mark's expulsion accounts are the most extensive miracles in his gospel. They are symbols of divine power; but they are also signs that the Kingdom which is present in Jesus himself triumphs over the rule of Satan. The exorcisms are a central part of Jesus' combat against Satan and confirm that Jesus' own Kingdom has indeed arrived. The Marcan stories make use of contemporary idiom regarding exorcisms and the possession of demons in sickness. It is all the more note-worthy then that Jesus uses none of the contemporary exorcists' spells and rituals. It is simply the power of the Son, rather than any incantation, which expels them.

Whereas the healing of the sick and the expulsion of demons confirm the message of Jesus, his miracles over nature reveal his divine glory. The disciples alone, not the people at large, were witnesses of the stilling of the storm and the walking on the waters. These events were meant to open their eyes to the fact that this Friend and Master in their midst was no less than the Lord all-powerful over nature. In contrast with accounts of hellenistic miracles, Mark records no ritual formulas or magic in Jesus' won-ders, but only his word—which is usually a brief command (1:25; 2:11; 3:5; 5:8, 41; 11:14, etc.). Especially in the nature miracles, certain details must have appeared in the course of the development of the traditions. Their very style shows that they are not to be analysed with a view towards learning exactly 'what happened', but rather to be taken as affirmations of faith. We must always keep in mind the deeper significance of these stories : Jesus himself initiates the struggle against evil in order to emerge vic-torious. Significant, too, is the atmosphere of peace and the awareness of God's presence which seems to surround the miracles. 'Peace, be still!' Jesus said to the winds and the sea, 'and the wind ceased, and there was a great calm' (4:39). The man who had been possessed by a legion of devils was found sitting peacefully 'clothed in his right mind' (5:15). When the paralytic took up his pallet and began to walk, all were amazed and glorified God (2:12) —'We never saw anything like this!' When Jesus heals the daughter of Jairus, or Peter's mother-in-law, or the possessed boy, each time Mark refers to his 'raising up' of the afflicted person—a suggestion of Jesus' own resur-rection.

So we come to see where Mark has been leading us in stressing the humanity of Jesus at the same time as he shows us his powerful deity: his message is to show that the risen Lord of glory is one and the same as Jesus of Nazareth. The Jesus who submitted to suffering is one and the same as the triumphant Messiah. The entire gospel of suffering is set within a frame of glory. It begins with the ushering in of the messianic age as the Holy Spirit descends upon and anoints Jesus (*Mark* 1:10; cf. *Acts* 10:38), and it ends (in the later ending) with his own ascent to the right hand of God (16:19).[4] The suffering within this frame is the passageway to glory. The first announcement of the passion is followed by the transfiguration (8:31–9:8), and the farewell—the 'eschatalogical'—discourse on the eve of the passion is a prevision of the triumph which lies beyond death (ch. 13). The passion narrative ends with the rending of the temple veil (15:38) a symbol of the ending of the time of Judaism and a beginning of God's manifestation to the Gentiles through his Son. The death which was the climax of his suffering and of his Secret was also the full revelation of the Son of God.

## II. MATTHEW

Matthew's gospel has been called the 'gospel of the Church' and, indeed, no other gospel so reveals how an evangelist has written in and for his Community. We must see Jesus' preaching and works in the setting of the later community. And if this would seem to detract from valid historical and future perspectives, one must try to grasp the *intention* of the author, his efforts to bring to bear a deeper, newer prospect on the traditions concerning Jesus.

**Matthew's Milieu**

Matthew has a special interest in the role and fate of Israel in history. But, he also feels that there is a single

67

people of God in *both* Testaments which amounts to the true Israel. God exercises his Lordship in an uninterrupted saving pattern in the two covenants. One should speak, then, not of an old/new Israel but of a false/true people. Matthew exposes one aspect of this in describing Israel under judgment. This is notably evident in the parable of the Wicked Tenants (21:33–43) with its warning that the Kingdom will be given to another people of God, a new messianic community in place of the unbelieving Jews. Matthew's narrative of the passion accentuates the collective responsibility of the Jerusalem Jews in rejecting Jesus. The responsibility for Jesus' death rests wholly with the people of the Old Covenant; this reaches a climax when they accept responsibility in 27:25. There is a graphic paradox: the Jews demand Jesus' death, while the Gentiles affirm his innocence. The Jews are no longer *ho laos theou* (the people of God) but *Ioudaioi*, merely a race. They are contrasted with the Roman soldiers who confess that Jesus is the Son of God (27:54). The Messiah of Israel thus becomes the Messiah of the pagans. For Matthew, the gift of the Kingdom lies in recognising Jesus as Messiah. The response given him decides true membership in the Community.

Connected with the question of Matthew's milieu are the two apparently contrasting viewpoints on the scope of Jesus' mission. Two texts proper to Matthew limit the mission to Israel (10:5f.; 15:24), whereas 28:19 is clearly the great missionary command with all nations as its goal. This discrepancy has been variously explained. It could reflect the early christian tradition that the entry of the nations would not result from a mission *to* them, but of *their* coming to Zion as pilgrims. Or, Matthew 28:19f. would be a development of 10:5, the commission to the disciples, in the light of the death and resurrection of Jesus. Jesus himself will now go to the nations in the

68

person of his messengers and bring them the Kingdom. Thus, the universal mission becomes part of the Parousia which was initiated by his death and resurrection. Jesus confined his lifetime commission to the Israelite community, knowing that *God's* act of power would bring the Gentiles into the Kingdom. When he gives the command to 'make disciples of all nations' in 28 : 19, this implies that *God* no longer limits his saving grace to Israel but turns his mercy to the whole Gentile world.

## A Portrait of Matthew's Jesus

Because Jesus is the Lord of the Kingdom, Matthew gives a 'hieratic' picture of him rather than a markedly human one. He is the Jesus whose divine power ever shines through—as if the evangelist has always in the back of his mind the great picture of the final Judge. He sees Jesus as the *Kyrios* living in his Church, as the Son of Man of the End-time to come in glory with his angels. The disciples in Matthew do not call Jesus *didaskalos* ('teacher'), but *Kyrios*—understood as a divine title whose use is legitimised from Scripture. It is the distinction between those who acknowledge him in earthly life and those who refuse to follow him, and thus call him merely 'rabbi'. For the Community recognises the active Lord in their midst *within* the figure of the earthly Jesus. The one presented to them in the final scene as the all-powerful Lord is inextricably linked with the image of the Man of Nazareth. Just as Matthew sees more vividly than the other synoptists the presence of the Community behind the disciples, so too does he see the presence of the living Lord of the Community behind the earthly Jesus. Everything which the Lord does in his Church has its origin in his earthly life.

Even in the infancy gospel there is an interest in community : from the beginning Jesus Messiah is the representative of God's people and, in his life, reflects the history of Israel. Matthew's genealogy (1 : 1–7) does not seek to *prove* the Davidic descent of Jesus; it has, rather the theological intent of situating him within the divine plan of salvation : he emerges as the heir and as the fulfilment of God's purpose. The passage 1 : 18–24 answers the question raised by v. 16 of the genealogy ('Joseph, the husband of Mary, of whom Jesus was born, who is called Christ'). It makes two points : that Jesus was virginally conceived by the action of the Holy Spirit, and that Joseph, divinely enlightened, became the legal father of the child; in this way Jesus is truly 'son of David'. Having thus presented the Messiah Jesus in the light of his virginal and Davidic birth, Matthew goes on to depict his mission in an aura of light and of suffering. In anecdotical form he conveys what Luke has done through the mouth of Simeon (*Luke* 2 : 34f.) : the call of the pagans to salvation (the Magi), crisis and rejection in Isreal (massacre of the Innocents, flight into Egypt, obscurity in Nazareth). All these episodes are centred in biblical texts which bring out their theological significance.

In the Magi from the East, guided by the star (*Num.* 24 : 17) and adoring Jesus in Bethlehem (*Mic.* 5 : 1), Matthew sees the pagan world attracted by the light of the Messiah and coming to pay homage in the city of David. The homage is described with the help of the scriptural theme of the kings of Arabia bringing their presents to the King Messiah (*Is.* 60 : 1–6; *Ps.* 72 : 10f., 15). In the Flight into Egypt, Matthew's interest bears on the return involved; he quotes Hosea 11 : 1—'Out of Egypt have I called my son'. Thus he sees in the episode a parallel to the Exodus which makes the infancy of Jesus a symbolic accomplishment of the destiny of Israel. Jesus is the Son *par excellence*, truly meriting the title 'son' already given to Israel. In calling him from the land of exile, God calls together with him the messianic people of which he is the inclusive representative (*Matt.* 1:1–17). His return is the divine guarantee of the deliverance many times promised.

The citation of Jeremiah 31:15 enables Matthew to evoke, beyond the massacre of Bethlehem infants (*Matt.* 2:13–18), the Babylonian Exile; this great crisis in the history of Israel has its reflection in the destiny of the child Jesus. The comparison of Jesus with Moses, frequent in the New Testament, is evident in Matthew 2:19–23 for v. 20 echoes Exodus 4:19—like Moses, Jesus can return after the death of those who have sought his life. Here again Matthew's chief interest is in the prophetic oracle (2:23). In *Nazōraios* ('He shall be called a Nazarene') he probably sees an echo of the Hebrew participle *nasur* ('preserved') as an allusion to the Servant of the Lord (*Is.* 42:6) and to the messianic Remnant (*Is.* 49:6—'the preserved of Israel'). Jesus, for Matthew, is thus the anti-type of the Remnant come back from the Exile in humble circumstances, but yet preserved by God as the hope of messianic salvation.[5]

In his infancy gospel Matthew has shown that the son born to Mary is indeed the Son of David but he has shown, too, that beyond this, he is the Son of God. For this Son of Mary, conceived by the Holy Spirit (1:18–20), is to save his people from their sins (1:21) and is named by God himself (in Scripture) 'God-with-us' (1:22f.). And God declares: 'Out of Egypt have I called *my Son*' (2:15). It is the same Son of whom he had said: he will shepherd 'my people' Israel. A christological truth stands forth: Jesus, the Messiah, is the Son of God, the eschatological Shepherd who will save God's people from their sins.

In the body of the gospel Matthew is silent about anything that would suggest an emotion or weakness or ignorance in Jesus (compare *Matt.* 13:58 with *Mark* 6:5; *Matt.* 14:17 with *Mark* 6:38), whereas he accents the power and sovereignty of Jesus (cf. 4:23; 8:24; 15:30).

He accentuates the magnitude of the miracles, and what separates Jesus from the people (e.g. 8 : 18–27). He raises Jesus above emotions of anger or tenderness, stresses his supernatural knowledge and control of destiny. The boisterous and throbbing crowd scenes of Mark give way to moments when the onlookers fade into the background, leaving individual suppliants face to face with the majesty of Jesus. As the most Jewish of the synoptists, Matthew shows Jesus as fulfilling Old Testament figures. In the infancy narrative, he is already shown as the new Abraham, Moses, and Israel. The Temptation, the Sermon on the Mount, the Feeding of the Multitude also point to a new Moses. Most of all, Jesus is called 'son of David' because he fulfils the promise of a deliverer to sit forever on the throne of David, although it is made clear that the Jewish expectations of the son of David were inadequate (22 : 42–45; 26 : 64).

Yet, at the same time, this Jesus is the King of lowliness, as Matthew shows by quoting Zechariah with its reference to the 'lowly king'. The adjective *praüs*, 'humble', describes the messianic *basileus* (king). Matthew alone reports Jesus' word to the heavy-laden (11 : 28–30). Here we see his gentle approachability as he appeals to the burdened, for it is also an exhortation to the Community to follow the will of God in their suffering. When he says, 'Learn of me . . .', Jesus is referring not only to his doctrine, but to his Person and to the cross he embraced. He not only teaches the will of God, but follows it himself in humility and obedience. His very first spoken word in Matthew indicates this when he answers John the Baptist that it is 'fitting' that he submit to baptism in order to accomplish justice—i.e. God's will (3 : 15). The passion narrative itself underlines particularly that Jesus' career is a work of obedience freely consented to. He accepts his passion voluntarily and introduces it, mindful that he is accomplishing Scripture. No wonder that his sympathy is with the poor and oppressed (8:17; 9:10–13; 11:1–6) and that his Kingdom is open to 'such as these' (5:4–12; 18:1–5).

All comes down to an answer to the question: 'Who is this man?' In 12:22–42 Jesus is not only son of David but also son of God. This appears right from the beginning in the genealogy, the reflection-citations,[6] and the baptism scene. By the title, 'Son of God', the community expresses its faith in him. For Matthew, divine sonship is the most profound of the mysteries of Jesus' person. Peter's acknowledgment of the Messiah (16:13–20; cf. *Mark* 8:27–30) has been transformed by Matthew into a profession of christian faith. Jesus does not correct Peter, but tells him he has spoken a revelation from the Father. In Matthew's account, the juxtaposition of titles of honour (Son of man; Son of the living God, vv. 13, 16) is not repetition, but is intended to interpret the mission of Jesus as the Son of God by a confession of the absolute faith of the community, which can *develop*. Throughout the gospel he employs abundant titles of messianic significance. His 'reflection citations' contribute to his picture of Jesus as one who fulfils the former covenant's promise of the Saviour; Jesus' person and career are an accomplishment of what the prophets announced.

Interesting is Matthew's use of the Isaian Servant prophecies. He introduces Isaiah 53:4, 'He has taken upon himself our infirmities', after the miracle cycle. Matthew (even changing the text of Isaiah) shows that, for him, it is not a matter of the Servant of God suffering in expiation of man's sins. Rather, Jesus is the obedient servant who executes the good will and mercy of God in relieving the sickness and infirmity of men (8:16f.). Likewise, in quoting Isaiah 42:1–4 (*Matt.* 12:18–21), he is referring to Jesus' quiet humility in refusing to allow his miracles to be published abroad. Thus, Matthew's citations of Isaiah play no special part in his theology but are simply in the context of Jesus' healing activity and his lowliness in caring for the disabled. The Emmanuel prophecy, at the start of the gospel (1 : 23) is realised through the guiding help of the Risen One, and through his presence amidst those who are gathered together in his name (18 : 20). And all the traditions which Matthew takes up relative to Jesus flow from his having experienced the living Lord at work in his Community.

## The Community or Church in Matthew

Because this book is concerned not alone with Christ but also with christian living, it is fitting, when touching on this ecclesial gospel, to say a word about Matthew's understanding of the Church. In fact, it becomes exceedingly difficult to distinguish between the disciples and the Community (or Church) because in Matthew's eyes they blend into one. This is evident in the instructions given to the disciples in Matthew 18 which really form a *Gemeindeordnung*, a 'Community Rule'. Moreover, it is here that Matthew also brings together his significant ideas on the Church: true greatness in the Kingdom (vv. 1–4), scandal (5–10), the Lost Sheep (12–14), brotherly care and correction, authority in the Church (15–18), association in prayer (19f.), and forgiving offences (21–35). For Matthew, the Church is a sociological reality centred on God with Jesus as its model. It is a family of children of the Father. Jesus is present in the *midst* of his Church—an idea framed by the Immanu-el promise of 1 : 23 and the promise to be 'with us always' in 18 : 20. We find he is *with* his followers, *present* in his missionaries (10 : 40), in all in need (25 : 35–45), in all received in his name (18 : 5), and in the assembly (18 : 20). When the disciples are persecuted, it is because they represent Jesus and imitate also his sufferings. Matthew

74

too seems to see the community as a ship beaten by the waves, as he shows in the story of the stilling of the storm (8 : 23–27; cf. *Mark* 4 : 35–41). In Matthew, this episode becomes a paradigm of discipleship for, even more than in Mark, his boat becomes a *navis ecclesiae* and the cry *Kyrie sōson* ('Save, Lord') is at once a prayer and a confession of discipleship. 'Those of little faith', the *oligoi pistoi,* are those in the boat of the Church. Matthew knows that, like the disciples in the gospel, his community has but 'little faith'; he himself had experienced the 'false prophets' of 24 : 11f. The men who 'marvel' are those who learn of the good news in the preaching. But they do not know quite as Matthew does the lack of love and faith which menaces the interior of the Community in the apostolic Church.

The Church is not a secluded cenacle of the elect who are self-assured of salvation. It is a mixed body, comprised of men and women who are fully human, who will have to face a separation between good and evil at the last judgment. It is the completion of the disciple-group which Jesus formed around him during his ministry, to continue his mission with an ideal and a dedication identical with his own. This is why he gave authority in his own person to the closest of his disciples : he wanted them to preach and direct in his stead. The word *ekklēsia* occurs in the gospels only in Matthew 16 : 18 and 18 : 17, though it is frequent in the rest of the New Testament. (It has been pointed out that those who would argue that Jesus did not speak of a 'church' still must explain the wide use of the term by the early Christians.) Matthew uses the term *ekklēsia* to designate the messianic community as distinct from the Old Testament community. This is the force of Jesus' saying to Peter, '. . . *my* Church', in 16 : 18. For Matthew, only one standard settles membership in this messianic community : to have brought forth fruits of the Kingdom

(21:43), to have done the will of God (5:16; 7:21), to have attained to the higher righteousness (5:20) and shaped one's life-course to enter the Kingdom by the narrow gate (7:13). 'Let your light so shine before men that they may see your good works and glorify your heavenly Father' (*Matt.* 5:16).

Matthew's Church is seen in the perspective of the coming judgment, and the task of discipleship is interpreted accordingly. The seven Kingdom-of-God parables (ch. 13) combine both ecclesial and eschatological motifs. Jesus rules over the Church, and from the Church over the world, thus realising the Kingship of God in the present period of salvation. The Church is the link between accomplishment here and now and final consummation. The members of the Community are the personal members of the Church who have submitted to God's rule in Jesus. They keep it warm and alive as *persons*, rather than as an institution. In short, the Church is a preliminary stage and school preparing for and already representing the future *basileia* or Kingdom.

## The Great Commission, Matthew 28 : 18–20

This text, the final word in the gospel, has been seen to recapitulate the whole of Matthew, besides being one of the most comforting assurances which the Christian could hear that the risen Jesus lives on among us. Looking first at the literary value of the passage, one notes that it is connected with Daniel 7:14 and the image of the Son of man there. It is not a direct quotation of Daniel, but rather presents a similar combination of authority, dominion and recognition by the nations. The form is like a *Gottesrede*, a 'divine discourse', just like Yahweh's exhortations to observe the commandments in Deuteronomy. The sayings could have arisen as independent sayings or confessions of faith (cf. *Eph.* 5:14; *Phil.* 2: 6–11). Although Jesus speaks as the *Kyrios* here, the kernel of his message is not his own person but the missionary command. He uses the language of Matthew and of the Lord living in Matthew's community. There are also the Matthaean concepts of Jesus' sovereignty, the universal destination of the gospel, the prominent role of the disciples. The sayings have not been spoken by Jesus on earth, but have been constructed by the apostolic Church, and are redolent of that Church's faith in the risen and living Lord. They are, however (like the Johannine discourses) authentic expressions of his mind, framed by men confident of being moved by the Spirit of Jesus.

Jesus' saying that 'all power has been given to me' is directly influenced by Daniel 7:14, where we read that power was given to the Son of man. But in Daniel it is a matter of earthly power over humans, whereas in Matthew it is divine power in heaven and on earth. 'Power' (*exousia*) in the New Testament includes divine commission, authorisation, and strength from above. It is inseparable from the proclamation that the Kingdom is near. 'Go, therefore, and make disciples of all nations'—*panta to ethnē* implies, as we have seen, that God no longer limits his saving grace to Israel but turns his mercy to the Gentiles. Here (vv. 19–20a) we have Jesus' 'order of mission', whereas in the preceding verse (18) we had the word of 'revelation'. *Mathēteuein* normally has the meaning 'to be a disciple'; here, it takes on the meaning, 'to make disciples'. It suggests here finding membership in a community rather than any vague religious assent. Salvation will come to the peoples through their union in Jesus. While in Daniel the nations are ordained to serve the Son of man, here they will be invited to become disciples of Jesus. It is not a process of subjection, but of being drawn to Jesus through persuasion and grace. 'Teaching them all that I have commanded you': the baptised, the one taught or the 'disciple', is he who observes Jesus' commands. 'All' his commands consists of the true life of God's people, as in Deuteronomy. God, through Jesus, is the true lawgiver.

Finally, we have Jesus' great promise of v. 20b: 'Lo, I am with you always, to the close of the age (the end of time)'. Here, in his very last words, Matthew opens out into the perspective of the Community, and the one who has spoken all the words of the gospel preceding this verse remains present to the community. They are not really left alone (cf. *John* 14:18). Matthew does not speak of a 'departure' or of a 'farewell' of Jesus. Rather, he places the Community at the heart of the universal power of the resurrection. The 'end of time' which he has in mind designates the time of the Community (cf. 13:39f.; 24:3). It corresponds to the 'hereafter' of 26:64, where Jesus tells Caiaphas, 'hereafter you will see the Son of man seated at the right hand of Power . . .' Jesus is promising his help as God himself, echoing all his assurances throughout the gospels: 'Fear not!'; 'I am with you!', 'It is *I*!'. Whereas Luke closes with a farewell blessing and the ascension (*Luke* 24:51), here in Matthew Jesus assures us that he will be abidingly present in the congregation. Moreover, what is promised is not his static presence in one chosen group, but his dynamic and helping presence for a world-wide mission. It is the mission of salvation: the name of *Immanu-el*, 'God-with-us', is perfectly realised in the name and work of *Jesus*, 'God saves'.

Thus Matthew 28:18–20 both assigns to Jesus the functions of Yahweh in the Old Testament and sums up Matthew's view of the *Kyrios* in the New. He has universal lordship, he gives commands that determine the whole life of God's people and their relationship to him, and he promises to be the sustaining Lord at all times. Will he not keep his word? 'Where two or three are gathered in my name, there am I in the midst of them' (*Matt.* 18:20).

How faithfully he has kept his word! For we have all experienced it in our deepest hearts: the kingdom of God is truly in our midst (cf. *Luke* 17:21).

## III. LUKE

Like Matthew, Luke was a second-generation Christian, writing after the fall of Jerusalem (A.D. 70). His Jesus, too, is of course, Jesus of Nazareth, but also, at the same time, he is the risen Lord, the Saviour. As a Gentile convert, Luke is not exercised, as was Matthew, by the relationship of Christianity to Judaism; for him, the break with Judaism is an accomplished fact. He does not look for an imminent return of the Lord (nor does Matthew for that matter); his two-volume work (gospel and Acts) is written for Christians who live in the post-apostolic age. Indeed, the Parousia is, in a true sense, a present reality, present in the risen Lord. Christ, the source of salvation, is in the christian community. The present moment is the time of fulfilment. This explains the frequency of the adverbs *nun* ('now') and *sēmeron* ('today') in the gospel (and Acts)— e.g. 2:11; 3:22; 6:21–25; 9:33; 12:52; 19:5, 9; 23:43. The 'today', the 'now' of Christ's presence is the time of salvation. And now life is poured out in the Holy Spirit.

Luke is the theologian of salvation history. For him, that history falls into two periods: the period of Israel; the period of Christ and of his Church.[7] The first, the time of the Old Testament, is the time of preparation for the culminating event of Christ's coming: 'The law and the prophets were until John; since then the good news of the kingdom of God is preached' (16:16). The second period begins with Jesus and is supremely the whole time when he, as exalted Lord, is present in the Church. This is the perspective of Luke's great work. After his account of the infancies of John and of Jesus, he turns to the preaching of the kingdom of God in Palestine, first by the precursor and then by the Messiah; and at the close of the work he has Paul proclaiming the same kingdom at the centre of the Roman world (*Acts* 28 : 30f.). The gospel tells of the mission of Jesus and of the saving event of his death and resurrection; it ends with his glorification in the ascension. Jesus had come as the Messiah of his people and had found himself rejected by them. But his mission had not failed: he had brought salvation to a new Israel—repentance and forgiveness of sins must be preached in his name to all nations, beginning from Jerusalem (24 :47).

## Universalism

Luke may be called the evangelist for all men, writing in a way that all men can understand. He knows that the risen Lord, so present to him and to his community, yearns to be present in every community of men. The note of universalism sustained throughout the gospel is first sounded in the infancy narrative. The angels heralding the birth of Jesus call for peace on earth 'among men with whom (God) is pleased' (2 :14); this peace comes in the person of God's own Son, 'a light for revelation to the Gentiles' (2 :32; cf. *Is.* 42 :6; 49 :6). Isaiah is also quoted in the words of the Baptist: 'All flesh shall see the salvation of God' (3 :6), and it is in support of this view that Luke extends his genealogy of Jesus back to Adam, parent of all flesh (3 :23).

To Jesus—and to the Christian who would follow him—no one is a 'foreigner'; no one is despised by him, and nothing is too mean for his all-embracing love. The last commission of Jesus is that 'repentance and forgiveness of sins should be preached to *all* nations, beginning from Jerusalem' (24 :47), a commission which Luke has shown in Acts as being already fulfilled, with the message offered to the Jews too, for it is *universal*, and which he himself is helping to fulfil even in writing his gospel. It 'seemed good' to Luke (1:3) to bring home his message of universalism most closely by including in his gospel, as none of the other evangelists do, the parable of the Good Samaritan (10:30–37). Surely Jesus felt that only through this poignant, vivid story, drawn from the everyday world of his people, could he convey to them the truth that all barriers, all distinctions of persons, fall before the absolute demands of *love*. By writing his gospel for all men—out of the love in his own heart—Luke had indeed learned well this vital word of his Lord, a word bringing newness of life and peace.

### Christ the Lord

Unlike the other synoptists, Luke regularly calls Jesus *ho kyrios* ('the Lord')—it is a deliberate use of a christian title. His infancy gospel, whose purpose is emphatically theological, justifies the use of the title. These two chapters are dominated by the idea of messianic fulfilment. The different scenes build up to the climax of the entry into the Temple, for Luke saw in that event the formal manifestation of Jesus the Messiah. At an early stage we learn that the child of Mary will not only be the Davidic Messiah of Old Testament expectation (1:32–34); for the power of the Holy Spirit will make of him Son of God in a new and unexpected sense (1:35). In the Visitation episode, Elizabeth greeted Mary as the mother of her *Lord* (1:45). The angel's message to the shepherds is an announcement of good news and joy to all the people of Israel: 'This day' (2:11)—the long awaited day of Israel's salvation—has dawned; a newborn child is the Saviour (*sōtēr* is used of Jesus only here in the Synoptics, but Luke employs it again in Acts 5:31; 13:23). This Saviour is 'Christ the Lord'—the title *Christos Kyrios* occurs once only in the Septuagint (*Lam.* 4:20) and nowhere else in the New Testament: he is the Messiah endowed with lordship and dominion (cf. *Is.* 9:5). But the splendour of the angelic manifestation at his birth was not reflected in his person: he was an infant, lying helpless in a manger, a babe who must be circumcised on the eighth day (2:21). It was the father's right to name his child and in this case, too, the heavenly Father had bestowed the name, indicated beforehand by the angel (1:31). The name of Jesus ('Yahweh saves') suited perfectly the character of that Saviour announced to the shepherds, him who was Christ the Lord.

It is nowhere laid down in the Law that the firstborn should be taken to the Temple and presented there, yet the fact that Jesus was so presented (2:22–40) is obviously of great importance for Luke. We should realise that *eplēs-thēsan*, 'accomplished' (v. 22; cf. 1:23, 57; 2:6, 21), has more than the banal significance of the completion of a specified period and, in the context of the infancy gospel, suggests the end of the time of waiting and the arrival of the messianic age. In v. 23—'Every male that opens the womb shall be called holy to the Lord'—*hagion*, 'holy', is unexpected. The verse is a rather free citation of Exodus 13:2, 12 but the word 'holy', which does not occur in the Exodus text, has come from Luke, who has inserted it also in 1:35b—'therefore the child to be born will be called holy'. Its presence in the latter case is due to the influence of Daniel 9:24—the consecration of a 'Holy One' which wil mark the inauguration of the messianic age—while its occurrence in 2:23 establishes a link between Daniel 9 and another messianic text, Malachi 3, for this last text stands behind Luke's description of the Presentation. Since in 1:16f. and in the *Benedictus* he presents the Baptist as the messenger, the Elijah, who will prepare the way of Yahweh (*Mal.* 3:1, 23), it must follow that the 'Holy One' who is presented in the Temple is none other than the *Lord*: 'Behold, I send my messenger to prepare the way before me, and the Lord whom you seek will suddenly come to his Temple' (*Mal.* 3:1).

Simeon, the righteous and devout, finds his cup of joy filled to overflowing because he has gazed upon the 'salvation of God', the Messiah whom God had sent to save his people. And not his own people only: salvation is destined for the Gentiles too (2:29–32). Yet, though this infant has come as the Saviour of his people, he will be rejected by many of them, for he will stand as a sign of contradiction, a stone that can be a stumbling block (*Is.* 8:14f.) or cornerstone (*Is.* 28:16) according as men turn their backs on him or accept him (*Luke* 2:34f.). In his presence there can be no neutrality, for he is the light that men cannot ignore (cf. *John* 9:39; 12:44, 50), the light that reveals their inmost thoughts and forces them to take part for him or against him.

The incident of the boy Jesus lost and found in the Temple (2:41–50) is related in the form of a pronouncement story, finding its climax in the question of Jesus (v. 49). His query, the first and only words of his recorded in these chapters, might be paraphrased: 'Where would you expect a child to be but in his father's house?' This episode may be regarded as a prolongation of the Presentation: the child who has been presented is now, as Son of God, at home in the Temple.

It emerges that, throughout these chapters, Luke has wished to present Jesus as a transcendent, divine Messiah. The titles given to him (Great, Holy, King, Light, Glory, Son of God, Saviour, Christ the Lord, Lord), when taken together, point in that direction. In short, we might say that the assimilation of Jesus to Yahweh is the final word of the Christology of Luke's infancy gospel.

**The Saviour**

If Luke's message is concerned with the gifts which

the Lord's coming meant for the world, its specific impact is to be found even more directly in the presentation of the Saviour himself amidst his own. For, in Luke's eyes, Jesus was simply Saviour of men. It is in this capacity that the evangelist, who had never met Jesus, had come most fully to perceive and to receive his Lord. He saw that the whole ministry of Jesus was marked by understanding, forgiveness, and merciful compassion, all flowing from the exquisite sensitivity of Jesus. As we have noted in the passage which Jesus cited at the beginning of his ministry (*Is.* 61 : 1f.; *Luke* 4 : 18f.), the works proclaimed there are the works of a Saviour, the very deeds which he himself will perform : preaching good news to the poor, proclaiming release to captives, restoring sight to the blind, freeing the oppressed. Although the title 'Saviour' is used only once in his gospel (in the annunciation to the shepherds, 2 : 11), yet, throughout, Luke portrays the poor, the captive, the blind, the oppressed—of many kinds, of all sorts and conditions of men and women—as being touched by the gentle, saving power of Jesus.

Perhaps nowhere more than in the wonderful passage on the 'woman of the city who was a sinner' (7 : 36–50) do we see Jesus as Luke saw him. The Lord does not hesitate between the self-righteous Pharisee and the repentant sinner and his words are clear and to the point : 'I tell you, her great love proves that her many sins have been forgiven' (7 : 47). Luke alone records the words of Jesus to the 'good thief' (23 : 43) and his prayer for his executioners : 'Father, forgive them, for they do not know what they do' (23 : 34). He alone tells of the look that moved Peter so deeply (22 : 61). Everywhere, at all times, there is forgiveness. It has been well said that the gospel of Luke is the gospel of great pardons.

But the sinner, the outcast, humble people, the distressed and the poor were asked simply for one thing :

to place all their trust in a loving Father who provides for them so much more than for the birds of the air and the lilies of the field (12 : 22–32). And this could be asked of them because they had been given One who had been hailed as Saviour at his birth and whose last message was of salvation, and of forgiveness in his name to all nations (24 : 46f.). Luke, who was deeply sensitive to sickness and wholeness, to disquiet and joyful peace, and to the most elementary human needs, Luke was perfectly attuned to this Saviour.

### Rich and Poor

There is great gentleness, but there is nothing soft or easy-going about this Jesus of Luke. Indeed, there is something almost shocking about his call for total renunciation, his invitation to give up all one has. This demand is prepared for by sharp warnings on the danger of riches; Luke is far more emphatic than the other evangelists on this score: 6 : 24–26; 12 : 13–21; 14 : 33; 16 : 9, 11, 19–31; 18 : 22. The parable of the Rich Fool (12 : 16–21) gives the moral: 'So is he who lays up treasure for himself, and is not rich towards God.' A choice must be made, for no man can serve God and mammon (16 : 13). On the positive side, there is the fact that Jesus lived among the poor. At his birth Luke tells of the shepherds who came to him (2 : 8), and not of the Magi of Matthew. His mother and Joseph gave the offering of the poor (2 : 24). In short, it is above all in the humble birth of the Son of God and the penury of his life that *voluntary* poverty is exalted: 'Foxes have holes and the birds of the air have nests; but the Son of man has nowhere to lay his head' (9 : 58). And the example was efficacious, for Simon and James and John—and so many others—left everything and followed him (5 : 11).

It is to be expected, then, that Luke should insist on renunciation. Confidence is not to be placed in riches

(12:13–21) but in God who will provide (12:22–32): 'Sell your possessions and give alms' (12:33). The followers of Jesus must renounce *all*: 'Whoever of you does not renounce all that he has cannot be my disciple' (14:33), and the ruler who comes to him is bidden: 'Sell all that you have and distribute to the poor . . . and come, follow me' (18:22). In both these texts, and in 5:11, 28, Luke stresses the completeness of the renunciation (cf. *Mark* 10:21; *Matt.* 19:21). He, too, is the only one of the synoptists who includes the *wife* among the possessions of this world which call for renunciation or detachment on the part of the perfect disciple (14:26; 18:29).

There is another form of renunciation which the Lucan Christ demands; it is evident, for instance, in the parable of 12:42–48. The parable deals with alternative modes of conduct facing a servant whom his master placed in charge of his affairs while he himself was absent on a long journey. Especially significant, in v. 42, is the change of 'servant' (*doulos*) to 'steward' (*oikonomos*) (cf. *Matt.* 24: 45). When Luke wrote his gospel, hellenistic Christians viewed their leaders as God's stewards (cf. 1 *Cor.* 4:1f.; *Tit.* 1:7; 1 *Pet.* 4:10). They were God's deputies, acting not in their own name but in his. Hence, they were not masters of the community but men dedicated to its service. As stewards, God's stewards, they were more than ever *servants* (cf. *Luke* 6:39–45; 22:24–27). In Acts 20:17–35 Paul movingly outlines, in personal terms, the quality of community service. For Luke, service is the essence of office in the Church. And Jesus had asked for the setting aside of all ambition, for the renunciation of any desire to lord it over others.

**Prayer, Joy, Peace**

Luke is the gospel of prayer, and the supreme example of prayer is given by Jesus Christ himself. This fact is not

86

neglected by Matthew and Mark. According to the three synoptists Jesus prayed in Gethsemane; he prayed after the first multiplication of loaves (*Mark* 6:46; *Matt.* 14:23); he prayed in Capernaum after he had cured many (*Mark* 1:35). But Luke speaks of the prayer of Jesus in eight further circumstances. He prayed at the baptism (3:21), he retired into the desert to pray (5:16), and before choosing his apostles he spent the whole night in prayer (6:12). He prayed before the confession of Peter (9:18) and later he told Peter that he had prayed specially for him (22:32). He prayed at the Transfiguration, and it was the sight of him in prayer that moved his disciples to ask to be taught how to pray (11:1). He prayed on the cross for his executioners. Indeed, we might add that the surrender of his life to the Father was a prayer (23:46). Jesus often recommended prayer to his disciples: persevering prayer like that of the importunate friend (11:5-13) or of the widow before the unjust judge (18:1-8). They must pray to obtain the Holy Spirit (11:13) and, in short, they ought to pray at all times (21:36). Their prayer must be true prayer, like that of the tax collector (18:13).

The personal example of Jesus is nowhere clearer than in Gethsemane. At his hour of trial (22:39-46), the Lord chose to drink the cup, he chose the cross; the disciples must pray that they, too, in their turn, will make the right choice. Here is the culmination of the prayer of Jesus: in anguish, vividly foreseeing and humanly shrinking from the horrors of the passion, burdened above all by his love for his people and for all men, he prayed more earnestly. He himself in his hour of trial, this 'temptation', put into practice his own recommendation to his disciples. If Paul could understand so clearly that the power of God can support our weakness (cf. 2 *Cor.* 12:10; *Phil.* 4:13), Jesus himself has experienced, with a clarity we cannot imagine, that weakness and that strength.

87

This passage on the agony of the Saviour should not only remind us of the cost of our redemption but, above all, ought to be a powerful encouragement for us. Because, indeed, our High Priest is no stranger to suffering; he knows the demands it can make on our humanness and he can fully sympathise with our human lot (cf. *Heb.* 4:15; 5:7–9). And, in our own prayer, we should keep in mind the precious observation of Luke: 'being in an agony, he prayed more earnestly' (22:44), and of Matthew: 'he went away and prayed for the third time, saying the same words' (26:44). The evangelists have given us these words. '*Abba*, Father, all things are possible to you; remove this cup from me; yet not what I will but what you will' (*Mark* 14:36; cf. *Luke* 22:42; *Matt.* 26:39). The prayer of Jesus was an *earnest* prayer, yes, but not a prayer of many words. It was a cry from the heart.

The coming of the Saviour has created an atmosphere of joy and Luke is keenly aware of it. The annunciation of the birth of John includes a promise of joy (1:14), a promise that is fulfilled (1:58), and the unborn child leaps for joy in the womb at the presence of the mother of the Messiah (1:41, 44). At the greater annunciation the angel bids Mary rejoice (*chaire* = rejoice!) and her thankful joy finds expression in the *Magnificat* (1:46–55). The birth of Jesus is an event of great joy for the angels who proclaim it and for the people he had come to save (2:10, 13f.). Later, the crowds rejoiced at the works they had witnessed (13:17). The seventy-two disciples returned, rejoicing, from their mission; Jesus pointed out to them the true motive of joy (10:20) and he himself 'rejoiced in the Holy Spirit' (10:21). Zacchaeus received Jesus joyfully (19:6). The disciples rejoiced on the occasion of the entry into Jerusalem (19:37) and after the ascension they returned to the city with great joy and praised God in the temple (24:52). The parables of chapter 15 depict the joy of God at the finding of a lost sheep, the return of a sinner.

Peace follows on joy, the peace which Jesus gives (7 : 50; 8 : 48), the peace that came into the world at his coming (2 : 14, 29). The song of the angels celebrating the birth of the *Rex pacificus* (2 : 14) is echoed by the disciples when the King of peace enters the holy city in triumph (19 : 38) —the city that did not receive his message of peace (19 : 42). It is this same gift of peace that the risen Christ gave (24 : 36), the peace which the disciples spread throughout the world (*Acts* 9 : 31). But peace and joy, both, are the fruit of prayer, of close personal union with Jesus Christ the Saviour.

## IV. PAUL

Paul, of course, is the earliest christian theologian whose writings we possesss; it would have seemed logical to begin this short survey with him. The synoptists, however, as evangelists, were more concerned than he was with the traditions about Jesus, and so it was best to begin with them. At the same time, a great deal of 'Paulinism' is common, apostolic Christianity. Paul's debt to his Christian predecessors includes: the apostolic *kerygma*, the concepts of Jesus as Messiah, Lord, and Son of God, the Church as the New Israel, the sacraments, and the expectation of Christ's imminent Parousia. Paul's 'gospel' is the good news of salvation which God has achieved through the incarnation, death, and glorification of Jesus Christ, and which he offers to all who have faith; his theology is that gospel as explained in his letters. 'Justification' by faith, though it is his most distinctive doctrine, does not epitomise Paul's gospel; the only term that can do so adequately is 'salvation'. Salvation is *from* sin but also *to* reconciliation and righteousness; it is a present experience, a communion with Christ, life in the Spirit. Salvation points to a Saviour —Paul's gospel is Christocentric.

If Paul was the most influential figure in apostolic Christianity, it was because he always was conscious of being precisely an *apostolos*—'one sent'. 'He worked harder than any' of the others (1 *Cor*. 15 : 10) because he knew in his own life the burning longing to spend himself for Jesus. He had been completely transformed by his 'Damascene revelation' (though, of course, the full implication of that experience needed time to sink in, cf. *Gal*. 1 : 16f.), so that for him to live *was* Christ. He continually preached 'the word of the cross' because he knew the power and effects of pain, of evil, and of human weakness—and knew, too, the greater power of love so manifest in Christ's supreme gesture of love.

**The Lord**

The crucified and risen Lord is the centre of Paul's preaching. It was his theological task to understand the divine activity both in Christ and in christian existence from the standpoint of his faith-experience that God in Christ had brought about salvation. He had to grasp and present the truth that this salvation is a present reality, although the fulfilment is still to come. God's saving activity is manifest in the resurrection of Christ. The end-time is already begun.

*Kyrios*, 'The Lord', had come to designate Jesus Christ as the one to whom the community prayed and who encountered them in worship. It is Paul's title *par excellence* for Jesus. The title asserts that the exalted Christ is much more than an instrument of salvation history in the past, much more than an object of future hope; he is a living reality in the present. By the designation 'Son of God'—used relatively seldom but significantly—Paul describes the 'history' of Christ from pre-existence to the Parousia. The title indicates the connection between God's activity and the Christ-event; it points to God at work through Jesus Christ. Since the death of Jesus on the cross is central to Paul's soteriology, the man Jesus is decisively important for Paul's Christology, though he seldom refers to his life and teaching.

The first Christians, who believed that the risen Christ had been established as heavenly Lord, and experienced the activity of the Spirit in their midst—the principle of the new life which the Lord had made possible—understood that the End-time had already broken in. Paul's theology is built on the primitive community's experience of salvation. The coming of the Son of God into this passing world—his cross and resurrection on the one hand and the expectation of his imminent coming on the other— means, according to Paul, that the present is already the time of salvation and that the existence of the believer is determined by this reality of salvation. The presence of salvation is manifest in the fact that the risen Christ is present, through his Spirit, in his community, and rules the life of the Christian. Hence, only in the authentically christian life of the community is salvation manifest and, in a real sense, a *fact*.

## Salvation

Paul paints a gloomy picture of man without Christ, in a state of hopelessness. Created in the image of God (*Gen.* 1:27), man is fallen man (*Gen.* 3): his mode of being is less than fully human. Fallen man still has the possibility of being authentically human, but this is an ontological possibility (that which is possible in principle for man as man). Fallen man does not really have the ontic possibility (actually and in the concrete) of being authentically human; he does not have it in his power to become so.[8] But the situation is not hopeless. Christ has brought into the world true, full, humanness again. He gives to men the ontic possibility of passing from 'death' to 'life', of becoming authentically human: fully the image of God, truly sons of God. Through faith in Christ man can indeed turn from death to life—for 'Jesus . . . was raised up for our justification' (*Rom.* 4:25). Man under faith is subject to the righteousness of God (1:17); he is made righteous.

Rather than a quality or something a person has as his own, righteousness is a relationship; a man is 'righteous' to the extent that he is acknowledged to be such. Righteousness is a legal term which, in the development of Jewish piety came to be also an eschatological term, implying future vindication by God. Yet it retained a judicial aspect that is not characteristic of the christian reality. Paul fitted the metaphor to a christian context. He gave the term the nuance of salvation; thus, in Romans 1:17, *dikaiosynē theou* ('the righteousness of God') may be rendered: 'God's salvation'. He declared that righteousness is imputed to a man already, in the present, on condition that he has faith. God does not regard man as if he were righteous but makes him righteous by granting him his forgiveness and by removing him from the environment of sin. And Paul insists on the utter gratuity of justification. In direct contrast to the view of Judaism he asserts that justification comes by or from faith and absolutely not by works of the Law—it is sheer gift. If 'the righteousness of God' is God's salvation, then the verb 'to be justified' (*dikaiousthai*) is 'to find God's good pleasure'. Righteousness has its only origin in God's act of grace accomplished in Christ.

When Paul declares: 'We hold that a man is justified by faith apart from works of the Law' (*Rom.* 3:28), it is true that the concept of justification is directed against the basic concept of Judaism and judaising Christianity, according to which one finds grace by the observance of the Law— by 'works of the Law'. But, the teaching has wider implications. Justification cannot be won by works of the Law—

or by any works. For justification by faith is justification by faith *alone*, meaning the utter incapacity of man for self-justification. We are justified, made upright, by God's grace, by his good pleasure: therefore every human achievement is excluded when it is a matter of justification. Yet there is a sense in which we may say that God does grant his grace on the basis of achievement. 'But now it is not my achievement, but the achievement of Christ on the cross. Faith is not an achievement in itself; rather, it is the hand which grasps the work of Christ and holds it out to God. Faith says: Here is the achievement—Christ died for me on the cross (*Gal.* 2:20). This faith is the only way to obtain God's grace'.[9]

Justification is a manifestation of the divine mercy: 'God shows his love for us in that while we were yet sinners Christ died for us' (*Rom.* 5:8); it is forgiveness for Christ's sake. But as well as forgiveness, it is an 'antedonation' (a donation in advance) of God's final salvation. It is the beginning of a movement towards a goal, towards the hour of definitive justification. Sanctification will be the development, in the course of a christian life, of the seed planted at the moment of justification. And that gift can be lost. Justification places an obligation on the believer and leaves room for salutary fear and for hope—a hope that is firmly grounded (*Rom.* 5:8f.). Justification is not a covering up of the past; it is an antedonation of the full salvation; it is a new creation; it is the new life in Christ.

The believer does not stand alone in relation either to the other members of his community of faith or to those outside it. The obligation placed on the believer covers our attitude of mercy towards others in a lifetime of development. For, as God's justification has intervened on our behalf and liberated us, so ought we likewise to enable others to be free. After all, the very righteousness and faith which we may seem to have in their eyes are only there as a consequence of God's action, and are only really fulfilled in our relating to other people.

Paul tells us, several times, that the bestowal of justification takes place in baptism. Does not this conflict with the notion of justification by faith? The fact of the matter is that the expression 'by faith' implicitly includes baptism. The connection of justification with baptism is so obvious to Paul that he does not think it necessary to draw attention to the fact every time he speaks of justification. But he can, and he does, speak of them in the same terms and in the same breath: 'In Christ Jesus you are all sons of God, through faith. For as many of you as were baptised into Christ have put on Christ' (*Gal.* 3 : 26f.). The formula 'justification by faith', should not be taken in isolation, but should be seen as one expression of the meaning of the rite of baptism; it stresses that God's grace in baptism consists of his granting undeserved pardon. Faith and baptism are not in conflict, but are closely associated. There is no baptism without faith—not inner assent only, but faith in heart and outward confession in the baptismal rite. That is the meaning of Romans 10 : 9f.—'If you confess with your lips that Jesus is Lord and believe in your heart that God raised him from the dead, you will be saved. For man believes with his heart and so is justified, and he confesses with his lips and so is saved.'

Paul shows how baptism, the sacramental initiation into christian life, brings about a death and a renewal. He shows that the death and resurrection of Christ on the one hand, and faith and baptism on the other, are so intimately associated that all four meet in the birth of a Christian: 'Do you not know that all of us who have been baptised in Christ Jesus were baptised into his death? We were buried therefore with him by baptism into death, so that as Christ was raised from the dead by the glory of the Father, we too might walk in newness of life' (*Rom.* 6 : 3f.).

94

Identified with Christ, the Christian dies to the Law and to sin (*Gal.* 2 : 19; *Rom.* 6 : 6, 10). Identified with Christ in his resurrection, he shares in the life of him who has risen from the dead. But christian life cannot be lived in isolation; it is, essentially, a being-with-others. Baptism is, in a sense, a corporate experience; or, more accurately perhaps, it is an incorporation: 'For by one Spirit we were all baptised into one body—Jews or Greeks, slaves or free— and all were made to drink of one Spirit' (1 *Cor.* 12 : 13). The Christian is incorporated into 'the body of Christ', into a community of salvation. God's gift of salvation is incarnational not only at its source but in its manifestation. Authentic christian life is authentically human life : a life lived among, with, and for other men and women.

## In Christ Jesus

Man makes himself open to the effects of the Christ-event through the experience of faith, a vital personal commitment. This experience is not something external to a man but affects his inmost being : it is an intimate union with God in Christ. Somehow, the Christian exists and lives as a Christian in virtue of the life that comes to him from the risen Christ—God has brought it about that he has life in Christ Jesus (1 *Cor.* 1 : 30); he is created anew in Christ (2 *Cor.* 5 : 17). The prepositional phrase *en Christō* ('in Christ') which occurs frequently in Paul's writings, points—when taken in a vertical sense—to a relationship with Christ in person, an incorporation that becomes a symbiosis of Christ and the Christian. To live in Christ, to exist in Christ, means that the life of a Christian is a life flowing from his union with Christ who is its source and author by his living presence in the believer.

This follows, perhaps more obviously, from another expression—the obverse of the other and its complement

—which occurs less frequently : Christ lives, is, in the Christian. Paul can say : 'it is no longer I who live, but Christ who lives in me' (*Gal.* 2:20). He can ask the Corinthians to remind themselves, to bring themselves to a fuller realisation of the fact, that Jesus Christ is in them (2 *Cor.* 13:5; cf. *Rom.* 8:9–11; *Eph.* 3:17). Thus, if the Christian exists and lives in Christ, so, too, Christ lives in the Christian. From different points of view both formulas express the same relationship, the union of Christ with believers. One is reminded of the Johannine *menein* ('to abide'). We hear in John that just as the Son is in the Father, and the Father is in the Son (14:10f.), so the disciples are to *abide* in the Son as he *abides* in them (15:4–10). It would seem that the two great theologians, each in his own way, are struggling to put into inadequate human words the ultimately ineffable reality of union with Christ.

The Christian is altogether dependent on Christ : all comes from him. There cannot be a Christian except in terms of Christ : after all, that is what the name implies. Paul can declare that, in Christ, all differences go : all Christians form *one* in Christ. 'As many of you as were baptised into Christ have put on Christ. There is neither Jew nor Gentile, there is neither slave nor free, there is neither male nor female; for you are all one in Christ Jesus' (*Gal.* 3:27f.). This text focuses our attention on the other dimension of the formula 'in Christ'—the horizontal dimension. The Christ-life in the Christian finds expression, incarnational expression, in christian living. One force alone can overcome the divisions inherent in inauthentic humanity ('Jew and Gentile . . . slave and free') : the power of love. It is the hallmark of the life of Jesus and must mark the life of the Christian; it alone 'binds everything together into perfect harmony' (*Col.* 3:14). Love necessarily involves others; only in community can a life that is characterised by love be lived. A Christian cannot be autonomous nor live his life in isolation; others are essential to this mode of being. The christian community enables the individual to be authentic.

Obviously in Galatians 3:27f. Paul is concerned with the ideal: the fully christian community where differences really do not exist. But he remained always the realist. Though he declared: '. . . there is neither slave nor free, there is neither male nor female; for you are all one in Christ' he, nevertheless, took for granted the inferior status of women in his society, and accepted the fact of slavery (1 *Cor.* 7:24); nothing was to be gained by an assault, then and there, on such entrenched social attitudes and institutions. But the ideal remains: it is meant to be striven after and given shape.

## The Body of Christ

The most typical Pauline figure to express the union of Christ and Christian is 'the body of Christ'. His meaning is that somehow Christ and the Christian share a union that implies one flesh; a union that is not so much corporate as corporal. We tend to equate the Body of Christ with the Church. It is necessary to be clear that, in Paul's writings, the theme of the Body developed independently of that of the Church; they merge only in the Captivity epistles. The Head theme, too, appears at first independently of the Body theme. In Colossians and Ephesians, for the first time, the themes of 'body', 'head' and 'Church' are linked, and the Church is identified with the 'Body of Christ'. But this was very probably a later development, by a disciple, of Paul's thought.[10]

We can profitably begin to study Paul's concept of the Body by noting the realism of his view of the Eucharist. In 1 Corinthians 10:16 he asks, rhetorically (as of something self-evident to the Christian): 'The cup of blessing which we bless, is it not a participation in the blood of

Christ? The bread which we break, is it not a participation in the body of Christ?' Through the eucharistic experience we become associated with Christ, and our union with him should be understood in a very realistic sense. Then Paul goes on to affirm that, if the christian community can form 'one body' it is precisely because it partakes of the personal body of Christ : '*Because* there is one loaf, we who are many are one body, *for* all partake of the same loaf' (10:17). He, logically, insists that Christians should realise that they are bound together through their common union with Christ. The Christian's union with Christ is brought out too, rather unexpectedly, in 1 Corinthians 6:15 when Paul is warning against the defilement of man's body by sexual licence. Again he appeals to a known fact : '*Do you not know* that your bodies are members of Christ? Shall I therefore take the members of Christ and make them the members of a prostitute? Never! *Do you not know* that he who joins himself to a prostitute becomes one flesh with her? For, as it is written, "The two shall become one flesh". But he who is united to the Lord becomes one spirit with him' (1 *Cor.* 6:15f.). The Christian becomes one spirit with the Lord—and yet it is a relationship analogous to the 'one flesh' relationship of man and woman. It is not easy to be more realistic than that. Christians are baptised 'into one body'—into Christ—and so find unity among themselves (1 *Cor.* 12:12f.). Through incorporation into him in baptism, through union with him in the Eucharist, the unity of the christian body, called to join themselves individually to him, is achieved.

In Colossians and Ephesians the independent themes of body, head and church are drawn together. The Church is identified with the Body of Christ, and Christ is the Head of the Church. This rather awkward development brings out what was already present in Paul's thought. Salvation is not an individualistic experience for the Christian : he is incorporated into Christ not in isolaton but in union with his brethren, the one family of God. This corporate union of Christians must grow to fill out the total Christ, the *plērōma* ('fullness') of the cosmic Christ. And Christ is the Head, for 'on him the whole body depends' (*Eph.* 4 : 16). In Christ, the glorified Lord, 'the whole fullness of deity dwells bodily' (*Col.* 2 : 9) and Christians, in their turn, are 'filled' in him and from him (2 : 10). And so the Church can be called the 'body' of Christ: the expansion of his risen body by the union with him, through baptism, of Christians. The Church is his 'fullness', for in the Church he exercises and manifests the power of life and sanctification; it is the sphere in which the divine life that passes through Christ comes to full flower (*Eph.* 1 : 23). From this point of view, Christ is the head of the body, head of the Church; it is from the head that life flows into the body (1 : 22). This is but another way of saying that the Church, in its life, is the sanctifying activity of Christ manifest to the eyes of men.

The Head belongs to heaven, and since the Church receives its life from the head, the Church is, in this respect, a heavenly reality. And it is in heaven that, at the end, the marriage-feast of Christ will be celebrated because then will his Church appear, glorious and without blemish, 'as a bride adorned for her husband' (*Apoc.* 21 : 2). But before she can come to that she must be purified by him, cleansed of every stain. It is still the time of purification. And the Church is no vague personification. It is a living organism, made up of men and women, of beings who are not only human but fallen—though redeemed. The Church on earth, though animated by the life of Christ, is still the Church of sinners. Even in the face of the sublime Pauline doctrine, this is something we may never forget. And we are reminded of it by Vatican II's *Constitution on the Church*: 'The Church, with sinners clasped to her bosom, is at once holy, and in constant need of cleansing, thus she pursues a ceaseless course of penance and renewal' (art. 8). All of us, fellow members, share the same human limitations. Yet the love of Jesus is living in our very weaknesses; and our perceiving this makes the Church truly one of fellowship in him.

## V: JOHN

John has indicated, quite firmly, the purpose of his gospel: 'These (signs) are written that you may believe that Jesus is the Christ, the Son of God, and that believing you may have life in his name' (20:31). Obviously, he has sought to stress faith in the person of Jesus Christ and in his salvific power. The foundation of that faith is his own presentation of the facts, his choice among all the many signs which Jesus had wrought (20:30). He sets out to bring men to believe that this man of flesh and blood, Jesus of Nazareth, is the Messiah of Jewish expectation—and something far, far more than that. He is 'Son of God' in the sense of the christian profession of faith which surpasses all Jewish expectations. 'That you may believe' is not only addressed to potential converts; it also envisages those who already believe, inviting them to 'go on believing', to attain to a more profound and stable faith. This faith is directed to the living and glorified Lord preached by the Church, living in the Church. He is the Saviour, the Lord of glory . . . and none other than the Jesus of the gospel. Faith in him has power to bestow salvation, life, 'in his name'. Faith is faith in the person of Christ, a Christ who is Saviour.

The Johannine world is characterised by a division into light and darkness, life and death. Yet, it is clear that John's dualism has nothing to do with a philosophical speculation on good and evil, but is a component of salvation history. The warfare between light and darkness in this world is not cosmic, but is a struggle within man in his search for truth and light. In the Johannine view, truth in its entirety has come with the coming of the Son of man. In him the meeting of God with man takes place: he is the communication of divine life. John stresses equally the divinity and the humanity of the Saviour: the truth, light, and life which men need have been brought from above by the Son, but they are given because he is one with mankind, a mankind that can, through him, enter into the divine sphere. 'The reality of the incarnation is not simply an affirmation of christian dogma, but constitutes the essence of salvation.'[11]

For John the story of Jesus is that place in history where the ultimate truths about God are to be found. More than the synoptists, it is he who gives us an awareness of this through his theme of *life*. John had more to tell about Jesus than any gospel could hold. This is why he emphasised the coming of the Spirit, promised not so much to supply for Jesus' absence as to complete his presence. This Spirit had matured John himself, and his work is characterised by his experience of the Spirit. He saw the divine light which all along had irradiated the human Teacher from Nazareth.

**The Word**

When he identifies Jesus as the creative Word of God, source of the light that is man's life, John presents him as the revealer of God. But his conception of revelation is dynamic—the idea of the Word is eminently soteriological. The revelation made by the Word gives knowledge of God; the revelation is found in the example and invitation of a life that has been lived, the life of the Son of Man. Because the incarnation is the supreme grace of God, the Word is pre-eminently the revelation of God's love; hence John's stress on love. It is the essence of discipleship, of what it means to be a Christian.

The incarnation is a beginning. It has to be fulfilled in

the work for which the Son has been sent into the world: the glorification of the Father that in turn is his own glorification. The 'hour' of Jesus, the hour of his suffering and death, is one phase of his 'glorification', the other phase being his resurrection and return to the Father. In contrast to the synoptists, who reflect the common tradition, John has underlined the glorification aspect of the passion story. It is an hour of triumph because, despite appearances, it is the world that stands judged and the power of evil broken. The incarnate Word has glorified God by his words and deeds; God in turn has glorified him by the same words and deeds. The 'signs' of Jesus comprise his words and works: the words give determination to his works and show them to be the works of God. These 'signs' of Jesus are the communication of God to men, and so they are truth and life, abiding realities. The glory of Jesus is something that has been seen by men and in him they have found the glory of God.

The pre-existence of the Johannine Christ is affirmed in the Prologue (1:1f.) and in the testimony of the Baptist (1:30). It is asserted by Jesus himself ('where he was before', 6:62), ('before Abraham was, I am', 8:58), in the great prayer to the Father (17:5, 24), and indirectly in many other texts where his pre-existence is assumed. It is present in the *egō eimi* ('I am') sayings. Indeed, the strongest expression of Jesus' claim to be the divine redeemer in the strict sense is found in the absolute usage of *egō eimi*: 'You will die in your sins unless you believe that I AM' (8:24); 'I tell you this now, before it takes place, that when it does take place you may believe that I AM' (13:19.)[12] The source of these confident assertions of pre-existence lies in the Christology of the primitive Church previous to John. Only an acceptance of pre-existence can explain Paul's identification of the legendary Rock, which accompanied the Israelites in the desert, with Christ (1

*Cor.* 10:4). Only this can account, too, for his assertions in 1 Corinthians 8:6, Galatians 4:4, and Romans 10:6f. John is not introducing a wholly new idea but is developing an aspect of the Christology of the early Church.

**Faith**

Faith, playing a supremely important part in John's theology, is, of course, equally emphasised by Paul, but the accent is different. For one thing, John prefers the verb 'to believe' while Paul favours the noun 'faith'. Perhaps John wants to stress that faith is less an internal disposition than an active commitment; but surely Paul would fully concur in this. More significant is the fact that, for Paul, faith in the crucified and risen Lord is all-important. John projects this faith into his account of the earthly work of Jesus and shows it unfolding in personal encounter with the redeemer during his life in the world. However, John is careful to bring out its bearing on the time after Easter in Jesus' concluding statement (20:29). But it is in his exposition of the christian faith as it was at the time of the ministry that John strikingly and effectively describes the beginning and the growth of faith, the motives that inspire it, the dangers it runs. He can show that Jesus himself demands faith as the one thing necessary for salvation, and can make it clear that faith is faith in Jesus as the one in whom God has revealed himself. And he also brings out that faith is rooted in this historical and incarnational revelation. It is precisely because of this incarnational aspect that Paul and John are at one in asserting that faith must become effective in love. 'For in Christ Jesus neither circumcision nor uncircumcision is of any avail, but faith working through love' (*Gal.* 5:6). And, in John, fraternal charity becomes the 'new commandment' of Christ (13:34f.).

The most distinctive, and the most frequent, Johannine

expression is *pisteuein eis*, 'to believe in'. This usage brings out the most marked characteristic of Johannine faith: faith is directed exclusively to the person of Jesus. To believe means to receive and accept Jesus' self-revelation; it means to attach oneself to him, in personal union, in order to receive from him eternal life; it means a total commitment to him. It is so much more than trust or confidence in him. The believer can have the fullest assurance as he finds, in the very object of his faith, the deepest motive and the surest foundation of his faith. For this Son is attested by the Father, attests himself in God, and is continually attested in the apostolic testimony.

The personal union of the believer with Christ is also expressed by other terms which can stand for the Johannine faith. It emerges clearly in the parallelism of 6 : 35 that 'to believe' in Jesus is *to come to* him: 'I am the bread of life; he who comes to me shall not hunger, and he who believes in me shall never thirst'. Faith can also be described as 'hearing' the voice or the words of Jesus, hearing and obeying. The believer *abides* in the word, and in Jesus himself (8 : 31). Believing is also seeing. More than any other New Testament writer John has laid stress on faith as vision; it is a true vision of God, of Truth. Faith and knowledge are often associated, but they are not identical. 'Faith', whose object is a Person, can certainly grow into 'knowledge' for, in biblical thought, 'to know' is always an act which institutes or reinforces fellowship. Knowledge comes through faith, and faith should grow into knowledge—more intimate fellowship with Father and Son. And because the revelation of God in Christ is pre-eminently the revelation of his love, there is the closest possible connection between faith and love.

**The Spirit**

In John, the Spirit is presented as the divine power that

continues and completes Jesus' ministry, as the perpetuation of Jesus' presence among his followers. The Spirit is the principle of the divine sonship that Jesus has made possible for men; John's emphasis is on the Spirit as sanctifier and as principle of the life of the Christian. The activity of the Paraclete (John's designation of the Spirit) is to reveal the mind of Christ. We live not by the words of the 'historical' Jesus, but by the words of Jesus as made known through the Church enlightened by the Spirit.

All this becomes more obvious and, indeed, self-evident, if we accept that, for John, the Paraclete is 'the personal presence of Jesus in the Christian while Jesus is with the Father.'[13] Thus, the one whom John calls 'another Paraclete' is another Jesus. 'As yet the Spirit had not been given, because Jesus was not yet glorified' (7 : 39)—if, then, the Spirit can only come when Jesus departs, the Spirit/Paraclete is the presence of the 'absent' Jesus. As Paraclete, the glorified Lord is abidingly present in his Church. In this way, the later Christian is assured that he is no further removed from the ministry of Jesus than the earlier Christian, for the Paraclete dwells within him as fully as Jesus 'abode' in his disciples. John's theology of the Spirit meant that his eschatology could hardly be other than 'realised'. Hence it appears that it was not so much the 'delay' of the Parousia as the Church's consciousness and experience of the presence of the Holy Spirit that was responsible for the development of 'realised eschatology', the possession of eternal life here and now.

Men find in the Church not only the words of Jesus but also his works of salvation; and the works of Christ perpetuated in the Church by the Spirit are chiefly the sacraments, which draw their efficacy from the Christ-event. The presence of the Spirit is manifested in christian life, specifically in fraternal love. John's concept of judgment is in line with his realised eschatology : while not denying a final 'judgment', he insists on the present reality of judgment, on the importance of the existential moment of decision. The coming of Jesus is, and remains, an occasion of judgment; men must decide whether to accept him or reject him. In making this decision, man judges himself. The 'division' caused by the appearance of the Light continues into John's Church and into the Church of our day.

## CHAPTER IV

# Life More Abundantly

'Life' is everywhere for sale today. Wholesale and retail, it is advertised; in all honesty, or by hook or by crook, it is made to submit to being purchased. 'Life', in its alluring zest, is held out to society in countless forms through the mediating hands of words, pictures, and sounds. But there is something wrong. 'You turn things upside down! Shall the Potter be regarded as the clay, that the thing made should say to its Maker, "He did not make me"?' (*Is.* 29:16). Yes, there is something wrong, and things are turned upside down. For in the end, after searching so feverishly for 'life', man finds only Death. It is not only that he meets bodily death at the end of his days. Rather, it is the more tragic experience of finding that being alive is death-like because it is void of meaning.

Moreover it is not mankind in the abstract or a rather generalised experience that we speak of. It is painfully close to home, lurking in the hidden, daily moment of all of us who call ourselves Christians. It may take the form of boredom, or hopelessness, or that passive form of existence which is merely 'lying around'. It brings about a kind of empty feeling—like death; it crops up as life without fulfilment, existence without purpose or dimension. Why? Jesus has already answered us, had we but ears to hear. Because, he tells us, though you search high and low and in every possible material thing for the meaning of existence, you will not come to *me* that you may have life (cf. *John* 5:39f.). We would suggest that existentialist parallels can foster meditation on certain aspects of the gospels, lighting up the one authentic meaning of 'existence': 'He who has the Son has life' (1 *John* 5:12).[1]

## Life in Oneself

We must go straight to the heart of 'life' in the Bible in order to explain the notion of 'Existence'. Biblical man was deeply appreciative of the material goods of creation and had wholesome views on the value of being thoroughly human. He set great store by progeny and prosperity in this life. But in the end he came to see that to really *live* was simply to be forever in companionship with God. To live was to 'be with God'; and however final physical death might be, this fellowship with God was still more powerful and permanent. It was life forever, in this world and in the world to come. 'My flesh and my heart may fail. But God is the strength of my heart and my portion for ever' (*Ps.* 73:26). For *God* to be one's portion forever meant that life on this earth had already that deeper quality which belongs to his own Kingdom. And it is this deeper dimension of life here-and-now which lies behind the frequent reference to 'eternal life' in the gospels. Eternal life is the *true* life, the real life. It is that special quality which transforms totally our everyday lives, simply because God has become man in Jesus.

Now it is this 'real life' which corresponds to Heidegger's fundamental term for existence: *Existenz* in German, which is best rendered 'exist-*ing*'. His 'authentic existence' finds its ultimate fulfilment in the 'eternal life' which Jesus offers in his person. According to the existentialists, the existent is either himself, as a unique person, or he is not himself, being absorbed into the world of things. This is the same distinction as that between 'authentic' and 'inauthentic' existence, and between having life in the Son and not having life in the Son. Moreover, just as authentic *Existenz* must exercise freedom and break away from being moulded by external standards, so too does the following of Jesus demand a choice. One must be either for the Light or against it, in Johannine terms. And the man who chooses against it brings judgment upon himself, for his real self becomes harnessed to, and even swallowed up by, the darkness outside him.

The person who lives authentically continually 'stands-out' (the root meaning of ex-sistence) and emerges from where he is at any given moment. Indeed there is something dynamic in this—a 'going out'. Jesus has put it in christian terms by his absolute demands, such as those in the Sermon on the Mount—demands which are impossible by human standards, but which are made possible through the strength he himself gives to meet them. The authentic Christian keeps on reaching out to be 'perfect as your heavenly Father is perfect' (*Matt.* 5:48), even though constantly made aware of his own weakness before the 'narrow gate' and the 'hard way' that leads to life (*Matt.* 7:14). As the true existent, he abides by this way—precisely because he is always on the way to somewhere else. And if he hesitates and questions what the way is, the Christian already has the answer of Jesus: 'You know the way . . . I am the way' (*John* 14:6). He is the Way, because he is *Life*. This is the heart of christian *Existenz*, and we can hear the voice of the Teacher behind us declaring: 'This is the way, walk in it' (*Is.* 30:21). Thus the Christian is always 'standing out', always on the way to one Goal.

This quality of being whereby man transcends himself at each moment is one of the basic characteristics which distinguishes him from other kinds of being, such as plants or animals or mountains. According to the existentialists, man 'thrusts himself into the possibilities of existence'. For the Christian, this is another way of saying that he takes the step of daring to *believe* where he cannot see and cannot know. Jesus himself has made this comparison between his followers and other creatures of God in his unforgettable words about the birds of the air and the lilies of the field, telling how his Father always cares for these though they do nothing to 'earn' it. Now in pointing to these as examples, Jesus is not saying that we shall be free of tribulation or must approach each day with a kind of lackadaisical attitude, refusing to earn our daily bread. No: he is saying that amidst the very real cares and crosses and labours of every day, we must have the daring of 'little children' to call upon our *Abba*, Father. We must be confident of the Creator's providence, given to us through the care of his Son: 'I *know* him in whom I have believed' (2 *Tim.* 1:12). It is what Kierkegaard calls the 'leap of faith'. It does not mean that the believer is delivered *from* the conflicts and pain of the world, but rather that he is delivered *amidst* them by the Saviour who has overcome. 'In the world you will have tribulation; but, be of good cheer, I have overcome the world!' (*John* 16:33).

The existent is a unique being, 'irreplaceable and never interchangeable'. This uniqueness possesses the quality of 'mineness': it knows itself as an 'I'. How in keeping with the whole biblical doctrine of man! The Old Testament never speaks of some mystical absorption by which man loses his identity in God. Rather, the person is very conscious of his individual role before God, as so many of the psalms show, with their personal discoursings before Yahweh. The prophets were strikingly individual characters, conscious of God's special Word sent uniquely to them. One like Jeremiah was also capable of lamenting the weakness of his selfhood before God (cf. *Jer.* 20:7). But, from the beginning, there was the marvellous truth that 'male and female', man and woman, were created as equals and individuals before Yahweh, however much this original idea may have suffered in practice. And this uniqueness and dignity of the human person, exemplified by all the notable Old Testament personages, reached its peak in the New Testament. The very fact of the Incarnation confers infinite value on the individual. Flowing from and confirming this, of course, is the most joyous good news of the entire gospel: the love which God through Jesus has for each one of us personally, a love even unto death.

Jesus explicitly said that he came in order that his sheep might have *Life*, and have it 'more abundantly' (*John* 10:10). That is, that they might have life to the full, or 'fulfil-ment'. The search for fulfilment has gone hand in hand with the cry for 'life' throughout the centuries. For the existentialist, to exist as a self, to live authentically without being divided against one's true self, means to stand in the possibility of finding this self-fulfilment. But the existentialist, so aware of the paradox and tension that is part of human life, also grasps the supreme paradox of Christianity in regard to such fulfilment. The arrival at 'selfhood' comes only through 'giving up' oneself! 'Whoever seeks to gain his life will lose it, but whoever loses his life will preserve and gain it' (*Luke* 17:33). It is the mystery which Paul experienced: because he knew he had been 'crucified with Christ' so that it was no longer he who lived but Jesus in him (*Gal.* 2:20), he could be most certain of his own identity as the Apostle ('one sent') of the risen Christ. 'By the grace of God I am what I am!' (1 *Cor.* 15:10)—thus Paul's most direct declaration of his *Existenz*. We shall now see, however, how this fulfilment by 'losing oneself' comes not so much through one's individual life, as through life among others.

## Life in the World

The freedom of selfhood—of being an authentic Christian—is never absolute, because of the external circumstances and particular situations in which we are placed. The 'yoke' and the 'burden' upon us as followers of Jesus may be, as he says, 'sweet' and 'light' because they are his (*Matt.* 11:29). Nevertheless, they remain a yoke and a burden, and we are constantly being made aware that God's ways differ from our ways, being as high above them as the heavens are above the earth (*Is.* 55:8f.). Existentialists use the word 'facticity' to describe the limiting factor in existence. It refers to the awareness of one's own being as a fact to be accepted; it is the givenness of our existence here and now into which we are 'thrown'. It is part of man's finitude which cannot be overcome; hence, there is always a tension between possibility and actuality in living. Whether it be experienced as personal weaknesses or an external 'thorn in the flesh' (cf. 2 *Cor.* 12:7) or the 'daily cross' involved in following Jesus, the Christian too is aware of this tension in his efforts to follow his Lord. It is hard to find simplicity—singleness—of heart. Man simply cannot understand certain elements of mystery both within himself and in the world around him which refuse to yield to his analysis and to his grasp. But the resolution of the tension for the Christian is repeated many times in the Bible: acceptance of the will of God which always, though it remains a mystery, 'works all things together for good' (*Rom.* 8:28). This quiet acceptance which is part of 'becoming as little children' in the Kingdom, makes it possible to perceive that there is one who can deliver us from the tension of being mortals in this world, one whose very name means 'Saviour'.

Through him, though the Christian is called upon (he is an 'existent') to live in this world, he is never merely part of the world. Jesus prays for his own who are 'not of the world' even as he was not part of it (*John* 14:14). He goes on to pray not that they may be taken out of the world, but only that they may be kept from the 'evil one'. This can be compared with the existentialist description of man as 'being-in-the-world' as distinct from being pulled into 'innerworldly being' involving the loss of his true nature through surrender to the subhuman elements in the world. It is the same distinction which runs through the whole of John's gospel between the 'Spirit that gives life' and the 'flesh that is of no avail'. However, quite apart from this pejorative meaning of 'the flesh' in John, we must constantly be made aware of its counterpart in the whole of biblical teaching: man is a whole person, body and spirit, and he cannot be in the world or interact with his environment without his body (as existentialist teaching also holds). Christianity pulses with living breath: 'the Word became *flesh* and pitched his tent among us' (*John* 1 : 14).

## Life Amidst Others

The incarnate Jesus has spoken to us the one word needful, the one thing he asks in our being Christians: 'A new commandment I give to you, that you love one another, as I have loved you' (*John* 13 : 34). His teaching finds many parallels in the existentialist's awareness of interpersonal relations. I must meet persons in the world, not as objects belonging to the world, but as co-existents. To treat another as an object would be to enslave him, whereas we are to follow the example of the Lord who 'no longer calls us servants, but friends' (*John* 15 : 15). I may have 'concern' for *things* in the world, the object of my concern remaining external to me and but an instrument. One could say that the Pharisees cared about their community in a very impersonal, legalistic way because their concern—indeed anxiety—was with the fulfilling of the minute prescriptions of the Law itself. In contrast, the commandment of Jesus corresponds to what the existentialists would call 'solicitude'. Solicitude contains the relationship between one existing self and another in wholeness and openness : seeing the other as a distinct person.

*I-Thou.* This leads to one of the most fruitful concepts in existentialist thought : Martin Buber's understanding of the 'I-Thou' relationship. The primary word 'I-Thou' can only be spoken with the whole being related totally to another person, making possible genuine solicitude for him.[2] This is in contrast to the 'I-It' relationship, which can never be embraced with the whole being and exercises merely concern for external instruments. Buber recognises that the distinction between the two is not always absolute, and the 'I-Thou' can degenerate into the 'I-It'. However, the reverse can also happen in that it is possible for an impersonal or self-seeking relationship to blossom into a true 'I-Thou' bond.[3] And the character of this genuine relationship consists largely of 'dialogue', a willingness to listen and receive as well as to speak and give. In biblical terms, it is God's love for men that has given an 'I-Thou' relationship with the Father himself. The idea of man's privilege of communion with God underlies the entire Covenant concept of the Old Testament. And then, because God so loved the world that he sent his only Son (cf. *John* 3 : 16), and gave him up to death on a cross, this became the new Covenant sealed by his own blood. In simpler, everyday terms, this means that Jesus abides with us always and walks hand-in-hand with us as our friend. He speaks to us the primary word 'I-Thou'.

Jesus not only taught the I-Thou relationship in his own terms of the Kingdom; he also actually lived it in his own meetings with others. He continually sought out people and engaged in dialogue with them; while doing so he always saw them as distinct persons. We need but think of the special solicitude and gentle devotion he showed towards women, who were accorded a decidedly inferior status in the society of his day. There was his unprecedented invitation to all the 'poor', the outcasts, exemplified by his table-fellowship with tax collector and sinners. How clearly Jesus speaks the word I-Thou when he bids the unpopular tax collector Zacchaeus to scramble down from his vantage point in a sycamore tree and receive the Lord as his own guest!

*Distance.* But Buber also brings out another important aspect of that 'being-with-others' which is the personal element in the world around us. This is the truth that a genuine relationship between persons also implies distance. To seek union with another to the exclusion of his or her own individuality cannot be part of a genuinely loving relationship. The loved one must be allowed the absolute freedom to be himself, the scope to preserve his unique 'otherness'. Otherwise, the love becomes a possessive relationship: true, good need turns into 'neediness', and the one seeks to change the other in order to mould him to fit one's own image or fill a lack. This idea of 'distance' finds its parallel, too, in Christianity in that Jesus, whether in his earthly life or in his continuing presence in the Church, never rigidly imposes himself on others. His followers are always left free to choose for or against him; it is in freedom that they answer his call 'Follow me!' And, as we have seen in the case of Paul, to truly answer this call and lose one's entire life in Christ means to actually find that life and live to the full the personhood which the Creator has given to each of his children. The manifold different ways and vocations through which one can be led to Jesus and live a 'christian' life are an indication of the unique personhood which he fosters.

There are other aspects of this notion of 'distance' that can be seen in biblical terms: there is the familiar and sometimes painful experience of God's 'distance' from us —those barren times in our lives when we feel we cannot reach through to him. There is also the frequent need to 'go to a place apart' to pray, as Jesus did, in order to find the stillness and aloneness in which to experience God's nearness anew. Such 'distancing' always serves to strengthen both the individual Christian and his I-Thou relationship with Jesus. It is like the 'pruning' of the branches of the Vine, in order that they may bear more fruit (*John* 15 : 1f.). It is a preparation for the gift of the Spirit as the 'comforter', the presence of Jesus himself in our aloneness (*John* 16 : 7). This Spirit is associated with the sacrament of confirmation, and it is one of the most beautiful thoughts of existentialism that, in the interpersonal relationship, I am 'confirmed' by the other. This means again and again that there can be no 'I' without a 'Thou'. We may think of this in terms of the strength of friendship. Or we may think of it in terms of the 'faith' relationship with God : to place all our trust in him means to be in turn strengthened and confirmed by him. And for the Christian, of course, the most profound sense of being 'confirmed' comes through Jesus' repeated assurance throughout the New Testament : 'Do not be afraid . . . it is I !' It is the I-Thou condescension of the Saviour.

*Availability.* A further aspect of the I-Thou relationship is what Gabriel Marcel terms 'availability' : the willingness to put oneself completely at the disposal of the other and be unreservedly open to him. The *un*available person, in contrast, is absorbed with himself and closed against the other. He is convinced that his existence is something that he 'has', that he possesses by his own right; because he is so anxious to maintain this and defend himself, he cannot really be available to others. In christian terms, the mistake of such an unavailable person is his forgetting that, apart from Jesus, he is nothing and can do nothing (cf. *John* 15 : 5). Our existence is a gift to us, and we can draw Life only from the Vine in whom we abide. 'What have you that you did not receive?' (1 *Cor.* 4 : 7). A person can become 'unavailable' because he is saddled by some of the obstacles to the growth of God's seed, his word of love, illustrated in the explanation of the parable of the Sower. Above all, he can become crippled by *fear*—the fear which 'has to do with judgment' (1 *John* 4 : 18), making him react in self-defence against imagined threats to himself in life around him.

The 'available' person on the other hand has found that perfect love 'casts out fear', by leaving no room for it. He has been able to reach out beyond himself in openness to the other without fear that something will be taken from him. And he has been able to do this through a radical awareness of his own dependency on God, having nothing belonging to himself which could be taken away. 'We have this treasure in earthen vessels, to show that the transcendent power belongs to God and not to us' (2 *Cor.* 4 : 7). Availability makes one person present to another and depends on a person's 'coming out' of himself towards the other. After Zacchaeus had scrambled down from his tree, he *received* Jesus joyfully. Freed by his dependency on God from the fear of being 'invaded', the available person is willing to receive. This is the most perfect form of giving because it is to place oneself completely at the disposal of another's will : 'Behold, I am the handmaid of the Lord' (*Luke* 1 : 38). It is to allow Jesus and his Father to make their home with us (*John* 14 : 23). And the New Testament teaches clearly that the way of openness, the way towards genuine human existence, lies through being able to expend oneself. It is not enough to be generous. One must sell *all* that one has for the sake of a greater treasure in heaven in following Jesus; indeed, one must leave behind home and lands and family for his sake (cf. *Mark* 10 : 17–31). The true disciple and Christian will be able to say to his fellowmen: 'I will most gladly spend and be spent for you' (2 *Cor.* 12 :15).

*Community.* It is the fellowship of 'available' persons committed to the I-Thou manner of relating to one another that builds up the genuine christian *community*. The community rests on fidelity: faithfulness to the engagements we have assumed. Paul exhorts the Colossians to 'continue in the faith, stable and steadfast, not shifting from the hope of the gospel which you have heard' (*Col.* 1 :23). The Christ of the Apocalype lays upon the community no other burden than to hold fast the teaching which they have already received, until he comes (*Apoc.* 2 :25). And the God of the entire Bible is he who always keeps the promise he has made to his people from the beginning, though his words be fulfilled in ways they do not expect, and though their perfect fulfilment must await the future with the *eschaton* and *parousia*.[4] His people, in turn, have the responsibility to see that their community is authentic; in other words, it must allow his members freedom to become the unique persons they are meant to be.

An inauthentic community is governed by the pressure of uniformity: the crowd, the mass, the herd, 'they', cannot tolerate differences, suppress the genuinely human. The existentialist says that it is only by breaking out of this inauthentic and distorted being-with-others that a genuine community can arise. The Church today could well be mindful of this. It could recall that the first Christians had to have the courage to break away from established religious norms in Judaism in order to follow the 'more excellent way' of Jesus and his supreme 'law' of love. The New Testament is full of references to the ostracism and persecution they were called upon to suffer, as well as Jesus' assurance amidst it all.: 'By your patient endurance you will gain your lives' (*Luke* 21 :19). But such external persecutions as

Christians then suffered at the hands of their enemies are, in a sense, less vicious than those the present Church must encounter at the hands of the 'establishment'—indeed, sometimes, of her own institution. We must have the courage to perceive and to live anew the simple but stark demands of the gospel in their purest form. In the midst of apostolic works we must pause just to sit quietly at the feet of Jesus and listen to *his* teaching, as did Mary of Bethany. An inauthentic christian community must repeatedly deny Jesus, as did Peter.

## Life in God

The existentialists, and others too for that matter, use so many 'words' to describe the experience of being, so many concepts to measure the potential within each individual. But because of man's radical 'facticity' and the limitations inherent in his very being, existentialist philosophy (like many christian ideals) tends to remain in the realm of abstract ideas. And it continually encounters the tensions of human existence. For all the positive attitude towards man which such philosophy offers, for all the optimistic help it tenders towards self-fulfilment, one still must ask: does anything really make sense in existence? Must the psalmist perpetually ask, 'How long, how long, O Lord?'. And must teachers of wisdom such as Qoheleth always conclude that there is nothing but 'vanity' and 'striving after wind' beneath the sun (Qoh. 1:14)? But, in another sense, Qoheleth does have the answer after all when he concludes finally that wisdom is out of *his* reach, for the work of God cannot be understood any more than the way in which his Spirit quickens a child in the womb can be fathomed (Qoh. 11:5). 'That which is far off is deep, very deep; who can find it out?' (7:23).

This is very similar to Kierkegaard's teaching on man's existence before God. For him, the dilemma of existence has no rational solution, for its paradox cannot be resolved in 'rational' terms (as Paul knew that the 'letter' of the Law would not suffice). Moreover, this dilemma of existence has no human solution, for man's mortal and earthbound nature makes it impossible for him to bring about his own salvation. This is why the Old Testament is filled with the longing for God himself to intervene as Saviour, to step into the treadmill of existence on earth and bring about his Kingdom. And this is why the very name of the One who did intervene means 'God saves'—'salvation' for us nowadays meaning essentially a life filled with meaning. Thus, with no rational or human solution to the dilemma of existence, Kierkegaard finds the only answer to lie in a still greater paradox. This is the absolute paradox, the *skandalon*, or stumbling block of Christianity and the Incarnation itself. Christianity is indeed the 'great offence', for Christ crucified is 'a stumbling block to Jews and folly to Gentiles' (1 *Cor.* 1 : 23). Jesus himself is a 'sign of contradiction' from the beginning (*Luke* 2 : 34), and his teachings are couched in paradox. He came to appeal not to cold reasoning but to the heart. He called for the leap of faith, and the Christian must necessarily 'walk by faith, not by sight' (2 *Cor.* 5 : 6). Like Anselm, each Christian must say, not 'I understand in order that I may believe' but rather, 'I believe in order that I may understand'. Only believing in Jesus—beyond the great paradox of Christianity—can ever satisfy the contemporary thirst for existence (cf. *John* 6 : 35).

The 'leap of faith' also brings about what Kierkegaard calls the 'moment before God', a moment when eternity crosses the threshold of time. This is very reminiscent of the distinction made between 'final' and 'realised' eschatology in Johannine thought : as we have already implied, the life which Jesus brings in his person both awaits a future consummation and yet is already present here and now.[5] The believer is not delivered from time and its conflicts: 'in the world, you *will* have tribulation'. However, he has a dimension of eternity in his life, brought out in John by the very term 'eternal life', indicating something not quantitative but qualitative. It is this sense of a deeper dimension beyond our everyday rather superficial existence which gives meaning and purpose to our lives. Through Jesus we are continually made aware that his Kingdom is not 'of this world' (*John* 18:36) and that we have on earth 'no abiding city' (*Heb.* 13:14). It is this dimension of eternity in Jesus which transforms such ordinary things as water and bread and wine into Life-giving sacraments.

For Kierkegaard, then, this 'moment before God' is that in which authentic existence is attained, for it is also the moment of self-knowledge. It was in their moment before God that Adam and Eve knew themselves to be naked (*Gen.* 3:7). It was in his lifetime's moment of knowledge and complete obedience to the Father's will that Jesus, the new Adam, knew who he was and the mission for which he was sent. And it is the moment when each Christian realises that 'for me to live is Christ' (*Phil.* 1:21) that makes him most fully the person he is. In Kierkegaard's view, to will to belong to Christ, to will to be a Christian, is to will oneself. It is to will the *summum bonum*, the 'one thing needful'. The paradox is that this highest thing involves the utter scandal of the cross and the lowliness and hiddenness of God's Kingdom, given only to 'little ones'. It is these who have truly authentic existence, these alone who have enough simplicity and pureness of heart to see God himself in the face of Jesus (cf. *Matt.* 5:8; 2 *Cor.* 4:6).

'Unless a grain of wheat falls into the earth and dies, it remains alone; but if it dies it bears much fruit' (*John* 12:24). Jesus' parabolic reference to his own imminent death contains the kernel of Christianity and its paradox. The road to Life leads through death; the meaning of liv-ing is grasped in die-ing. And so, Heidegger's teaching on the ultimate meaning of *Existenz* will not be foreign to the Christian. What Kierkegaard had called the 'moment before God', Heidegger calls the 'moment before death'. Death for him is not something negative: anticipation of it can bring wholeness to life because life is given unity by this boundary upon it. This should also be the christian attitude towards death: something positive, something capable of bringing forth 'much fruit'. Not only is physical death to be viewed in this way, but also the endless daily trials which are themselves forms of 'dying'. Suffering is the way to peace and wholeness. The psalmist says, 'It is good for me to have been afflicted, that I might learn your word' (*Ps.* 119:71). The school of suffering taught obedi-ence to the Son of God (*Heb.* 5:8); and he said repeatedly that it was necessary for him to suffer in order to enter into his glory (cf. *Mark* 8:31; *Luke* 24:26).

The mystery of bodily death terminating life remains, however, the decisive moment both for the 'existentialist' and for the 'Christian'. But whereas both must maintain positive attitudes towards it, the Christian (in contrast to Heidegger) must see death not so much as a 'boundary' in a terminal sense, but as a new horizon. Indeed, he must see it as the open door to the fullness of Life for which his entire earthly existence has been searching. It is not so much death in itself which gives a whole, unified existence to the Christian; rather it is the resurrection. Just as John saw Jesus' death, resurrection, and ascension to glory as a single moment, so too the Christian is to see the life to come as a continuation of the process of dying. And, of course, it is Jesus who has made this possible for us (cf. *John* 11:25).).

Paul taught that even to be a follower of Jesus means

in one sense to have died: to be baptised into Jesus meant also to be baptised into his death, and hence to be united to his resurrection life (*Rom.* 6:3–8). The Christian has died, and his life is 'hid with Christ in God' (*Col.* 3:3). And so the 'moment of death' is for us the moment of true life simply because it is the moment of perfect communion, fellowship, with Jesus and his Father.

We are thus led back again to man's tireless search for life. We have placed side by side the existentialist and the Christian answers to life's dilemma, and we have seen that their positions become essentially united in that single 'moment' of the End before God. True life, then, is only the life which God himself gives; for the Christian this means 'eternal life' here and now made possible through the incarnate Word. And so we could say that the true Christian—the really believing Christian—is an authentic existent. But it does indeed all come down to a single moment, a moment of existential decision, whether one thinks of it in terms of a daily happening, or the end of life, or the final coming of the eschatological Kingdom towards which God's Reign on earth is moving. The existentialist would say that it is the moment when one's past, present, and future are gathered into the unity of *self*. The Christian must say that it is the moment when he in faith commits himself to be gathered into Jesus—and through him, is 'gathered into the barns and nets of God' (in the words of the old Irish hymn). This 'moment' is, in fact, every *now*: 'Now is the acceptable time, now is the day of salvation' (2 *Cor.* 6:2): The moment of existentialist self-fulfilment is the moment of christian salvation—of being saved from oneself by Jesus. In him alone, the Bread of Life, can be found that 'life more abundantly' for which we hunger. To find oneself in Jesus is to experience at last *Existenz*: 'Abide—live—in Me, and I in you' (*John* 15:4).

# CHAPTER V

# Christian Freedom

'F o r freedom Christ has set us free' (*Gal.* 5 : 1). Paul, the former Pharisee, believed passionately in *freedom*. He had known, too long, the slavery of a rigid religious system, the bondage of a religion of law and precept. Christ had set him free from all that, and he gloried in his freedom. He ached for his disciples to value the freedom that was theirs; he was sad, and angry, when freedom was not truly appreciated: 'stand fast, therefore, and do not submit again to a yoke of slavery' (5 : 1). He understood very well the awesome responsibility of freedom and scrupulously respected the conscience of his disciples: he would not compel them—they must make a personal decision. But christian freedom is never licence to do as one pleases; it is always motivated—and constrained—by love. 'For though I am free from all men, I have made myself a slave to all . . .' (1 *Cor.* 9 : 19). We shall look at St Paul's conception of freedom in Christ.[1]

## Freedom from Sin and Law

Paul knows that man was created in the image of God (*Gen.* 1 : 27) and as such stands apart from and above all other creatures. But he stands always in dependence on his Creator and is, or ought to be, conscious of his creaturehood. Man lives his life, and is truly man, if his mode of being is fully human. But man is fallen man (Gen. 3); left to himself his mode of being is less than fully human. In Jewish thought awareness of this sad state led to the emergence of the mythological figure of the last, the second,

Adam, the perfect man of the future, as the criterion, the standard, of true humanity. Paul, however, looks not to a mythological Adam, but to the concrete figure of Christ. He has brought again into the world true, full, humanness, and only against him can humanness be measured.

We can turn again to existentialist categories and may effectively express Paul's thought in the language of Heidegger. Man, every man, has the possibility of being authentically human. But it is an ontological possibility (that which is possible in principle for man as man). The two basic possibilities for man are: he can be at one with himself or he can be estranged from himself; he can be authentically human or inauthentically human. The tragic reality is that fallen man does not have an ontic possibility (actually and in the concrete) of being authentically human; he does not have it in his power to become so. 'Wretched man that I am! Who will deliver me from this body of death?' (*Rom.* 7:24), the despairing cry of fallen man. However, the situation is no longer desperate. Authentic humanity *is* a reality: Christ—though he only— is authentically human. And to the extent that his mode of being is in harmony with that of Christ, man, in his measure, may be authentically human. Christ empowers man to pass to this mode of being; he places man in the ontic possibility of authentic existence—'thanks be to God, through Jesus Christ our Lord' (*Rom.* 7:25).

*Sin.* Paul envisaged all mankind under the baleful power of *sin*: 'all men, both Jews and Greeks, are under the power of sin' (*Rom.* 3:9). 'Sin' is to be distinguished from 'sinning'—that is, from individual sinful acts (e.g. 3:23). 'Sin' is the environment in which man lives. It is a condition of mankind which follows on a decision taken in opposition to the will of the Creator; the contribution of successive generations has aggravated the situation. Human society is inauthentically oriented. The individual is set in a corrupt environment and, inevitably, is influenced by it; man is dominated by his 'world'. The world's understanding of man is tailored to fit man's concrete mode of being, but this is an inauthentic mode of being. Always, however, man retains the ontological capacity to choose authentic existence. Yet the pressure of his environment limits his ontic possibility to inauthenticity only; left to himself, he has no real choice.

God has restored to man the possibility of genuine choice, making authentic existence an ontic possibility for him. He did this by sending his Son who, *fully* human, alone exemplifies what man should be, and makes it possible for man so to be: 'You, who were dead . . . God made alive' (*Col.* 2 : 13). Authentic humanity lives again in lives modelled on that of the truly authentic Man. We shall see that authentic existence is a being-with-others. The christian community, authentically oriented, has its own environment, sheltered from the pervasive atmosphere of sin. Only within the Christ-community does the individual find freedom from sin.

One way in which man can make his mode of being inauthentic is by defining his possibilities in terms of things —as for instance, if his whole interest is concentrated on the possession of money, social status or the like. Thus, man submits himself to what is essentially lower than himself and makes himself part of an alien world of being. In relation to man all 'things' have an essentially utilitarian value. Heidegger defined 'thing' as 'being-to-be-used', and it is a term that can cover any non-human reality. In regard to things, man makes an authentic decision when he recognises that they are merely to be used; he makes an inauthentic decision when he accords them any greater value. It is on this principle that Paul so radically criticises the Jewish attitude to the Law. And it is this, too, that explains his apparently contradictory stand in relation to the Law.

*Law.* In Romans 8:2 Paul characterises the Torah as 'the law of sin and death', while in 7:12 he has declared that 'the law is holy, and the commandment is holy and just and good'. Is there any way of reconciling such statements? Bultmann has provided the key: 'Paul does not criticise the Law from the standpoint of its *content*, but in respect of its *significance* for man'.[2] Paul had respect for the Law; his quarrel was with the place it had come to hold in the lives of Jews. For the Jew the Torah (including both the written Torah and the oral law: the *Halakah*) expressed the fullness of the divine mind. Indeed, Law and Lawgiver were practically identical. In this situation the Torah took on an absolute value, and man could concern himself exclusively with the Law (to the practical neglect of God).

One who adopted this Jewish attitude to the Law was, in practice, defining himself in terms of a 'thing'. And he limited his possibilities by limiting, drastically, his field of choice: the Law decided—man submitted. In this way man found security, but it was a crippling security which limited his right to decide. Furthermore, this attitude was deceptive: man relied on the Law (*Gal.* 3:10) as a means of life (3:21) whereas, in fact, his slavish reliance on it meant death (*Rom.* 8:2). Worst of all, guided exclusively by the Law, man sought authenticity within narrow, precise limits —and found a 'righteousness' that was his own, and not God's. All this goes to explain why, for Paul, the Torah, though 'holy and just and good', remained decidedly a 'thing'. It was not absolute in any sense, but had a merely educative value. It was a 'pedagogue' (*Gal.* 3:23–25) which guided the first faltering steps of man groping for authenticity. The Christian, who looked to Christ and *imitated* him, had outgrown the need of a *paidagōgos*. For if Paul had respect for the Law in itself ('holy, and just and good') he was quite sure that, in the time of fulfilment, it no longer had any place. In Galatians (as in Romans) Paul contrasts Law and gospel and in doing so he is not being abstract or theoretical : he looks to biblical tradition. On the one hand Israel, at Sinai, received the Law; and in Jewish eyes, the winning of 'righteousness' before God, with the help of the Law, is the proper goal of all religious practice. On the other hand Paul knows from the same biblical tradition that Abraham *believed* and that his faith was, by God, reckoned to him as righteousness (*Gal.* 3 : 6). The Law rested not on the principle of faith, but on the principle of works (3 : 12); the gospel, which the Apostle proclaimed as the fulfilment of the promise, rests on the principle of faith. Paul concedes that in the time of promise faith and Law could have existed side by side, but he maintains that, in the time of fulfilment, it is no longer possible for them to exist together— because the Law has been abrogated by Christ.

The question then arises that, if the law has been abrogated by the gospel, should we still call the latter the *nova lex*, the 'new law'? For the Apostle, Christ is 'the end of the [Mosaic] law' (*Rom.* 10 : 4), and if he speaks in Galatians 6 : 2 of a 'law of Christ' (cf. 'law of faith', *Rom.* 3 : 27; 'law of the Spirit', 8 : 2) what does he mean by the expression? The fact is that now the term 'law' has taken on a radically new quality : it is the 'law of the Spirit' (*Rom.* 8 : 2). It gives 'life in Christ Jesus' and had set the baptised free from the law of Sin and Death. This Spirit-law of Christ is an imperative flowing from the indicative, the living reality, of new being in Christ. The new existence of the baptised in Christ involves a personal commitment to him; the imperative urges the implementation of the new existence, through christian living, in christian 'work', which has nothing to do with 'the works of the law' but is 'the fruit of the Spirit' (*Gal.* 5:22). And according to Galatians 5:14, every christian imperative is concentrated on the *basic* imperative, to love others. The 'law of Christ' is observed in and through *agapē* (6:2).

There has, however, been a radical break with the past. 'The *nova lex* of the New Testament does not stand in continuity with the Mosaic law, abrogated by the gospel, even when there are inclusive contacts, as in the demands of the Decalogue which also are valid for the Christian—not even when the demands of its second part are "summed up" and "fulfilled" in the commandment of love (*Rom.* 13: 8–10; *Gal.* 5:14) . . . The obedience of the baptised to the law of Christ is *usus practicus evangelii* [the practical living of the gospel], not a life under law. It implies that the gospel [and not the law] expresses the will of God.'[3] Christ is 'the end of the law, that every one who has faith may be justified' (*Rom.* 10:4), he has 'abolished in his flesh the law of commandments and ordinances' (*Eph.* 2:15). In the emphatic teaching of Paul and his disciples, the Law is once for all superseded by the gospel, which is the 'law' of Christ, the visible dynamic of being-in-Christ.

## Christian Community
*Collectivism.*  A fundamental characteristic of man's mode of being is defined by Heidegger as 'being-with-others'. On this level, too, man is forced to the choice between authenticity and inauthenticity because he is necessarily in contact with other persons. For Heidegger, man makes himself inauthentic by submerging his individuality in the amorphous, depersonalised mass which he terms '*das Man*': he becomes one of 'the crowd'. He thereby insulates himself against the challenge of his existence and avoids being pressed to the point of true decision. His decisions are made for him, by the society in which he is merged, by 'public

opinion'. In this atmosphere of collectivism Heidegger could see no scope for authentic existence. At best, one could opt out of society.

*Community.* Paul did not succumb to such pessimism. In place of collectivism, he saw community. It is his presupposition that all men are brothers, children of the one Father. In this situation man has two basic options open to him : openness to others or withdrawal from sharing with others, from concern with others. Inevitably, then, inauthentic existence is characterised by egocentrism, by isolation. Paul lays stress on the acceptance of responsibility as the criterion of authenticity, but this responsibility, instead of being an egotistic affirmation of self as an individual apart from others, manifests itself in the apparently conflicting demands of individualism and community.

*Life-in-Christ.* The new mode of existence that man achieves in Christ is not wholly his own. It is a participation, a sharing in which others are essential. Paradoxically, Paul's understanding of sin is a help to understanding his idea of community. Man is not only born into a disoriented society—made so by the sin of preceding generations—but he contributes to that disorder by his own sins. As a Christian he belongs to a community that is, in principle, rightly oriented to God. In fact, through the failure of individuals, sin gains an entry into this sphere which ought to be immune to its influence. The individual sins of each Christian provide a bridgehead for sin and make it that much more difficult for the other members of the community to be their true selves—hence Paul's stern attitude towards the toleration of incest in Corinth (1 *Cor.* 5 : 1–5).

In short, then, my freedom to realise my potentialities, and become truly human, is conditioned by the authenticity of the other members of the community. Christian freedom, and its necessary correlative of responsibility, highlights in a concrete way the interdependence of Christians on one another. But all this is in the realm of interpersonal relationships, for the great danger of a christian community is to see itself as, in some way, distinct from its members. This danger is all the more real because, as a human, visible reality, the christian community must of necessity be institutionally organised. Too easily the community is assumed to have a value in itself which the members are ordained to serve. Uniformity in thought and action becomes a virtue and the individual finds himself cast in a mould, and his authentic development is inhibited. In truth, the *christian* community exists for the sake of the individual. And its response to God is nothing other than the response of its members.

The individual must always be conscious of the community, but must never become lost in it. What Paul demands of his converts is, paradoxically, a completely *altruistic individualism*. Their commitment to Christ is achieved in isolation, through the loneliest decision a man can make, the act of faith. Their growth in that commitment is to be an intensely personal development of the unique potentialities that God gives to each individual. Yet their attention is never to focus on themselves. Their whole being must be alert to detect and minister to the needs of others. All this is possible only to the extent that the community is a *loving* community. Otherwise, there will be selfishness on the one hand, and the individual will be hampered by the institution on the other.

*Forms of Community.*   There are two specifically distinct forms of community; it is of paramount importance to know in which category the christian community fits.[4] The action-community is one whose *raison d'être* is the performance of a series of related actions. Such is an army which exists to carry out a plan of defence or attack; or a business company which exists in order to produce and market a product. In an action community the individual takes second place to the plan and organisation which represent the common good of that community. The role of authority is to formulate a course of action and to see that it is carried out. Over against the action community is the community of being, or the formation-community—a community whose members gather together not in order to do something but in order to become something. A simple example of this is the fitness club, whose members join together in order to become fit and healthy, or in order to remain in condition. The 'common good' of a community of this nature is the success of the individual. The fitness club exists to help its members to become fit. Its success is measured only in terms of the personal success of its members; the common good is the achievement of the individual member.

*The Church.*   In the New Testament it appears clearly that the Church in respect of its members is not an action community, but a community of those in process of formation.[5] Paul shows his complete awareness of this fact: 'Not that I have already obtained this [fullness of life] or am already perfect; but I press on to make it my own, because Christ Jesus has made me his own. Brethren, I do not consider that I have made it my own; but one thing I do, forgetting what lies behind and straining forward to what lies ahead, I press on toward the goal for the prize of the upward call of God in Christ Jesus' (*Phil.* 3:12–14). As a formation community, the Church is not an army (despite the unfortunate designation of the 'Church-militant'), and it is not big business, with a product to sell. Unhappily, it has too often assumed the aspect of both the one and the other. Its authority structure is still basically that of an action community. Policy is decided at headquarters and commands and directives are passed down to the rank and file. And the 'gospel' can be made to seem a marketable commodity; one needs better business techniques in order to 'sell' the product. Somehow, the individual tends to get lost though he may be noticed with approval when he notably conforms, or with disapproval when he dares to make up his own mind and deviate from the official line.

Whatever happens in practice, the Church is meant to be, and ought to be, a formation community. And here the individual comes into his own: *this* community is for the sake of the individual. The characteristics of the Church, as a formation community, have been finely sketched by Jerome Murphy-O'Connor:

> The formation community is first and foremost a community of opportunity. It is a setting which aids something to happen to the member. Since the formation community with which we are concerned is the Church, this 'something' is the deepening of faith, hope, and love, the intensification of identification with Jesus Christ. In other words, the community provides the conditions which enable man to become what God originally destined him to be, that is, fully and consciously human. This, it should be remembered, is the fundamental lesson of the incarnation. God *became man* in Jesus Christ. As followers of Christ we in turn must become men. True humanity is not something given. In man there is no inexorable programmed evolution to maturity as in the case of the animals. What makes Christianity unique among world religions is the fact that it has given man a concrete model for his inarticulate, sometimes unconscious aspirations. Jesus is the invitation of the Father, but he is also the perfect fulfilment of God's

design for his human creation. In his humanity he is the living demonstration of the consequences of acceptance of the divine invitation.[6]

Because the christian community is such, recognition of Christ as the divine offer of friendship is the only condition for membership in it. This recognition is not only a grace—it is also conversion. Of course, the conversion is not complete in itself, and one must work towards its deepening. To achieve this the believer must, in the first place, be protected from the power of sin. In principle, at least, he finds this protection within the community and finds, too, the mutual support that is the bulwark of christian freedom. The community is a human society, with a purpose. If it is to be effective it must have leadership: the ideal towards which it aspires must be incarnated in a symbolic centre which draws the individual members into true community. This is precisely the function of authority in a formation community.

*Following Christ.*    The goal of the members of a christian community is to follow Christ as perfectly as possible. Hence, they must know Christ as a real person. Paul makes us understand that to live in Christ is to follow him wholeheartedly, to consent to imitate him. This is the plan of God who has predestined us 'to be conformed to the image of his Son, in order that he might be the first-born among many brothers' (*Rom.* 8:29). Or, to put it another way, the Father has chosen Christians to bear the family likeness of his Son, that he might be the eldest of a family of many brothers and sisters. Jesus himself had declared that his disciples, like true children of their heavenly Father, must strive to be like that Father (*Matt.* 5:48; *Luke* 6:36). Paul, in his turn, exhorts Christians: 'therefore be imitators of God, as beloved children' (*Eph.* 5:1).

But though we can turn to our Father without fear and trustfully, we have never seen him (cf. *John* 1 : 18), and we cannot imitate a model we have not seen. We must turn to the image of the Father in the Son. Christ must be the centre around which our lives evolve and develop.

This is what Paul urges: 'Be imitators of me, *as I am of Christ*' (1 *Cor.* 11 : 1). Not only does the Apostle state, in as many words, that christian living is the imitation of Christ, he has let us know that he himself had taken Christ as his model. And it is because he is fully conscious of being an imitator of the Lord that he can confidently ask his Corinthians to imitate himself. He wants them to take the first steps in the christian life: let them pattern their lives on his, then. Two factors are involved here: not only that imitation demands direct experience but that there is a deep human need for a concrete demonstration of the real possibility of a preached doctrine. Paul was fully aware of this and so proposed the concrete reality of his own life (cf. 1 *Thess.* 1 : 6; 1 *Cor.* 4 : 16f.). This was Paul's supreme and most effective exercise of his apostolic authority. 'A little reflection shows that it could not be otherwise in a christian community. A christian community is founded on the incarnation, an act which introduced a new mode into God's relationship with mankind. No longer can that relationship simply be spoken about, in the mode proper to the old dispensation which has been superseded. It must be reincarnated. It is only in this perspective that a traditional statement such as "the voice of authority is the voice of God" can be given *specifically christian* interpretation. In the Old Testament God spoke, but in the New Testament he conceived and uttered a Word, the person of Christ. The word that the bearer of christian authority "speaks" is his own personality as transformed by Christ. Unless he is "another Christ" no one has genuine authority in a christian community.'[7]

## Christian Freedom

Freedom, which is absolutely essential for authentic existence, has two correlative facets: freedom from restraint and compulsion, and responsibility. Paul's stand against the Jewish attitude to the Law was a defence of the first aspect. While he accepted the goodness of the Law and its valid educative role—it was a *paidagōgos*—he rejected the view that saw it as the inflexible manifestation of God's will. In his eyes, it was a guideline, to be given due weight—but it did not command obedience. Paul never speaks of man obeying 'the Law' or of obedience to a 'commandment'. Obedience is man's response to God's offer of salvation—*faith* is obedience.[8]

Paul, in fact, would repudiate the idea of giving obedience to what were intended to be simply guidelines. Any binding directives Paul himself issued were in the realm of social organisation (e.g. 2 *Thess.* 3 :6, 10f.; 1 *Cor.* 7 :17; 11 :34; 16 :1). In strictly moral matters he refrained, absolutely, from laying down any precept. His concern was with the authenticity of the act which must spring from a personal interior decision on what is fitting for a Christian to do. The freedom that is essential to such an act is destroyed by any form of compulsion—such as a binding precept. Paul's view is very clearly expressed in Philemon. He tells Philemon, bluntly enough, what he *ought* to do, but he refuses to command him. 'Though I am bold enough in Christ to command you to do what is required, yet for love's sake I prefer to appeal to you' (vv. 8f.). His real concern is expressed a few lines later : 'I preferred to do nothing without your consent in order that your goodness might *not be by compulsion but of your own free will*' (v. 14). Paul has no doubt about his own authority, and could command if he had wanted to. But he regards a command that *must* be obeyed as a form of compulsion, a limiting of the *free decision* that is essential for authentic growth; and he will not issue a binding directive in the area of moral decision.

Paul saw that the Jewish attitude to the Law hampered free decision and authentic growth. When he learned that one of his own Churches, the Galatian community, was in danger of falling under the sway of judaisers and was looking to the false security of observance, he reacted violently. One of the great object lessons of the New Testament, unhappily almost entirely lost on Christians down the centuries, is the astonishing fact that the one and only time that Paul 'pulls rank'—when he, in Galatians 1-2, spells out his apostolic authority and insists that it came *directly* from the Lord—he does so in the interest of *freedom*! He insists on his authority, not to browbeat the Galatians, not to awe them into submission, but in an almost desperate effort to get them up off their knees, to get them to accept the burden of responsibility and to take the risk of making decisions. They were welcoming the judaisers, who offered them the security that came from clinging to the 613 precepts of the Torah, thus freeing them from the burden, and the risk, of personal decision. Henceforth, their life would be mapped out for them : they had only to do or to avoid what the Law prescribed. They were ready to shrug off their responsibility and let a moral directive carry the burden of decision.

Paul saw, what later christian communities were to discover to their cost, that this attitude made for immaturity and hampered love. It was a misunderstanding of the role of law. Law, in this view, can be the adequate expression of God's will and so man can limit himself, in his response to God, to what is prescribed in the Law. And this brings a false sense of security because, having fulfilled the Law, man assumes that he stands right with God. There is something really frightening in the realisation that an attitude which eventually was to become prevalent enough in the

Church to be regarded as 'normal', had not only been sharply criticised by Paul, but was the very attitude of the Pharisees repudiated by Jesus himself!

There is another enemy of freedom: exaggeration. This Paul found in Corinth. It is an interesting feature, and not at all surprising in view of his own profound feeling in the matter, that it is precisely in Galatians and Corinthians that Paul is most vehement because, in each case, he is defending the principle of christian freedom. He was conscious that freedom could be abused. Thus, he recognised that the attitude of the 'strong' at Corinth was based on a mis-understanding of christian freedom. The freedom that characterises christian living is twofold: it is both a freedom *from* and a freedom *to*. Within the christian community the Christian is free *from* sin and Law; ideally, this freedom can be absolute. However, to understand this new freedom as a freedom *to* do whatever one wishes is a grave error, to which the Corinthians had succumbed. It would seem that they regarded themselves as taken over wholly by the Spirit; they were now authentic men so that each and every act of theirs was authentic. Paul regarded this attitude as quite simply immature (1 *Cor.* 3:1; 14:20). He took up their vaunted slogan: 'All things are lawful for me'—and modified it:

'All things are lawful for me'—but not all things are helpful.

'All things are lawful for me'—but I will not be enslaved by anything. (6:12).

'All things are lawful'—but not all things are helpful.

'All things are lawful'—but not all things build up. (10.23.)

Only whatever is 'helpful' or 'builds up' is consistent with christian freedom. This is because freedom *to* must be understood in a communal context; it is a freedom whose exercise is designed to reinforce the bonds that bind men together in Christ. In other words, this freedom is circumscribed by 'love which binds things together in perfect harmony' (*Col.* 3 : 14). In Christ, one is freed for love, and love is real only in service. To absolutise freedom, to transfer to freedom *to* the absolute character of freedom *from*, is to lose it, to become *enslaved*. As Jerome Murphy-O'Connor has pithily expressed it : 'Freedom can be lost through exaggeration, never through renunciation.' I can, for instance, take a stand on my *rights* and exercise my 'freedom'—while someone is hurt thereby. I can renounce my 'rights', out of consideration for others. I am, in a sense, thereby a loser, but my renunciation is a real exercise of freedom. Consideration for the needs of others is always the primary factor in the Christian's moral judgment; it must also condition the exercise of his freedom.

## Guidelines

The attitude of Paul's Jewish contemporaries was one of complete obedience to the Torah. For them, the prescriptions of the Old Testament expressed the will of God and were therefore normative in the strictest sense. For Paul, the Law could not be regarded as the will of God. In his eyes, the precepts of the Old Testament were guidelines to be followed with great discretion in working out the christian response to the call of God in Christ. To say that the Law cannot be regarded as the will of God does not mean that it has no relevance. To say that the moral imperatives found in the New Testament are guidelines and not precepts does not mean that they can be ignored. Both the one and the other have an educative value, and this is operative only when they are confronted with the utmost seriousness. But there always remains responsibility, the exercise of a critical, personal judgment. 'Test *everything*; hold fast to what is good' (1 *Thess.* 5.21). The directive *must* be a factor in the moral judgment, but it must not predetermine the judgment.

Do Paul's moral guidelines have any relevance for us? Some of them, undoubtedly, coloured by the social situation of his time and also by his own eschatological perspective, his expectation of an imminent Parousia, no longer fit our conditions and have nothing to say to our contemporary being-in-Christ. Such are, for instance, his imperatives concerning women, slaves, and the State. However, on the whole, one can say that, not only do his guidelines have abiding value, but our neglect of them, or our hardening them into precepts, has impaired the quality of our christian living.

> What is certainly of perennial value in Paul is his insight into the meaning of being-in-Christ, because it provides an answer of unequalled profundity to the two fundamental questions that each generation must ask itself : what does it mean to be human? and what does it mean to live in community? His imperatives retain an immediate value for us today to the extent that they are related to his understanding of authentic christian existence. Directives designed to discourage selfishness, and to encourage the selfless service of others have a lasting value. They are just as relevant for us today as they were for the Pauline communities. They must not be given blind obedience, but unless they are taken with the utmost seriousness the Christian risks remaining blind to the forces that are operating within him, and drifts into the danger of confusing intensity with authenticity.[9]

**The Heritage of Paul**[10]

The significance of Paul and his theology for the Church can scarcely be exaggerated. As a 'chosen instrument' (*Acts* 9 : 15) his role was in no sense a happy chance. But we may well ask what would have become of the 'religion of Jesus' if this man had not emerged. Galatians—and to some extent Acts 15—provides the answer. Paul fought for 'the truth of the gospel' (*Gal.* 2 : 5,14), for the inner thrust of the kerygma. He had grasped, as did no one else in the early Church, the implications of the gospel and he fought with determination against any softening of them. If the 'perversion' of the gospel (1 : 7) had prevailed, Paul knew, instinctively, that the universalist drive of Christianity would be blocked : Christianity would have become a Jewish sect. Of course Christians would have acknowledged Jesus as the promised Messiah, but their religion would have been firmly bound to the religion of the Torah. Paul saw that the way to salvation, through the crucified and risen Jesus, is open to *all* men who have faith. He saw that the way of faith is a universalist way, no longer linked to the way of the Law ('without works of the law'). Through his *sola-fide* and *sola-gratia* doctrine, grounded in *solus Christus*, Paul would lead men into that freedom for which, according to Galatians 5 : 1, Christ has set us free. The way of faith is subject to no other condition than that of faith itself. For in Paul's view, faith in Jesus Christ is the one, the exclusive, way of salvation. But, if the *sola-fide* principle is indeed an exclusive principle, it is not an unrestricted principle : it is 'valid' only when it 'is working through love' (*Gal.* 5 :6).

The theological insights of Paul are not only of abiding validity : they exercise a continuous critical function. This is, of course, provided that the Church pays careful attention to them and does not distort the theology of the cross preached by Paul into a 'respectable' theology. The abiding critical function of Pauline theology for the Church and for the world is seen in his urgent and unmistakable reference to the death and resurrection of Christ as the fundamental and totally decisive saving event which always brings to naught every self-glorification of Church and world. For Paul insists on the 'scandalous' and 'foolish' *logos tou staurou* : the 'word of the cross' which the 'wisdom of the world' can neither verify nor falsify (1 *Cor.* 1 : 18–25). But this word is also a word of hope. Because of its close link with the kerygma of the resurrection it is a word which opens up a future to all mankind, as it looks beyond the boundaries of death and leads men beyond death.

The exclusive salvation-way of faith which is, in Paul's view, the way of liberation and of freedom, preserves the Church from ever-threatening legalism and turns it into an 'open system' in which the Pneuma can work. Happily, the Spirit again and again bursts through ossified structures, makes room for the exercise of freedom and maturity, and draws the Church's attention to the signs of the times. At the same time, the close linking of faith and kerygma in Pauline theology saves the Church from vagueness and irrelevancy.

Paul is not vague; he is a supreme realist. We cannot do without him. The truth is, the tragedy is, that we have not really listened to Paul—as we have not heeded his Lord. Paul has told us that Christ has made us children of God (*Gal.* 3 :26). He has told us that Christ has set us free (*Gal.* 5 : 1). As children of God, we must find the courage to stand fast in the freedom which Christ has won for us. It is not enough for us to be careful not to betray our freedom through irresponsibility. We must take a stand against the 'yoke of slavery', any abuse of freedom in the world or in the Church. This is the precious heritage of the Apostle.

### Prayer

If christian living is an imitation of Christ, then prayer, based on the teaching and the practice of Jesus, must have a place in it. It is immediately obvious that Paul set great store by prayer. He speaks of 'unceasing prayer', prayer 'at all times', prayer 'night and day'. Of course, prayer had been part of his life as a Pharisaic Jew. But, just as his observance of the Law had given way to freedom in Christ, so, too, his more formal praying had yielded to the power of the Spirit of Christ. Now he sees that the very ground of prayer is the reality of divine sonship. And it is the Spirit who speaks to the heart of God's child and convinces him that he really is a child of God. The Spirit inspires him to turn to God in prayer and call him by the same familiar name that Jesus used: *Abba* (Rom. 8:15f.). Even then the Christian does not really know how he can make his prayer effective before God. But then the Spirit comes to the help of his weakness and intercedes for him 'with sighs too deep for tears' (8:26).

Already in the Old Testament thanksgiving was a distinctive feature of prayer. Thanksgiving always went along with profession of faith in God and with the recognition of his glory and of his goodness, because the acknowledgment of God inevitably gives rise to praise and calls forth gratitude for his generosity. Above all else, it is the merciful and saving work of God that fills the heart of the Israelite with overflowing gratitude. Thanksgiving is the public confession of determined divine acts; to thank God is to publish his goodness, to proclaim the marvels he has wrought, to bear testimony to his works. It is to be expected that Paul should very often give thanks to God and praise him. Regularly he begins his letters with thanksgiving—for the supreme gift of God in Christ, and for the acceptance of that grace by his converts.

The Lord had taught his disciples to ask (cf. *Matt.* 7:7-11); Paul prayed the prayer of petition. He prays without ceasing, making mention of those for whom he intercedes (*Rom.* 1:9), he asks that they may be established in every good work and word (2 *Thess.* 2:17), that God will grant them to dwell in harmony (*Rom.* 15:5), that he may fill them with joy and peace (*Rom.* 15:33; 2 *Thess.* 3:16). Paul in turn asks for the prayers of the brethren, that he and they together may practise mutual charity and fulfil the task of their apostolate (*Rom.* 15:32; 2 *Cor.* 1:11). Indeed, he invites them to '*strive* together with me in your prayers to God on my behalf' (*Rom.* 15:30). Suffering and affliction become shared prayer and a bond of union (2 *Cor.* 1:4-7). While Paul normally directs his prayer to God the Father, in the name of the Lord Jesus Christ, he also addresses prayer to Christ himself (2 *Cor.* 12:8) and he makes his own the earliest of christian prayers: the cry *Marana tha* (1 *Cor.* 16:22) 'Our Lord, come!' (cf. *Apoc.* 22:20).

In short, prayer is to be seen in close relation to all that has been said about our union with Christ, about his life in us, about our life in him. The more life-in-Christ is a reality for us, the more we see it as a sharing in the life of the risen Lord, the better we know Christ and strive to imitate him—so much the more will our prayer be spontaneous, simple, earnest. Knowledge of Christ, in the biblical sense of acceptance and commitment, is the wellspring of christian prayer.

EPILOGUE

# 'Pray at all times . . .'

We have closed our study of christian living with a glance
at St Paul's attitude to prayer. And we have seen that for
him, as for any Christian, prayer must have a place
in christian life, because prayer is union with Christ.
We may effectively close this book with a reflection on
prayer.

The Christian optimist—and a Christian of any other
kind is really a contradiction—will find that, even in the
darkest night, a candle of hope and promise will suddenly
shine out. And in our day we find (and who but an optimist
would have looked for such a thing?) a fresh and growing
interest in prayer. It is not an interest directly associated
with the liturgical movement though perhaps there is a
link. It seems to be something more basic, more personal: a
deeply felt *need*. We should be humbly grateful for this stir-
ring, this heartening touch of the Spirit.

## A Felt Need

One of the most precious gifts of God, of a loving Father,
is the need for prayer, a felt need. What one means by this
is an awareness, deep within us, that we are not self-
sufficient. It means a turning to a Father who understands,
who has given us his own Son. For indeed it would seem
that the prayer of a Christian is naturally and understand-
ably Christocentric. It springs, in the first place, from an
awareness of Jesus as a living Person, near at hand, a Friend.
It means taking him seriously, taking him at his word:
'Apart from me, you can do nothing' (*John* 15:5). It

means turning to him, leaning on him, being conscious of his support.

All this is, and must be, compatible with a knowledge of ourselves, a consciousness of our own frailty. But somehow we are not discouraged, we do not lose heart, because we are never alone. Jesus is there, close at hand. Like us in all things, he understands us. Perhaps only one who has an understanding friend who bears with one despite all one's failings, even (almost) to the very betrayal of friendship, can appreciate what such understanding means: the consolation, the comfort, of being understood just as one is. That is how Jesus understands us, and there is the greatest comfort in his understanding. Our reaction to it is prayer. It is not a prayer of many words for he has told us not to pray in that way: 'And in praying, do not heap up empty phrases' (*Matt.* 6:7). No, it is the prayer of love, of few words, prayer in the heart. It is a simple turning to Jesus, putting oneself in his hands. It is, like Mary's prayer, a letting it be done unto one.

## Unceasing Prayer

In this way prayer can be unceasing—because the awareness of our need is always with us. Day after day, hour after hour, minute by minute, our being, in a quiet, hidden way, cries out to the Lord. We are always responsive to his gentle touch. For if our understanding of christian life is that of John and Paul, then christian life is the most authentic reality within our experience. We view our christian becoming as a new birth, a new creation. We believe, with deep conviction, that the *life* which makes us Christians is, in some mysterious way, a sharing in the life of the risen Lord. We believe that we are branches of him, the true Vine, alive with his life within us. We share the conviction of Paul: 'I live, now not I—but Christ lives in me.' And, if this conviction is deep enough, we understand too the earnest desire of the Apostle to be dissolved and be with Christ, the far, far better thing. If in some measure we share the New Testament understanding of christian life, then Christ is real for us and we are bound to share some of Paul's deep feeling about the need for prayer.

But if we are not aware of a need for prayer, for simple but intimate communion with Jesus, then we have reason to feel concern about the reality, the quality of our christian life. On the surface, Paul's plea that we 'pray always', though it is an echo of the call of the Master (*Luke* 18:1), seems exaggerated. Yet if, as we have said, one takes seriously what Paul meant by christian life, then the abiding attitude of prayer becomes the *normal* attitude for the Christian. It is only because we do not have the same awareness as Paul that the idea of unceasing prayer seems unrealistic. And, of course, we have formalised prayer, formalised it in such a way that unceasing prayer is obviously an impossibility. If, however, the source of our prayer is the consciousness of our christian life, the awareness of our total need of Jesus, then all becomes simple. This is not to say that all becomes easy; 'simple' means uncomplicated. For there is nothing complex in our need itself, nothing complex in our dependence on the Lord. It is simply the reality of our christian being.

### Fellowship in Prayer

*The Friend.* Prayer is communion with a Friend. It is the beauty of true friendship that friends understand. My friend knows me, and accepts me as I am; otherwise the relationship is not friendship but something less, characterised by self-seeking. And Jesus knows me. He knows me as I am. He knows that I should make my own, now and always, the prayer of the tax-collector: 'Lord, be merciful to me, a sinner.' The fact that Jesus knows and understands me is my greatest comfort. I do not have to pretend, or even

147

make excuses. I can come to him as I am. My awareness of my own shortcomings, of my sin, is not complacency. I can be thoroughly ashamed of myself, and yet can come to him with simple confidence, because he will not throw my own shame in my face. I can be conscious of my sin, but that is no barrier. My coming to him, in sincerity, is a turning from my sin, an invitation to his forgiveness. Best of all, I can forget myself, my inadequacy, my failures, to lean on him. In this prayer of quiet confidence, my simple turning to the Lord, I find support and strength.

*The Mother.*   It seems that christian prayer most naturally finds issue in prayer to Mary. When we understand her place in the mystery of her Son and in christian living, prayer to her becomes the most natural thing in the world. And if she too is *real* to us, real as the Mother of her Son and as our Mother, our prayer-union with her has a special and lovely quality. She can tame our wilful hearts, she can impart to us something of her own delicacy. Above all she will fill us with her spirit of openness : I am the handmaid of the Lord . . . be it done to me. And she will teach us the reality of faith : Blessed is she *who has believed*. We so need faith, need it in our life, need it in all the areas of our christian living. Our Mother can teach us what real faith is, for she knows. Best of all, if we turn to her simply and trustingly, she will show us the face of her Son and help us to know him. We will find that prayer to her leads naturally to prayer to him. For our prayer of communion with Mary must lead to union with her Son.

*Communion.*   In prayer, too, we can find communion with those we love. This again follows from the reality of christian life. We not only pray for others, we can pray with them. This becomes most fully true where friendship finds spontaneous expression in prayer. When friends are united in a bond that is indeed *agapé*, love in Christ, they find union in their mutual belonging to Christ; they meet in him even when they are absent. And so we are back to the vital meaning and reality of christian life, the Lord himself. For if, in a true sense, all Christians are branches of him, the Vine, awareness of this fact must greatly strengthen the basis of friendship and give it a new dimension. Prayer can be a meeting-place of minds and hearts.

### Silence, Faith, Love

The deepest prayer of all is the prayer of silence. So much has been written about distraction in prayer, and too often in a context of formalised prayer that is itself the biggest distraction! The Lord warned us against many words. This is not only because empty phrases tend to be just that—empty, but also because our many words can hinder us from hearing. We all know the person who is so engrossed in talking that he never listens. 'Behold, I stand at the door and knock.' We can fail to hear that knock. We can miss the gentle voice of our Friend. We need to listen. And what we hear will not always be what we would wish to hear. Perhaps, after all, this is the main reason why we want to pray *in prayers*: we are afraid to listen, afraid of what might be asked of us. And we shall find that Jesus will ask almost contradictory things. We can be asked to die to ourselves, to lay down our lives, in so many ways. Now it will be to open our life to take another into it; and now it will be to stand apart, to set aside a treasured contact and association, to give another full scope for growth and fulfilment.

There is prayer that is faith, like the deep prayer of Mary. It is prayer that issues in peace and joy. Here, indeed, one touches the profound reality of christian life. Faith in the Lord, a confident leaning on him, a calm assurance of his love: this is the spring of all prayer. Prayer comes from hope, and hope takes its stand on faith. And prayer matures hope and strengthens faith. One who has come to know the Lord, who has communion with him in prayer, knows something more than hope—or perhaps, knows what hope really is: a firm anchor, a conviction that one is with the Lord; and a calm certainty that one will be with the Lord forever. Faith and hope and prayer: they go together, flowing from and playing upon one another.

Prayer is love. Our heavenly Father is the loving *Abba*, who looks with tenderness upon his children, who listens to them, speaks to them. Jesus is our friend who has shown us how utterly he loves us—*eis telos*. And he has sent his Spirit within us to help us to pray when we know not how to pray. Prayer with others can stir us to a deeper, purer love for them. The prayer that is love can move us to lay down our lives, can raise us above our innate, deep-rooted selfishness, can stir us to do what we had felt we never could bring ourselves to do.

## Pain

There is prayer that is born of pain. We have all experienced how, in times of sorrow or trouble, we tend to pray even if, before, we had not prayed very much. Too often, this is transient and fades as the sorrow eases. But there is pain that can work a transformation, a pain that purifies and uplifts. And the prayer that is born of this pain can be deep and abiding. Where the pain, the sorrow, would seem to stifle and crush us, the prayer that springs from it can change our life. This is the prayer of Gethsemane: 'Let this chalice pass from me.' Jesus is not asking to escape his fate. His prayer to the Father is to know if indeed his path can lie in no other way, to be assured that what seems to be asked of him is indeed what is asked. 'Not my will but yours be done.' Certain now of his way, Jesus goes serenely forward to suffering and death. In our Gethsemanes, when we must know if *this* cup is really held out to us, if we must drink of it, the prayer of Jesus himself is our only prayer: 'Thy will be done.' And for us, too, it will bring peace, peace in the midst of what will remain a hard saying. For we have to remember that Jesus went on to suffer and die.

Clearly there are many kinds of prayer, many ways of praying; and we are fortunate indeed if we see the need in our lives for prayer. For this need, born of an awareness of the reality of our life in Christ, will lead us to the right prayer. Perhaps our humblest and simplest prayer ought to be: 'Lord, teach us to pray.'

# BIBLIOGRAPHY

Benoit, P., and Boismard, M.-E., *Synopse des Quatre Évangiles*, II, Paris : Cerf 1972.

Bultmann, R., *Theology of the New Testament*, 2 vols., London : SCM 1952, 1955.

Brown, R. E., s.s., *The Gospel According to St John* II, London-Dublin : Chapman 1971.

Buber, M., *I and Thou*, New York : Scribner's 1958.

Caird, G. B., *The Revelation of St John the Divine*, London : A. & C. Black 1966.

Conzelmann, H., *The Theology of St Luke*, London : Faber & Faber 1961.

Cullmann, O., *The Christology of the New Testament*, London, S C M, 2nd ed. 1963.

Dodd, C. H., *The Founder of Christianity*, London : Collins 1971.

Dupont, J., o.s.b., Les Béatitudes, Tome II. *La Bonne Nouvelle,* Paris : Gahalda 1969.

Fitzmyer, J. A., s.j., 'Pauline Theology', in *The Jerome Biblical Commentary* II, edited by R. E. Brown, J. A. Fitzmyer, R. E. Murphy, London-Dublin : Chapman 1968, 800–827.

Flender, H., *St Luke, Theologian of Redemptive History*, London : S.P.C.K. 1967.

Fuller, R. H., *The Foundation of New Testament Christology*, New York : Scribner's 1965.

Harrington, W. J., o.p., *The Path of Biblical Theology*, Dublin : Gill & Macmillan 1973.

Harrington, W. J., o.p., *Parables told by Jesus: A Contemporary Approach to The Parables*, New York : Alba House 1974.

Harrington, W. J., o.p., Key to the Bible III. *Record of the Fulfillment*, Canfield, Ohio : Alba Books 1975.

Heidegger, M., *Being and Time*, New York : Harper & Row 1962.

Hunter, A. M., *Introducing New Testament Theology*, London : SCM 1957.

Jeremias, J., New Testament Theology I. *The Proclamation of Jesus*, London : SCM 1971

Jeremias, J., *The Central Message of the New Testament*, New York : Scribner's 1965.

Kierkegaard, S., *Training in Christianity*, Princeton : University Press 1944.

Kodell, J., o.s.b., 'The Theology of Luke in Recent Study', *Biblical Theology Bulletin*, 1(1971), 115–144.

Kümmel, W. G., *Die Theologie des Neuen Testaments nach seinen Hauptzeugen Jesus-Paulus-Johannes*, Göttingen : Vandenhoeck & Ruprecht 1969.

Macquarrie, J., *Existentialism*, Philadelphia : Westminster 1972.

Macquarrie, J., *An Existentialist Theology*, London : Penguin Books 1973.

Marcel, G., *Homo Viator: Introduction to a Metaphysic of Hope*, New York : Harper 1951.

Murphy-O'Connor, J., o.p., *Paul on Preaching*, London : Sheed & Ward 1964.

Murphy-O'Connor, o.p., 'Pauline Morality: The Human Options'; 'The Contemporary Value of Pauline Moral Imperatives'; 'Moral Discernment', *Doctrine and Life* 21(1971), 2–16, 59–71, 127–134.

Murphy-O'Connor, J., o.p., *What is Religious Life?*, Supplement to Doctrine and Life, 11 (1973).

Murphy-O'Connor, J., o.p., The Charism of the Founder, *Supplement to Doctrine and Life*, 12 (1974), 10–19.

Murphy-O'Connor, J., o.p., *L'existence chrétienne selon saint Paul*, Paris : Cerf 1974.

Mussner, F., *Der Galaterbrief*. Herders theologischer Kommentar zum Neuen Testament, Freiburg-Basle-Vienna : Herder 1974.

Ogden, S., ed., *Existence and Faith. Shorter Writings of*

*Rudolf Bultmann*, London : Fontana Books 1964.

Robinson, J. M., *A New Quest of the Historical Jesus*, London : S C M 1959.

Schillebeeckx, E., o.p., 'The Crisis in the Language of Faith as a Hermeneutical Problem', *Concilium*, Vol. 5, No. 9, May 1973, 31–45.

Stanley, D. M., s.j., and Brown, R. E., s.s., 'Aspects of New Testament Thought', *The Jerome Biblical Commentary* II, 768–99.

Stauffer, E., *New Testament Theology*, London : S C M 1955.

Taylor, V., *The Person of Jesus in New Testament Teaching*, London : Macmillan 1959.

Vawter, B., c.m., 'Johannine Theology', *The Jerome Biblical Commentary* II, 825–39.

Vawter, B., c.m., *This Man Jesus. An Essay Toward a New Testament Christology*, Garden City, New York : Doubleday 1973.

# NOTES

## INTRODUCTION (pp. 7-13)

1. By 'merit' is meant a *preoccupation* with 'good works', with running up indulgences and such like; in short, a certain book-keeping spirituality. This could lead to the impression, as in pharisaic Judaism, that the Lord somehow 'owed' salvation to the just man. 'Recompense' is a *gift* of a supremely generous Lord who calls his servants his *friends*.

2. See E. Stauffer, *New Testament Theology*, London : S C M 1955, 204,

## CHAPTER I, (pp. 14-34)

1. See J. M. Robinson, *A New Quest of the Historical Jesus*, London : S C M 1959.

2. J. Jeremias, New Testament Theology I. *The Proclamation of Jesus*, London : S C M 1971; C. H. Dodd, *The Founder of Christianity*, London : Collins 1971.

3. Elsewhere, C. H. Dodd makes an illuminating distinction between 'occurrence' and 'event'. An *occurrence* is the brute fact, the fact, let us say, of the crucifixion of Jesus: a routine Roman execution. What turned the crucifixion into an *event* is the meaning it bore, in faith, for the disciples—on the other side of Resurrection. Thus, an event is an occurrence plus the interest and meaning inherent in it. 'We might indeed say that an historical 'event' is an occurrence *plus* the interest and meaning which the occurrence possessed for the persons involved in it, and by which the record is determined.' *History and the Gospel,* London: Hodder and Stoughton, 2nd ed. 1964, 20.

4. It is not to be doubted that Jesus foresaw his suffering and death and spoke of this to his disciples. However, the formulation of his prediction, in the tradition and by the evangelists, has been coloured by the events themselves, and the details have been conformed to the story of the passion.

5. Where the crucifixion is clearly an historical event, a happening in time, the resurrection is an event beyond time (beyond death) and belongs to another order. In this sense, it is not 'historical', in the same way that the crucifixion is. It belongs to the new age and is thus 'eschatological'. The resurrection however is historical in that it impinges on human existence. It should be clear that, in making these distinctions, one does not, in any sense, question the *reality* of the resurrection. It is utterly real—but it belongs to another order.

6. In the gospels *others* address Jesus by various titles ('son of God', 'Son of David', etc); but only Jesus applies the title 'Son of Man' to himself. It is remarkable that even when 'Son of Man has, in the tradition, been inserted into a saying of Jesus, the title is still put on his lips.

7. When Jesus taught his disciples to address their Father by the Aramaic title *Abba,* he was presupposing an entirely new relationship between God and men. For *Abba* is intimate, familiar, the word which the little child will use of his father; it was never used by Jews with reference to God. But this was how Jesus addressed his father, in his full confidence of Sonship.

8. The earliest codification of rabbinical oral law is called

the *Mishnah* ('repetition'). The Mishnah is essentially a collection of *halakoth*—rules of conduct deduced from the Law—that are earlier than the year 200 A.D.

9. *The Revelation of St John the Divine*, London : A. & C. Black 1966, 170.

## CHAPTER II, (pp. 35–49)

1. J. Dupont, Les Béatitudes, Tome II, *La Bonne Nouvelle*, Paris : Gabalda 1969; J. Jeremias, New Testament Theology I. *The Proclamation of Jesus*, London : SCM 1971.

2. The 'tax collectors' of the gospels are subordinate officials who collected taxes and dues. The familiar term 'publicans' is not accurate because the *publicani* were high-ranking Roman officials who farmed the public revenues. The tax collectors of the gospels were unpopular and their work, which involved contact with Gentiles, made it impossible for them to keep the Law in the manner of the Pharisees. Thus, they were 'sinners', classed with those 'who do not know the Law' (*John* 7 : 49).

## CHAPTER III, (pp. 50–106)

1. See R. H. Fuller, *The Foundations of New Testament Christology*, New York : Charles Scribner's Sons 1965, 195–7; J. A. Fitzmyer, 'The Virginal Conception of Jesus in the New Testament', *Theological Studies* 34 (1973), 563f.

2. We should note, here and throughout this work, the historical contingency of the language of faith to which Edward Schillebeeckx has drawn attention. For that matter, there is the contingency of the historical events of Jesus : as a man he belonged to a given age and culture and played a given role in the history of his people. 'We must therefore be careful not to lose sight of this historical contingency of Jesus' appearance when we are speaking in the language of faith about Jesus as the Messiah, the Son of Man, the Lord, and so on. We should also not make the biblical expression of Jesus' words and actions in those concrete circumstances unhistorical and absolute by dissociating it from the historically conditioned linguistic categories of the period in which the

event of Jesus was expressed. The linguistic event should not, in other words, be raised to the level of 'timeless' categories. The multiplicity of christological dogmas, and the different definitions of the kingdom of God, redemption, and so on, in the New Testament itself should be a sufficient warning against this practice.' E. Schillebeeckx, 'The Crisis in the Language of Faith as a Hermeneutical Problem', *Concilium*, Vol. 5, No. 9, May 1973, 32.

3. Jesus used the parable, as a recognised teaching medium, to instruct, to challenge, and to provoke reflection. Mark, however, presents the parables as Jesus' way of addressing 'those outside', those to whom the 'mystery' of the kingdom had not been revealed (cf. 4 : 10-12). It is his way of insisting that only Jesus can grant enlightenment—to any who are open to receive enlightenment. See W. J. Harrington, *Parables Told By Jesus*, New York : Alba House 1974, 30–39.

4. Mark's work ends at 16 :8. The present ending (16 :9-20) is by another hand.

5. See M.-E. Boismard in P. Bensot and M.-E. Boismard, *Synopse des Quatre Evangiles*, Tome 2, Paris : Cerf 1972, 64–6.

6. In his 'reflection-citations'—so-called because they are personal 'reflections' of the evangelist—Matthew shows that Christ has fulfilled the Old Testament prophecies. There are eleven such distinctive quotations : 1 :22f.; 2 :5f., 15, 17f., 23; 4 :14-16; 8.17; 12 :17-21; 13 :35; 21 :4f.; 27 :9f.

7. The well-known theory of Hans Conzelmann that the Lucan *Heilsgeschichte* falls into three periods—i/ the period of Israel; ii/ the period of Christ; iii/ the period of the Church—has been convincingly disproved by Helmut Flender. Flender does agree with Conzelmann that Luke 16 :16 signals a division of epochs : the new replaces the old, the new including both the period of Jesus' ministry and the period of the Church. (H. Conzelmann, *The Theology of St Luke*, London : Faber & Faber 1961; H. Flender, *St Luke, Theologian of Redemptive History*, London S.P.C.K. 1967.) See J. Kodell, 'The Theology of Luke in Recent Study', *Biblical Theology Bulletin* 1 (1971), 115-44.

8. This existentialist terminology will be more fully explained and developed in chapters IV and V.

9. J. Jeremias, *The Central Message of the New Testament*, London : SCM 1965, 112.

10. It is widely held that Ephesians is the work of a disciple of Paul who sought to develop the ideas of his master in a markedly ecclesiological direction. There is less agreement that Colossians, too, is pseudonymous, but it seems likely that it is. Pseudonymity (the attribution of a writing, by the author, to another than himself) was a well-known and accepted literary convention in New Testament times, in both hellenistic and Jewish circles.

11. B. Vawter, 'Johannine Theology', *The Jerome Biblical Commentary II* edited by Brown, Fitzmyer, Murphy, London-Dublin : Chapman 1968, 832.

12. One must be clear that the absolute claim to divinity is a feature of the *Johannine Christology*. John has come to grasp the pre-existence of Christ, his relationship to the Father. During his ministry, Jesus did not, explicitly, claim to be divine.

13. R. E. Brown, *The Gospel According to St John* II, London-Dublin : Chapman 1971, 1139.

CHAPTER IV, (pp. 107–123)

1. See J. Macquarrie, *Existentialism*, Harmondsworth, Middlesex : Penguin Books 1973.

2. For Buber 'primary words' (and these are especially the primary words 'I-Thou' and 'I-It') are not isolated words, like 'I' and 'It' and 'Thou', but combined words that already imply the context of our being-with-others-in-the-world. If 'Thou' is said, the 'I' of the combination 'I-Thou' is said along with it.

3. In many cases, in fact, an 'I-You' relation is more appropriate than an 'I-Thou' relation. An 'I-You' relation is one that respects the personality and humanity of the other but does not seek to establish with him the depth and intimacy that are customarily associated with the notion of 'I-Thou'.

4. The Greek word *eschaton* means 'the end' (whence 'eschatology') : it is the End-time of salvation history when God's saving plan is rounded off. The *parousia* ('appearance') of the Lord marks the end-time : the being of a Risen Lord will be revealed to all as the meaning and climax of salvation history.

5. By definition, eschatology is the theological doctrine of the last things : it looks to the future. Thus, in the synoptics, 'eternal life' is something that one receives at the final judgment or in a future age (*Mark* 10.30, *Matt.* 18.8f.). For John, however, eternal life is a present possibility for men : 'He who believes in the Son has eternal life' (3 :36); who eats my flesh and drinks my blood has eternal life' (6 :54). This Johannine emphasis is referred to as 'realised eschatology'.

## CHAPTER V, (pp. 124–144)

1. In this chapter I am much beholden to my confrere, Fr Jerome Murphy-O'Connor, O.P., Professor at the École Biblique, Jerusalem. Apart from his published writings, I have had access to the MS of his forthcoming book, *Moral Imperatives in St Paul.* I gladly acknowledge my indebtedness to him and my appreciation of his generosity. His book has appeared in French : *L'existence chrétienne selon Saint Paul* (Paris : Cerf 1974).

2. S. Ogden, ed., 'Paul'; *Existence and Faith. Shorter Writings of Rudolf Bultmann,* London : Fontana Books, 1964, 159.

3. F. Mussner, *Der Galaterbrief,* Freiburg-Basle-Vienna : Herder 1974, 287. Mussner (77-290) has made a careful study of the relationship of Law and gospel in Pauline thought.

4. J. Murphy-O'Connor, *What is Religious Life?, Supplement to Doctrine and Life,* 11 (1973), 15–30.

5. By baptismal consecration, the Christian is committed to the following of Christ and to the service of Christ in his members. For the New Testament there is only one way of following Christ : total commitment to his person generating a love which puts one completely at the service of others. Every Christian *ought* to be actively concerned about the

plight of the sick, the poor, the underprivileged (cf. *Matt.* 25 :31–46). Thus, of course, the community must be, at the same time, an action-community. Yet, within the community, the Christian is meant to find help to become, to be, a Christion. One might say that the Church is an action community in respect of 'works'; but it is a formation community in respect of the members of the community. See J. Murphy-O'Connor, 'The Charism of the Founder', *Supplement to Doctrine and Life,* 12 (1974), 10–19.

6. *What is Religious Life?,* 22.

7. J. Murphy-O'Connor, *op. cit.,* 26f.

8. In *Rom.* 1 :5 *hypakoē pisteōs* ('obedience of faith') is an explicative genitive : the obedience which is faith.

9. J. Murphy-O'Connor, 'The Contemporary Value of the Pauline Imperatives', *Doctrine and Life,* 21 (1971), 70.

10. F. Mussner, *op. cit.,* 421-3.

**"Where are you?" Heidi whispered. She stepped back outside to scan the parking lot.**

A figure walked toward her. She studied him, but it wasn't the man she'd come to meet.

As he got closer, he lifted his gaze and connected with hers. Blue ice chips bored into her.

She whirled to go back into the restaurant, but a hard hand grabbed her ponytail and yanked her toward her car. She let out a scream and threw an elbow back. She connected, and her attacker let out a harsh grunt.

His grip relaxed a fraction, and Heidi lashed out with a foot, connecting with a hard knee. He cried out and went to the asphalt.

And she was free.

\* \* \*

**MILITARY K-9 UNIT:**
These soldiers track down a serial killer
with the help of their brave canine partners

**Lynette Eason** is a bestselling, award-winning author who makes her home in South Carolina with her husband and two teenage children. She enjoys traveling, spending time with her family and teaching at various writing conferences around the country. She is a member of Romance Writers of America and American Christian Fiction Writers. Lynette can often be found online interacting with her readers. You can find her at Facebook.com/lynette.eason and on Twitter, @lynetteeason.

### Books by Lynette Eason

### Love Inspired Suspense

#### Military K-9 Unit

*Explosive Force*

#### Wrangler's Corner

*The Lawman Returns*
*Rodeo Rescuer*
*Protecting Her Daughter*
*Classified Christmas Mission*
*Christmas Ranch Rescue*
*Vanished in the Night*

#### Family Reunions

*Hide and Seek*
*Christmas Cover-Up*
*Her Stolen Past*

#### Rose Mountain Refuge

*Agent Undercover*
*Holiday Hideout*
*Danger on the Mountain*

Visit the Author Profile page at Harlequin.com for more titles.

# EXPLOSIVE
# FORCE

## LYNETTE EASON

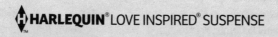

HARLEQUIN® LOVE INSPIRED® SUSPENSE

Special thanks and acknowledgment are given to Lynette Eason
for her contribution to the Military K-9 Unit miniseries.

Recycling programs
for this product may
not exist in your area.

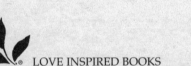

LOVE INSPIRED BOOKS

ISBN-13: 978-1-335-54397-4

Explosive Force

Copyright © 2018 by Harlequin Books S.A.

www.Harlequin.com

**Printed in U.S.A.**

But the Lord is faithful, who shall stablish you,
and keep you from evil.
*—2 Thessalonians* 3:3

Dedicated to the two-legged and four-legged heroes
who put their lives on the line every day.
No amount of thanks will ever be enough.

# ONE

First Lieutenant Heidi Jenks, news reporter for *CAF News*, blew a lock of hair out of her eyes and did her best to keep from muttering under her breath about the stories she was being assigned lately.

She didn't mind the series of articles she was doing on the personnel who lived on the base—those were interesting and she was meeting new people. And besides, those had been her idea.

But some of the other stories were just plain boring. Like the stolen medals. Okay, maybe not boring, but definitely not as exciting as some she could be working on. Like finding Boyd Sullivan, the Red Rose Killer. A serial killer, he liked to torment his victims with the gift of a red rose and a note saying he was coming for them. And then he struck, leaving death and heartache in his wake with one last rose and a note tucked under the arm of the victim. *Got you.*

Heidi shut the door to the church where her

interviewee had insisted on meeting and walked down the steps, pulling her voice-activated recorder from her pocket. She might as well get her thoughts down before they dissipated due to her complete disinterest. She shivered and glanced over her shoulder. For some reason she expected to see him, as if the fact that she was alone in the dark would automatically mean Sullivan was behind her.

After being chased by law enforcement last week, he'd fallen from a bluff and was thought to be dead. But when his body had never been found, that assumption had changed. He was alive. Somewhere. Possibly injured and in hiding while he healed. Reports had come in that he'd been spotted twice in central Texas. She supposed that was possible. But what if the reports were wrong? What if he'd made his way back here to the base so he could continue his reign of terror?

The thought quickened her steps. She'd feel better behind a locked door where she could concentrate on the story she was currently working on.

Someone on the base was breaking into homes and stealing war medals, jewelry and cash. Whatever small items they could get their hands on. But it was the medals that were being targeted. Medals of Valor especially. People were antsy enough about the whole serial killer thing. Having a thief on base wasn't helping matters.

She spoke into the recorder. "Mrs. Wainwright stated she hadn't been home at the time of the robbery. However, as soon as she pulled into her drive, she could see her open front door and knew something was wrong."

Heidi's steps took her past the base hospital. She was getting ready to turn onto the street that would take her home when a flash of movement from the K-9 training center caught her eye. Her steps slowed, and she heard a door slam.

A figure wearing a dark hoodie bolted down the steps and shot off toward the woods behind the center. He reached up, shoved the hoodie away and yanked something—a ski mask?— off his head, then pulled the hoodie back up. He stuffed the ski mask into his jacket pocket.

Very weird actions that set Heidi's internal and journalistic alarm bells screaming. And while she wanted to see what the guy was going to do, she decided it might be more prudent to get out of sight while she watched.

Just as she moved to do so, the man spun.

And came to an abrupt halt as his eyes locked on hers.

Ice invaded her veins, sending shivers of fear dancing along her nerves. He took a step toward her, then shot a look back at the training center. Back to her. Then at his wristwatch. With no change in his granite ice-blue eyes as he gave her one last threatening glare, he whirled and raced toward the woods once again.

Like he wanted to put as much distance between him and the building as possible.

Foreboding filled her just as a side door to the training center opened. A young man stood there, his uniform identifying him as one of the trainers. His eyes met hers, just like the hooded man's had only seconds earlier. But this time, she knew who the eyes belonged to. Bobby Stevens, a young airman who'd recently finished his tech training. He hesitated, glanced at her, then over his shoulder.

Her gut churned with a distinctly bad feeling. With everything that had happened on the base in the last few months, there was only one reason that the man in the hoodie would be so anxious to run when it looked like he would rather do her bodily harm.

She started backing away, her feet pedaling quickly. "Run, Bobby! Get away from the building. Something weird is going on!"

Bobby hesitated a fraction of a second, then took off toward her, looking determined to catch up with her. Her footsteps pounded as she put distance between her and the building and the man behind her.

Then an explosion rocked the ground beneath her and she fell to her knees, her palms scraping the concrete as she tried to catch herself.

Rolling, Heidi held on to her screams and looked back to see part of the building missing and fire spurting from the cavernous area.

And Bobby Stevens lying sprawled on the ground.

People spilled from the buildings close to her, many on their phones. No doubt calling for help.

Heidi managed to get her feet beneath her and scrambled to stand. She raced back to Bobby and dropped beside him, wincing as her knees hit the concrete.

Already, she could hear the sirens.

Calling on her past first aid training, Heidi pressed her fingers against his neck and felt a steady, if slow, pulse. He had a laceration on his forehead and his wrist hung at an odd angle.

His lids fluttered, then opened. His brows dipped and he winced.

"It's all right, Bobby," she said. "Help is on the way."

"What happened?"

"The building exploded, but you're going to be okay."

"Exploded? Why?" His eyelids fluttered. "Hurts." He tried to roll and groaned.

Heidi pressed her hands to his shoulders. "I know. Just be still."

"Hold my hand, please," he whispered. "I'm... cold."

She slid her fingers gently around his un-injured hand. "I'm here," she whispered. "Just hold on." Bobby's eyes closed, but he continued to breathe shallow, labored breaths. "You're going to be all right. Just hang in there."

In seconds, she felt hands pulling her away. First responders had arrived. Heidi backed up, keeping her eyes on the now-unconscious man who'd reached out to her as though she could save him.

"Are you all right?" the paramedic asked her.

She focused in on the figure in front of her. "Um...yes. I was farther away from the blast. It knocked me off my feet, but nothing else. I just ran back to check on Bobby."

"Your knees are bleeding."

She blinked and looked down. "Oh." Blood seeped through her slacks. And now that her attention had been brought to them, her knees throbbed.

The paramedic led her to one of the four ambulances now lining the street. "Let me just check you out and get these knees bandaged for you."

"Yes, okay. Thank you." She drew in a deep breath and let her gaze wander past the crowd that had gathered.

Was the bomber watching the building burn? Could he see the firefighters fight against the raging flames?

She had a bad feeling about this. A feeling that this was only the beginning of something that might be bigger than any story she'd ever worked on.

And she had a feeling that the man who'd done this would be back.

Because she'd seen him.

First Lieutenant Nick Donovan itched to get his hands on the person who'd just blown up part of the training center. Thankfully, it was an area of the building that wasn't being used at the moment and no animals had been harmed. Airman Bobby Stevens was reported to be in stable condition and was expected to make a full recovery. That was the only reason Nick's anger wasn't boiling over, even though his patience levels were maxed out.

Unfortunately, he and his bloodhound, Annie, would have to wait a little longer to do their part in figuring out exactly what had caused the explosion. Annie was trained in explosives detection, but right now, she couldn't get near the training center, even wearing the protective booties. The area was still too hot, and firefighters were still fighting the blaze. However, Annie and he *could* examine parts of the building that had landed yards away.

Office of Special Investigations, OSI, had arrived and would be taking lead on the case under the supervision of Ian Steffen. Nick also spotted FBI special agent Oliver Davison, who'd been a frequent visitor to the base—not only because of his search for the Red Rose Killer, but also to see his fiancée, Senior Airman Ava Esposito.

Of course, he would show up. At this point, anything bad that happened on the base was suspected of being caused by Boyd Sullivan. And Oliver was one of the most determined people on the elite investigative team formed especially to hunt Sullivan down and bring him to justice. Truth was, they all wanted the killer caught and were working overtime in order to do that.

Nick belonged to the Explosive Ordnance Disposal unit and had gotten the call shortly after the explosion happened. He'd raced from his home and arrived to find the organized chaos he was now in the middle of. If the EOD unit had been called, then someone thought the damage to the building had been caused by a bomb—and they wanted to make sure there weren't any more explosives waiting to go off. Which he would be happy to do just as soon as he could get close enough.

Security Forces with assault rifles flooded the area and stood ready should there be another attempt to attack, although Nick figured whoever was responsible was long gone. But Canyon Air Force Base had an action plan for this kind of thing and it had been put into place immediately.

From the corner of his eye, he caught sight of Heidi Jenks, one of the base reporters, talking to an OSI investigator.

He scoffed. Boy, she didn't waste a second, did she? He sure hoped the investigator knew how to keep his mouth shut. The last thing they needed was for her to write a story before the facts were even determined.

She ran a hand over her wavy blond hair and rubbed her eyes. He frowned. Where was her ever-present notebook? And why did she look so disheveled?

Annie pulled on the leash and Nick let her lead him over to a large block of concrete. She sat. And he stiffened at her signal, which indicated a bomb. While he didn't think the piece of concrete itself was going to explode, it obviously had explosives residue on it. She looked at him expectantly. "Good girl, Annie, good girl." He took a treat from his pocket and she wolfed it down.

He set his backpack on the ground and pulled out the items he needed to take a sample of the cement. Once that was done, he placed the evidence back in his pack and scratched Annie's ears.

"What was that?" a voice asked. A voice he recognized and sometimes heard in his dreams. Against his will.

He looked up and found himself staring at a pair of bandaged knees. The blood on the torn pants had a story to tell. Nick stood and looked down into Heidi Jenks's blue eyes. Eyes he could drown in if he'd let himself. But she was so off-limits in the romance department that he banished the thought from his mind as soon as it popped in.

"No comment."

"Come on, Nick."

"Just something I want to take a closer look at."

She turned away to look at the smoking building. Fire trucks still poured water onto it. It could take hours to put the fire out. "It was a bomb, wasn't it?" she said when she turned back to him.

He pursed his lips. "Why do you jump to that conclusion?"

"What else could it be?" She shrugged. "Why else would you and Annie be here along with other members of EOD? You're going to have to check to make sure there aren't any more bombs, aren't you?"

Nick knew Heidi because he'd read her newspaper articles and some of the stories she'd written. Most people would consider them to be fluff pieces, but the truth was, he could see her heart behind them. And whether he wanted to admit it or not, he liked it. He and Heidi had had a few conversations, and each time, he'd wanted to prolong them. Which was weird for him. He didn't do conversations with people like Heidi. Users who just went after the story without worrying about the fallout. Even though his gut told him she wasn't like that. But she had to be. Otherwise he could lose his heart to her. And that couldn't happen. No way.

"Good deductive reasoning," he told her. "But did you think it was possible that I just wanted to see what was going on?"

"No."

"Hmm. You're right. Annie and I'll have to check for more bombs as soon as we get the green light. And that's not confidential so I'm not worried about you saying anything."

She sighed. "Look, I know with all the rumors circulating, no one wants to talk to me, but this…this is different."

An anonymous blogger had been reporting on the Red Rose Killer, his targets and the investigation. Reporting on things that no one but those involved in the investigation could know. Rumor had it that Heidi was the blogger. As a result, she'd been mostly ostracized from anything considered newsworthy when it came to the Red Rose Killer. But Heidi was persistent. He'd give her that.

He nodded to the torn pants and bandaged knees.

"What happened to you?"

She glanced down. "I got knocked off my feet by the blast."

He raised a brow. "You were here?"

"Yes."

Well, that put a new light on things. "Did you see anything?"

"I don't know. Maybe."

"Either you did or you didn't."

A scowl pulled her brows down. "Then I think I did."

"What did you see exactly?"

She drew in a deep breath. "Like I told the OSI agent, I think I may have seen the bomber."

At Nick's indrawn breath and instant flash of concern, Heidi felt slightly justified in her dramatic announcement. She shrugged, not nearly as nonchalant as she hoped she came across. "Honestly, I don't know if he was the bomber or not, but I sure saw someone who looked like he was up to no good. He had on dark clothing and a hoodie—and a ski mask. Why wear a ski mask unless you don't want anyone to know who you are? Anyway, he took that off right before he turned around and looked at me."

"Tell me everything."

As she talked about the man in the hoodie with the ice-cold blue eyes running from the scene, Nick's frown deepened. "You might be fortunate he was in a hurry to get away."

"I think that's a reasonable assumption." Just the thought of him sent fear skittering up her spine.

"So, he knows you saw him."

"Oh, yes, he knows. OSI is rounding up a sketch artist for me to work with." She shivered and crossed her arms at the memory of the man's brief pause, as though he'd considered coming after her. Thankfully, he'd been in a hurry, more worried about getting away from the impending explosion. But she had seen his face. Well, some of it. The hoodie had hidden his hair color and some of his features, but she'd be able to identify those blue eyes anywhere and anytime.

"All right, stick close," Nick said. "I'm going to let Annie keep working and we'll see what she comes up with."

For the next thirty minutes, Heidi did as instructed and stayed right with him. Not just so she could collect facts for the story, but because she was just plain rattled. Okay, scared. She'd admit it. She was afraid and feeling decidedly out of her depth.

But watching Nick and Annie work was a good distraction. She felt safe with Nick in a way she couldn't explain, and she couldn't help admiring his strength and confidence, the total focus and dedication he had to his job.

Her father had been like that.

Before he'd died.

A pang of grief hit her and she shook her head. It had been two years and she still missed him like crazy. But he'd been a wonderful example of the ethical reporter she strived to be. She was determined to follow in his footsteps, determined to make him proud. Thinking of her father naturally sent her thoughts to her mother. A strong woman who'd loved her husband, she'd nearly been shattered by his death. His murder. He'd been killed by the big corporation he'd exposed as a front for the mafia. Killed by his best friend, who'd been the CEO of that corporation.

A lump formed in her throat.

Her parents had argued late one night. She'd come over for dinner and fallen asleep on the couch. When she'd awakened, she'd heard the harsh whispers coming from the kitchen. She'd stayed still and listened, hearing her mother begging her father to stop looking, to "give it up." Her father had been adamant. "I'm not looking the other way, Kate. I can't."

"I'm afraid, Richie," she'd whispered. "I'm truly afraid something will happen to you."

And it had. Not even two weeks later, a jogger had found his body washed up against the shore of a nearby lake. Her father had taken a bullet through the back of his skull. Executed. She lifted her chin. But his work would live on through her. The men who'd killed her father had been captured, tried and imprisoned—including the best friend who'd put the hit out on him. But it didn't bring her father back. It was up to her to carry on his work.

*Truth, baby girl. Nothing's more important than exposing lies and bringing truth to light. Keep your focus where it should be. Don't step on people to get to the top. Don't excuse people who do wrong no matter who they are—and you'll do just fine.*

Her father's words ringing in her mind, she watched as Nick finally stood from the last place Annie had alerted on and tucked a small bag into the larger one he carried. "All right," he said. "I think I'm done here for now."

"Did you find anything else?"

"I'll have to let the lab decide that." He dug a hand into his front pocket and rewarded Annie with a treat and a "Good job, girl."

His gaze slid to her and he opened his mouth as if to say something, then snapped it shut and gave her a grim smile.

He wasn't going to tell her anything. He didn't trust her. She gave a mental sigh and shrugged off the hurt. What did she expect with everyone thinking she was the anonymous blogger, posting about everything going on in the investigation of the Red Rose Killer? Things no one but the investigative team should know. The blogger had everyone on edge and pointing fingers.

While it was true she was upset she hadn't been assigned the story, that didn't mean she was going around shooting off her mouth about things she shouldn't. The fact was she didn't know anything. Other than what was reported in the papers—and by the anonymous blogger. But Nick didn't know that. He didn't know *her* other than from a short snippet of conversation here and there. They often ran into each other at the Winged Java café and he always made a point to speak to her—but he kept himself at a distance. Like he didn't want to get too close. For some reason, she wanted to change that.

His eyes narrowed on a spot over her shoulder. She turned to look. "What is it?" she asked.

"I thought I saw something move."

"Everything's moving around here. What are you talking about?"

"In the reserve just beyond the tree line." He strode toward it, Annie on his heels.

Heidi went after him, not about to miss out. Had the guy that set the bomb off stayed behind to watch the action?

But that wouldn't be smart.

Then again, where was the rule that said bombers had to be smart? "You think it could be one of the missing dogs?" she called after him.

Several months ago, after killing two trainers in the Military Working Dog program, Boyd Sullivan had opened all two hundred and seven kennels and released the animals. While the more highly trained dogs had stayed put, one hundred ninety-six dogs, some PTSD therapy dogs—and dogs with PTSD themselves—had escaped. Most had been found and returned to safety, but there were still twenty-one missing.

Nick reached the tree line and stopped, planting his hands on his hips. Heidi caught up and he shook his head. "No, it wasn't a dog. This shadow had two legs."

"Okay. You see him?"

"No." He sighed and rubbed a hand at the back of his neck. "Maybe I'm just imagining things. Like my nerves are so tight it's causing hallucinations."

"But you really don't believe that, so you want to keep looking, right?"

He slid a sideways glance at her. "Yes."

"Then I'm going with you."

"It's probably nothing."

"I'll just tag along and make that decision myself, okay?"

"No, not okay. Stay here."

"The longer you argue with me, the less likely you are to find out if you saw something."

He shot her a black look and turned on his heel to go after whatever it was he thought he saw.

She shrugged and fell into step beside him, doing her best to ignore the pain in her knees. They were going to be sore for a few days, so she might as well get used to it.

Usually Heidi didn't notice how small she

was in comparison to the men she worked with on a regular basis, but being next to Nick made her feel positively tiny. And feminine.

Which was stupid. Okay, not necessarily stupid, but seriously—why was she so hyperaware of him? Why did she notice every little thing about him? Like the way his blue eyes crinkled at the corners when he was amused. Or the way his jaw tightened and his lips flattened into a thin line when he was annoyed. Or how his dark hair was never allowed to grow too long. She shouldn't notice those things. But she did.

Nick was no more attracted to her than he was to the tree they'd just walked past, so she really needed to get over whatever it was she felt for him. The last thing she needed was to set herself up for heartbreak.

"I think he went this way," Nick said, pulling her from her thoughts.

She followed even though she didn't see what he did.

The farther they got from the kennel and all of the action, the more she thought he'd seen a bird or something. She hoped so, anyway. The adrenaline crash was coming now that the danger was over. It *was* over, wasn't it? "You see anything else?"

"No. I've lost sight of him."

"So it was definitely a him?"

"Yes."

Before she knew it, they were standing in front of her home. "Wait a minute, he came this way?" she asked.

"Yeah, that's what it looked like."

"This is my house, Nick."

"I'd better check the area. Stay put."

"You keep saying that."

"And you keep ignoring me."

This time she listened and let him do his job. With Annie at his heels, he walked around the left side of her home, then the right, which was next to the home that Staff Sergeant Felicity James shared with her husband, Master Sergeant Westley James. Felicity was still a target of the serial killer, but at least she had her husband to keep an eye out for her. Westley was part of the investigative team looking for Sullivan. A team Heidi really wanted to be a part of.

Nick returned with a frown.

"What is it?" she asked.

"I'm not sure. I thought I saw some footprints in the grassy area along your back fence, but I didn't see anyone."

"I see. That's a bit concerning, but it could be from anyone walking back there, using it as a shortcut."

"I suppose. Could be."

"Okay, well, I'm ready to call it a night," she said.

"I don't blame you. I'll wait here and make sure you get inside safely, then I'll head back to the training center. I don't think Annie and I can do much of anything else, but I'll see if OSI wants us to."

"I've given my statement, so they know where to find me if they have any more questions for me."

"Perfect."

He stood there a moment longer, looking down at her as though hesitant to leave. "Are you going to be all right?" he asked.

"I think so. Why?"

He glanced around one more time. "I don't like that we wound up here while we were following him. He disappeared too easily. Too quickly. If what you say is true, that guy got a good look at you."

"*If* it's true? Really?" She sighed. "I'll be fine, Nick. Good night."

A scuff of a foot just ahead and around the side of her house stopped her.

Nick turned toward the noise. "What was that?" he asked.

"I don't know. Probably nothing." Maybe. Without thinking, she slipped her hand into his.

He squeezed her fingers, then released them. "Stay behind me."

Not quite ready to argue with him, she followed his order as he and Annie led the way. They walked down the sidewalk in front of Heidi's home and were almost to the end of the small property when she saw the shadow skirting around the side of her house. "Hey! Can I help you?" she called.

The shadow took off.

Nick and Annie followed. The fleeing person wove in and out, between the houses, down alleys. Heidi fell back slightly as she realized there was no way she could keep up with Nick's long stride.

She didn't realize he'd stopped until she was almost next to him. Nick had the guy close to being boxed in a corner with no escape. There were buildings on either side of him and an open parking lot too far away from him to flee. He must have realized it the same time she did.

Because he spun and lifted his arm.

"He's got a gun!"

The words were barely out of her mouth before something heavy slammed into her, and she hit the pavement.

# TWO

Nick rolled off Heidi and leaped to his feet. He placed himself in front of her as he faced the armed man, disgusted that he'd had no time to pull his own gun—and it was too late to do so now with their attacker's finger on the trigger. "Drop the weapon," Nick ordered.

"Not a chance." The low voice trembled, but Nick couldn't tell if it was from fear or sheer determination not to be caught. The low ball cap and hoodie kept the man's features well hidden. "I'm getting out of here. And if you set that dog on me, she'll take the first bullet. Understand?" He slid sideways, toward the street.

"What are you doing here?" Heidi asked. "Did you blow up the training center?"

But the man wasn't interested in answering, just escaping past Nick. And as long as the man held a gun on him and Heidi, Nick wasn't moving. Also, with the threat against Annie, it was clear the man knew how dogs and their handlers worked. Nick wouldn't knowingly send Annie after him only to have the guy keep good on his threat to shoot her.

Two more steps brought the man to the edge of Heidi's house. He darted past Nick and Annie, his feet pounding on the sidewalk as he headed toward the parking lot. Nick pulled Heidi to her feet. "Are you okay?"

"Yes. I think that's the same guy I saw run from the training center. I couldn't see his face thanks to the hat and hoodie, but it looks like the same one my guy was wearing."

"Stay here. I'm going after him." He left Heidi as he turned and took up the chase once more. He followed on the man's heels. They would soon be at the fence on the other side of the lot and the guy would have nowhere to go.

But he was also armed.

Nick reported his whereabouts into the radio on his shoulder, requesting backup as he pounded the asphalt in pursuit. Heidi stayed behind him, yelling details to the Military Police dispatch.

Was this guy the bomber? Had he been hanging around to watch the chaos his explosion had caused? To gloat? Or was this someone else altogether?

Determined to catch him, Nick pushed himself harder. Annie stayed right with him, lunging at the end of the leash.

The guy disappeared around the building that backed up to the fence.

Nick followed, rounded the building…

And the guy was gone.

Nick skidded to a stop, slightly winded, but he would have gone a little farther if he could have seen who he was chasing. A piece of cloth on a bush caught his attention. He noted it, his eyes darting, looking for any sign someone might have a gun trained on him, while chills danced up his spine.

Footsteps sounded behind him. He whirled, weapon ready. Only to come face-to-face with Heidi. She flinched and he lowered his gun. "Sorry." Nick spun back to the area where he'd lost the suspect. Annie whined and shifted. "What is it, girl?"

Annie looked up at him, her soft, sad eyes asking permission. He glanced at Heidi. "Keep your eyes and ears open, will you? Let me know if anything catches your attention."

She nodded.

Nick slipped his weapon back into the holster and pulled a pair of gloves from the bag on his shoulder. He snapped them on, then reached for the piece of cloth and studied it. Had this been snagged recently? Or had it been there awhile?

It didn't look like it had weathered much. He held it out to the dog. "Annie, seek." She sniffed, lowered her nose to the ground, then lifted it to check the air.

"She can track, too?" Heidi asked.

"Sure. It's the same concept, and she's a smart dog. You can hardly train a bloodhound to sit, but tracking is so natural for them, the only training needed is for the handler." A slight exaggeration, but not much. He followed the dog cautiously while he spoke, scanning the area. His radio alerted him to backup closing in behind them and on both sides. The base had been shut down and security was tight. There was no way anyone would be able to get off or on the base for now.

But if whoever had been loitering around Heidi's house lived on the base, Annie would find him.

Annie padded her way to the fence at the far side of the parking lot and sat, looking back over her shoulder at him.

Nick squatted next to the animal and eyed the heavy-duty chain-link fence. "It's been cut." He sighed in disgust at the large opening. "This was his way out. He came prepared. He knew exactly where he was going."

"But where was he hiding? You checked my house."

"I'm guessing he jumped the fence into your

backyard when he heard me coming. Once Annie and I left, he simply hauled himself back over."

"My backyard? Nice." She grimaced. "But why would he wait so long to leave the base after setting off the explosion?" she asked. "He should have been long gone by now. Why would he be so stupid as to hang around and take a chance on being caught?"

He glanced at her and shook his head. He had his theories on that, but would keep them to himself for the moment.

"You said he knew his way around the base," she said. "That he was familiar with it. I would agree with that. So, why go this way? Why not simply run back to his home?"

"I said he was familiar with it. Doesn't mean he lives on it."

"True."

"Plus think about it…"

"What?" she asked.

"The dogs."

She raised a brow. "Of course. The base is full of them. He figured a dog like Annie could track him. If he left through the fence and had a car waiting…"

"Exactly. There might be some security footage, but since he kept his face covered, that won't help much."

"He took his mask off right before he turned and spotted me," Heidi said. "But even with the hoodie covering part of his features, I'd still be able to pick him out of a lineup. The guy you just chased? I don't know." She sighed. "Think your forensic people could find some prints or something?"

"On what?"

She shrugged. "I don't know. The fence maybe?"

"He had on gloves, I think." He tucked the piece of cloth into an evidence bag. "They'll try, but I'm not holding my breath." He stood.

His frown deepened and he remembered whom he was talking to. "This better not show up on the front page tomorrow."

Heidi stiffened and her lips turned down. "It's a story, Nick."

"And we don't have the facts yet so don't go printing that we chased the bomber. We don't know who we chased."

"I never said he was the bomber. But I *do* know we chased a guy with a gun."

"Heidi…" He sighed and pinched the bridge of his nose.

Backup arrived then, cutting him off, but he held her gaze for a moment longer before turning his attention to the OSI investigators clamoring for answers.

* * *

Standing back from the fence so she didn't trample any evidence, but close enough to watch the action, Heidi drew in a deep breath and tried to calm her nerves. She was glad Nick's attention was off her for the moment, but it did little to calm her.

She'd nearly been killed in an explosion, and someone had been lurking at her house and then held her at gunpoint—all in one night.

She ran a hand over her ponytail, hoping she'd hidden how shaken she'd been, how frightened. Pushing the residual fear aside, she pulled her voice-activated recorder from her pocket and hit Play. Holding the device to her ear, she heard herself call out to Bobby, then the explosion, the aftermath, Bobby begging her to hold his hand, her reassurances.

A tear slipped down her cheek and she sent up a silent prayer for the young man. She'd make her notes, then turn the recording over to OSI.

"Heidi?"

She stiffened at the sound of John Robinson's voice. Great. Of course *he* would show up. And of course, even in the midst of all of the chaos surrounding her, he would hone in on her like Annie on a bomb. No offense to Annie. She grimaced, then smoothed her features before turning to face her nemesis. John, the lead reporter for the Red Rose Killer case—and the bane of her existence at the moment—hurried toward her. She couldn't seem to escape the man.

"What are you doing here?" he asked. "You're supposed to be covering the break-ins and medal thefts."

"I am, John. I was on my way home when… things happened. What are you doing here?"

"Looking for you." He pulled out a pad and paper. "What *did* happen?"

Oh, no. No way was she letting him steal this story from her. "John, you're covering the Red Rose Killer, not everything else."

"I'm covering anything that could be related to him. I heard a couple of MPs speculating that Sullivan was back on base and causing trouble. So, see? This is my story. So…give me details."

"I'm still sorting it all out." She shoved a stray hair from her face. "I'm heading home. I'll see you tomorrow sometime."

"Heidi—"

She waved and started walking away from him.

"What's the rush?" he called. "You got to go get your blog post ready?"

Heidi froze, did a one-eighty and marched back to the man who'd been a thorn in her side from the day he stepped onto the base and into the newspaper office. She stopped in front of him, ignoring the stares from those who'd heard his comment. "Once and for all, John Robinson, I am *not* the anonymous blogger. So stop spreading that lie before I sue you for slander."

A hand curled around her right fist. A fist she didn't even remember making. Looking sideways, she found Nick beside her.

"He's not worth it," he said softly.

Drawing in a deep breath, she made a conscious effort to push down her anger. Nick was right. If she punched John, her career would be over. And she'd worked too hard to let him provoke her into losing everything. But she would *not* let him stand there and accuse her of being the anonymous blogger who was plaguing the investigation.

She pulled her hand from Nick's, and leaving John with his jaw hanging, she executed another about-face and headed toward her house. She was tired. Beat, actually. So exhausted it was all she could do to put one foot in front of the other. Not even the adrenaline sputter from the confrontation with Robinson did much to help her energy level.

Once she reached her home, she slipped the key in the lock, opened the door, and stepped inside.

Peace washed over her as she shut the door behind her. She drew in a deep breath and let the atmosphere calm her. Heidi loved her home. It may look boring and ordinary from the outside, but the inside was all her.

Blues and tans, with a splash of orange here and there, her home allowed her to breathe and cast off the worries of the day.

Except she couldn't stop thinking about Bobby and wondering if he had known the man who'd run from the training center only moments before it had exploded. Or was Bobby just an innocent caught up in a dangerous incident?

A knock on the door sent her temper spiraling.

She yanked it open. "I told you—" She snapped her mouth shut when she saw Nick standing there with Annie at his side. "Oh. I thought you were someone else."

"Robinson?"

"What makes you think that?"

A corner of his mouth tilted up. "Sarcasm looks cute on you."

This time it was her jaw that hung.

"Can I come in?" he asked.

She closed her mouth. "Of course." Stepping back, she let them enter, then shut the door. "Den is to your left."

"Thanks. Your place is similar to mine. Smaller, of course." Base housing for those who didn't live with family members was small. Hers was a one-bedroom residence, but at least she didn't have to do the dorm-style living other airmen were stuck with. "But it sure is nicer than mine. It's…calm and soothing. I like it."

"Thanks. That's what I was going for when I picked out the colors. The days around here can be so long and hectic that I wanted something that reminded me of the ocean. Peace and calm."

He settled on her tan couch and Annie curled up at his feet. "Are you all right?"

"I'm—" She stopped. "I was going to say 'I'm fine,' but I'm not sure that's true. I'm actually stressed and annoyed beyond everything with John Robinson. That man pushes me to the very edge." She shot him a look through her lashes. "Just in case you didn't pick up on that."

"I think I might have."

"Thank you, by the way, for keeping me from slugging him. I don't think I would have, even as much as I wanted to, but I can't say for sure that I would have walked away had you not been there."

"I don't think anyone would have blamed you, but yeah. You're welcome."

"I'll also admit I'm shaken from the explosion and the possibility of being shot, but mostly, I'm extremely tired of everyone thinking I'm the anonymous blogger." She let the last word out on a huff and sank into the recliner opposite the couch. At his startled expression, she wished she could retract the words, but it was too late now.

"And you're not? The anonymous blogger, I mean?"

She didn't have the energy to do more than scowl at him. "No, I'm not. I wouldn't do that. And besides, I don't even have the facts that are being reported in the blog. Every time I read it, I learn something new." She laughed. "That blogger is someone who has access to information I only wish I did."

His eyes searched hers and he gave a slow nod. "I think I believe you."

She wilted. "Really? You think?"

"Yes."

"Well...thanks. I *think*." She sighed. "If you believe me, do you have any thoughts on who it *could* be?"

"No."

"Not that you would tell me, anyway, right?"

He raised a brow. "I knew Boyd from basic training, but I didn't have much contact with him. I don't know who he hung out with other than what we've managed to dig up during the investigation—and, of course, the victims."

"That's probably a good thing. Not knowing

him too well, I mean. You don't want to be on his radar."

"No kidding. So…" He cleared his throat. "Now that we're away from all the craziness, would you tell me one more time what you saw tonight?"

Gathering her strength, she nodded. "I can tell you, but you can also listen to it."

"What do you mean?"

"My voice-activated recorder picked up most everything. I mean, the guy who ran out of the training center didn't say anything, but—" She stood. "Hold on and let me get my laptop. I'll start transcribing while you listen."

"You recorded it?"

"Not on purpose. I was walking and talking into it when I spotted the trainer coming out of the building. And then the explosion…" She waved a hand. "Just listen."

She brought up a blank document on her laptop, then hit the play button on the recorder. He listened while she typed as fast as her fingers could fly. If she missed something, she could always go back and fix it.

When the sound of the explosion came through, Nick flinched and rubbed a hand over his chin. He listened to her comfort Bobby. The screams of the sirens. He listened to it all. When it ended, he hit the stop button.

Since there wasn't a whole lot of conversation, Heidi was able to get the whole thing transcribed in one listen. She'd go back and add in her memories and perceptions later for the article. For now, she'd just lived through one of the scariest nights she'd ever experienced, and she was on the edge emotionally.

To put it simply, she wanted Nick to leave so she could crawl into her bed and hibernate until morning. And maybe cry a little. But instead of sending him on his way, she fell silent, not exactly sure that she really wanted to be alone after all. A knock sounded on the door. "Excuse me."

She rose, and he followed her. At her raised eyebrow, he frowned. "Can't be too careful."

Heidi peered out the side window. "Who is it?" she called out.

"Carl Trees. I'm the sketch artist," the man on the porch stated.

"I know him," Nick said. "He's legit."

Heidi opened the door. "Hi. Come on in." The two men greeted one another, and Heidi led them to the kitchen. "Have a seat at the table. Would you like some coffee or a bottle of water?"

"No, thanks. I'm sure you're tired and ready for this day to be over with."

Carl was right about that. She sat next to him

and he turned the laptop so she could see it. "All right," he said, "start with the shape of his face."

For the next hour, they worked on the sketch with Heidi doing her best to get the face as detailed as possible. Finally, she sat back and rubbed her eyes.

"That's him?" Nick asked. He stood behind Carl, looking down at the final rendering.

She studied the image on the screen. "As close as I can remember." The icy blue eyes stared back at her from the screen. "The eyes are spot-on, I know that." Carl had added a hoodie to the man's head, and Heidi shivered. "That's him."

Carl nodded. "Good job. Your descriptions helped a lot."

"Must be the way with words she has," Nick murmured.

"Must be." Carl shut his laptop and rose. "I'll get out of here and get this sent to the powers that be." He looked at Heidi. "If they catch him, they'll want you to point the finger at him."

"I know." She led him to the door. "Thanks for coming over here."

"Not a problem. Have a good night." Carl left, and Heidi shut the door behind him.

Nick placed his hands on her shoulders and turned her to face him. "I'm really concerned," he said.

"About what?"

"You. I think it's important to know whether the guy we chased was the same guy you just described to Carl."

She frowned. "I know. I think it was, but I'm not a hundred percent sure. There was a hoodie involved both times and it looked like the same one. The first time, I locked eyes with the guy running from the training center. They were blue and looked like they'd be right at home in the frozen tundra. The guy at my house had the hoodie pulled low and he kept his head down. I didn't see his eyes, so..." She shrugged and sighed.

"He might not know that. Or think that. I think the man you saw at the training center and the man who pulled the gun on us are one and the same. That's probably why he was here. Waiting on you. The fact that I was with you threw him off, and he decided he'd better retreat."

She grimaced. "I know. I've already thought of that." A shiver swept through her. She'd planned on a relaxing evening and an early bedtime. Now she wondered if she'd be able to shut her eyes.

Nick could tell his words had worried her in spite of the fact that she'd already put two and two together. He almost felt bad about saying something and confirming her fears. Almost. But she needed to be on the alert.

He'd been standing outside her home for the last twenty minutes, debating what he should do. He simply didn't feel right leaving her. Then again, she did live on a military base. If she needed help, all she had to do was holler.

But what if she couldn't?

He pulled his phone from his pocket and let his finger hover over Master Sergeant Westley James's number. After all, the man and his wife, Felicity, lived next door to Heidi. Surely, he could keep an eye on her. Still, Nick hesitated. He hated to bother him when he had his hands full with the investigation. Then again, it made sense. The man was right next door. Instead of dialing, he pocketed the phone and walked over to Westley's and knocked.

The curtain in the right window opened and Felicity peered at him. She disappeared and the door opened. "Hi, Nick."

"Hey." She wore loose-fitting jeans and a T-shirt that was probably left over from her days as a trainer. Now she spent her time behind the lens of a camera as the base photographer. The change seemed to agree with her. "Is Westley here?"

"I'm sorry, he's not. You want to come in?"

Nick shook his head. "That's all right. I'm concerned about Heidi and wanted to see if he'd be willing to keep an eye on her place tonight."

Felicity frowned. "I'm sure he would, but there's no telling when he'll be back. What's going on with Heidi?"

"We're pretty sure she saw the guy who blew up the training center and that he knows it."

Felicity's eyes widened. "No kidding. Well, I can understand why you want to take precautions. I'm sorry Westley isn't available to help."

"It's all right. I have one more option."

"Who?"

"Caleb Streeter."

She smiled. "He's a good option. And I'll be sure to keep an eye out as well. And so will Westley when he gets home."

"Thanks, Felicity." She shut the door and Nick dialed Caleb's number as he walked back over to Heidi's home. He stood at the base of her porch steps while the phone rang. Nick had just started to get to know the master sergeant who was now running the K-9 training center. He'd spotted him earlier in the midst of all of the chaos at the explosion site, but hadn't had a chance to say anything as he'd been swamped answering OSI's questions.

"Hello?" Caleb croaked.

"You awake?"

"I'd just dropped off. What's up, Nick?"

"I was going to ask if you'd help me out by keeping an eye on a friend's place for few hours tonight."

"Normally, I'd say yes, but I've got to get a few hours of sleep. I've got to be up and at the training center early to start assessing the damage and filling out insurance paperwork."

"How many hours do you need?"

A sigh filtered to him. "At least five. Only had three last night."

"When's your next day off?"

"It was supposed to be tomorrow."

Ouch. He was asking a lot of his friend, but everyone else he could think of was busy. "Okay, I'll take first shift. You get your five hours, then come over here. I'll buy you a steak dinner." He noticed Annie's ears perking up at the word *steak* and smiled.

"For two," Caleb said. "I'm taking Paisley with me." Paisley Strange was the girl Caleb was trying to get to know—and impress.

Nick rolled his eyes. "Fine. For two." He gave him the address and Caleb hung up. He noticed Felicity had come back outside and was sitting on the steps. He jogged over. "Hey."

"Hey. Is Caleb able to help you out?"

"Yes. For now."

She nodded. "Westley's still working. He

called and said he was going to be at the office for a while." She sniffed. "Still smells smoky out here."

"It comes in waves depending on the wind. I'm just going to hang around and keep an eye on things for a few hours. Do you mind if I use your rocker?"

"Make yourself comfortable." She stood. "This Red Rose Killer is about make Westley pull out what little hair he has."

"He's not alone."

She grimaced. "I don't understand how Boyd Sullivan can just disappear, show up to create havoc, then disappear again without a trace. It's ridiculous." Her lips tightened.

Nick grimaced. "And a bit embarrassing." He frowned. "The fact that we haven't caught him just confirms some of the conclusions we've come to. He's got help on the inside." He was fine discussing the case with Felicity as he knew she was privy to the information.

"I agree. But still, you would think he would have tripped himself up by now—or someone would have spotted him and turned him in."

"Even if someone spotted him, how would they know? He seems to be a master at disguises. Not to mention the fact that he'll kill to get the uniform he needs. He's smart and he's extremely careful."

"I remember Westley saying that Sullivan doesn't make a move unless he's sure he won't get caught."

"True." He frowned. "But we're not giving up. He *will* get careless and we *will* get him eventually."

"I know. That's what Westley says, too." She offered him a small smile. "Take care of Heidi."

"That's the plan."

"I'll watch out for her, too. Let me know if I can do anything."

"Could I get a bowl of water for Annie? I've got food with me."

"Sure. And a bottle for you?"

"That would be perfect. Thanks."

Once he and Annie had their water, Felicity slipped inside and Nick turned the porch light off. He took a seat in the wooden rocker.

After a long drink, Annie settled at his feet.

Time passed while Nick did as much work as he could using his iPhone. He requested one of the OSI investigators to stop by so he could give him the evidence he and Annie had collected from the bomb site. The investigator would make sure it was delivered to the lab for examination.

Once he had everything finished that he'd needed to do related to the explosion, Nick leaned his head back against the rocker and let his gaze linger on Heidi's home. She'd affected him in a big way. Those eyes of hers had brought forth emotions he'd thought he'd locked securely away a little over three years ago after Lillian Peterson had taken his heart and stomped all over it.

But with one outburst laden with frustration and truth, Heidi had snapped the lock like a toothpick. His heart had reacted and that scared him. He could face down guns and explosives, but a woman who had the potential to hurt him? No way. Normally, he'd run as far and as fast as possible. But he couldn't do that with Heidi. She might be in danger, and Nick simply couldn't bring himself to ignore that and abandon her when he could help.

So now he was completely unsettled.

The streetlamp illuminated a figure heading toward them, soft footsteps falling on the sidewalk. Annie sat up, ears twitching toward the noise. Nick focused on the shadow in the darkness, his hand sliding to his weapon. "Who's there?"

The figure stopped. "Nick? What are you doing out here?"

Isaac Goddard? Nick relaxed. The man was a senior airman and turning into a good friend.

"Hey, keeping an eye on Heidi Jenks. She's mixed up in everything that went down here tonight."

"I heard about that." Isaac walked over and leaned against the railing. "Glad no one was seriously hurt."

"Bobby Stevens ended up in the hospital but will heal. What are you doing out here?"

"Just walking. I couldn't sleep."

"Nightmares?" Isaac never talked about it, but Nick knew the man's PTSD, brought on after serving and being wounded in Afghanistan, kept him up most nights.

"Yeah."

"I'm sorry. Any word on Beacon?" Beacon was the German shepherd who'd been in Afghanistan the same time Isaac had been serving and had saved Isaac's life. Now Isaac was determined to bring him home. Unfortunately, red tape and bureaucratic nonsense had delayed that to the point where Isaac was ready to head back to the desert of his nightmares and find the dog himself.

"They found him," Isaac said.

"Wait, what?" Nick sat straighter. "They did? That's great."

"Yes and no. He was found injured and they're not sure he's going to make it."

Nick's hope for his friend deflated. "Oh, no. I'm sorry."

"I am, too. So right now, it's just wait and see." He shook his head. "I can't give up on him, Nick. He's as much military as I am. I was lying there, injured and bleeding, and he came up and settled down beside me. Like he was trying to let me know I wasn't alone."

Nick had heard the story before, but he let Isaac talk. It seemed to help him.

"He stayed right with me," Isaac said. "For hours until my unit buddies were able to get to me and pull me to safety."

"He's a hero, too."

"Exactly." Isaac sighed and rubbed a hand over his face. "Anyway, sorry. Didn't mean to talk your ear off. I'm going to keep walking. Maybe head over to the gym and work some of this energy off."

"Keep the faith, man."

"I'm trying. You keep it for me, too."

"You got it."

Nick watched his friend walk away and sent up a silent prayer for him.

Hours later, when Caleb arrived, Nick was still praying. About a lot of things. But mostly that the night would continue to be as quiet as it had been up to that point.

Caleb yawned and rubbed his eyes. "I'm

going to enjoy that steak dinner. I hope this is worth it for you."

Nick looked back over at Heidi's dark home. "It's worth it," he said softly. "Every single penny."

# THREE

Thankfully, the night had passed without incident. After pacing for a couple of hours, Heidi had finally checked the locks four times, glanced out the window to see her street quiet and motionless, and fallen into bed. To her surprise, she'd slept well and five hours later awakened with a new sense of purpose.

Before allowing herself to sleep, though, she'd worked on the story of the training center explosion and sent it off to her editor. The man was thrilled with the piece if his email this morning was anything to go by.

The fact that she could have been killed didn't seem to faze him. His "You're okay, right?" tacked on at the end of his gleeful thanks for a firsthand account of the incident seemed to be perfunctory. She imagined him scrolling through her story while asking that, his brain not even registering her response.

It was okay. She didn't need him to care about

her, she just needed him to recognize her work. When he'd given the Red Rose Killer story to John Robinson, she'd nearly had a coronary. But she was a good reporter and one day someone would notice that.

One day. As long as she kept working hard and proving herself. And she supposed she could start by figuring out who'd bombed the training center.

To do that, the first order of business was to visit Bobby Stevens in the hospital. Not only did she want to check on him, she'd admit she wanted to get his story. Having him tell his experience at the training center would make for a good story, ending with him being caught in the explosion at the training center. If she approached it that way, her questions wouldn't seem so intrusive or odd—or look like she was working on the Red Rose Killer story.

When she looked at her phone, she found a text from Nick that he'd sent after she'd gone to bed. Caleb Streeter is watching your house. Don't be alarmed if you see him parked across the street. Touched that he'd arranged protection for her, she texted him back. Thanks. Appreciate it.

She called the hospital and learned Bobby was able to talk in between periods of sleep. She hoped to catch him awake.

When she stepped out of her home, she stood for a moment on her front porch. The air still had a smoky scent to it and she shivered even though it promised to be a hot September day.

She glanced around looking for any indication the man from yesterday might be hanging around, but the only person she saw was sitting in a car opposite her home. Caleb. He lifted a hand in a short salute. She returned it and walked over to him. "Thank you for staying out here. You didn't have to do that."

He shrugged. "There's some scary business going down on this base lately. I'm happy to put in a few hours making sure nothing else happens."

"Well, I appreciate it."

"Where are you headed?"

"To the hospital. Thanks again and see you later."

"Sure thing." He took off, his headlights disappearing around the first turn.

Heidi couldn't help sweeping the area once more with her eyes. When nothing alarmed her, she climbed into her car and pulled away from the curb. It wasn't far to the base hospital, but she blasted her air-conditioning. The last thing she needed was to arrive with sweat pouring from her.

Minutes later, she pulled into the parking lot

and made her way toward Bobby's room, only to see First Lieutenant Vanessa Gomez near the nurses' station. The petite and attractive critical-care nurse had her dark hair pulled back into a ponytail and was focused on something on her laptop. Heidi walked over and smiled. "Hi."

Vanessa looked up. "Hi, yourself. I read about the explosion in the paper this morning." She frowned. "You were there and wrote the article as well? All last night?"

"Sleep was hard to come by, so I had nothing better to do. I sent it to my editor in time to be printed this morning."

"And you weren't hurt in the blast?"

"I had a scare and got a couple of scraped knees in addition to a few other bruises, but I'm fine. Much better than poor Bobby Stevens. He got the brunt of it, I think."

"At least he's alive."

"There is that." She paused. "Do you mind if I ask you a question about Boyd Sullivan?"

Vanessa's gaze grew hooded. "Depends on what you want to know."

"Just what you thought of him."

"You want to know what I think about a serial killer?"

Heidi wrinkled her nose. "Okay, so maybe I didn't phrase the question right. How do you know him? Why did he target you?"

"Now, that is a question I'd like the answer to myself." She sighed. "I met him one night when he got into a fight. He didn't want to go to the hospital and risk having his superiors find out about it so he asked me if I'd help him. I had a kit in my car and treated him. I was nice to him. He was nice to me. That was it. Or so I thought until I received a note and a red rose. I have no idea why he targeted me or what I did to make him mad." She shuddered and looked around. "But I feel safe here at the hospital. I'm always around people and I take precautions coming and going."

"How scary."

"Yes." Vanessa's gaze slid to the elevator. "Excuse me, I need to grab something from the cafeteria. It's going to be a while before I'll have a chance to eat again."

"Of course. Be careful."

Vanessa shot her a tight smile. "Always."

Once Vanessa was gone, Heidi found Bobby's room number and knocked. When she heard a faint "Come in," she stepped inside to find Bobby sitting up and eating a bowl of Jell-O while a game show played on the television opposite the bed. The remains of scrambled eggs and bacon sat on the plate in front of him.

"Hi, Bobby."

He set his spoon on the tray. "Hey, Heidi." He sounded surprised to see her.

The right side of his face sported a white bandage from temple to chin and his right arm had a cast from elbow to wrist. Other than that, he looked unharmed. "How are you feeling?"

"I have a headache and some other bumps and bruises, but overall, I'd say I'm a very fortunate guy." His eyes narrowed. "You were there. I remember seeing you."

"Yes. I saw the guy come out of the building."

Fear flashed in his eyes. "You yelled at me to run. How did you know it was going to explode?"

"I didn't. I just… I don't know." She shrugged. "Something felt off. This guy came out wearing a ski mask and I figured that meant he was up to no good. He didn't see me at first and took his mask off. When he realized I was there, he was furious, but the way he looked back at the building and decided to run… I really can't explain it."

"When the explosion happened, it knocked me off my feet," he said. "My whole body vibrated with pain—" He reached up and touched the bandage on his head. "You held my hand."

"You asked me to."

He nodded, then winced. "I've got to remember not to move my head." His expression softened. "Thank you for staying with me. I—uh—admit that I didn't want to be alone."

"I understand. I'm glad I could be there for you." She paused. "What else do you remember?"

It was like someone flipped a switch. His open, unguarded expression instantly shut down. "Nothing much."

He was lying.

"Come on, there has to be something."

"Nope. Just coming out of the building and you yelling at me."

"That part of the building is closed. What were you doing in there?"

He flushed. "I often walk through, checking to make sure everything is secure."

"I see." She paused and he started to pleat the sheet. "So, you have cause to believe something's going on in there that needs your attention?"

"What? No, of course not." He frowned at her. "It's just routine, okay? I do it on a daily basis." He shrugged. "It's quiet in there. Gives me a few minutes to clear my head and just take a break, you know?"

"So that's it?"

"Yeah. That's it."

He reached for the remote, so Heidi switched tactics. She had time to take it slow and pull as much information as she could out of him. In his time. She could be tenacious, but she had to be smart, too. There was more than one way to get an answer from someone. Most guys his age had an ego. "You know, people are going to think you're a hero."

"What? How do you mean?"

"I mean, you've been pretty brave through this whole thing. People might even believe you got hurt trying to stop the guy from blowing the center up."

"But I…well…really?"

"Sure."

"Oh."

"And they're going to want to know how you're doing."

He blinked and some of his chilly facade thawed. "Um. Okay. I guess." His curiosity seemed to take over. "How does this work?"

"I just ask you some questions and you answer. Then I run the article by you and if you approve it, I send it to my editor."

"And if I don't like something in it?"

"We change it so you do like it. I won't print it if you don't approve."

"I see." He thought for a moment. "What kind of questions."

"Questions like…" She looked at the game show he was watching on the television. "How good are you at solving those puzzles?"

His brows shot up and he smiled. "Not very good. I used to watch this show with my mother all the time. She's brilliant and can figure them out with the least amount of letters." He paused. "It's quite frustrating to play against her, actually. But fun, too. I always try to beat her and rarely can do it."

"Sounds like a good mom."

"The best."

"Is she coming to visit?"

He started to shake his head and then paused. "No. It's too far for her. She's in a wheelchair, with MS."

"Oh, I'm sorry."

A shrug. "Been that way my whole life, but didn't stop her from being a great mom. She's already called me several times and I know she'd be here if she could."

"I'm sure she would." Heidi nodded to the television. "Want to watch while we talk?"

Frowning, he tilted his head, then shrugged. "Sure."

Heidi nodded at the television. "Can you solve that one?"

He laughed. "No."

Caleb's phone call informing him that Heidi was leaving her home spurred Nick to action. "Where'd she go?"

"She said she was headed to the hospital. I can't follow her. I have to get over to the training center ASAP."

Hospital? Why?

The trainer who was hurt in the blast. She was going to question him. "Fine. Thanks for your help last night. Let me know when you're planning on that steak dinner."

"Will do."

Nick's next call was to Master Sergeant Westley James. He let the man know he was heading out to find Heidi, who was a possible witness to the bombing.

"Before you go, have you seen the paper this morning?" Westley asked.

"No, I haven't had the time." His gut clenched. What had Heidi done?

"There's a story on the bombing. Heidi Jenks wrote it."

"And?"

A pause. "The story is actually good. Facts and no opinions. Good reporting," he said with a faint smile in his voice, "in my opinion."

Nick paused. Wow. "Um…good to hear that." And a huge relief. "She said that's all she would write. She kept her promise."

Westley huffed. "I've known Heidi for a while now. At first, I was skeptical of her, but since I moved into Felicity's place next door to her

I've gotten a different perspective. She seems to be a good reporter who keeps her word. It's impressive. I'll have to admit that before getting to know her, I never would have believed it possible."

"You're not the only one."

"She's also started doing those personality pieces on enlisted personnel. I've read them and they're good. I've even learned a few interesting tidbits about the people I work with. It's nice."

"I'm glad to hear that." And he was. But he needed to get going if he was going to catch up to Heidi.

"Might change my mind and let her do one on me," Westley said.

"She asked?"

"Yes, but I said no at the time." He hesitated, then said, "She's a reporter, after all."

"Yes, she sure is."

To Nick's relief, the man made a sound like he was getting ready to wrap up the conversation. "All right. I know you're working with the investigative team on this Red Rose Killer case. I was talking to Justin and he said OSI wants you on the bombing as well. The evidence you and Annie found has been sent off and we're waiting to hear back. Until then, you might want to keep Heidi in your sights. If we've got a bomber out there who thinks she knows something, she could be in danger."

"Exactly." Which was why he needed to get moving.

"All right. Stay in touch and keep me updated, if you don't mind."

"Of course."

He hung up and whistled for Annie. She came running and stood impatiently at the door while he clipped the leash on her collar. "All right, girl, let's go make sure that nosy reporter doesn't get herself killed."

It only took him a few minutes to get to the base hospital. He left Annie in her temperature-controlled area of the car and headed inside the building. A stop at the information desk provided him the room number.

Once on the floor, he made a right at the nurses' station and found the room. The door was cracked open and he could hear voices inside.

"Come on, Bobby, please tell me what you know. Do you know who the guy was?" he heard Heidi ask. "The one who ran from the building?"

"No."

The trainer's low voice vibrated with tension.

Heidi sighed. "That explosion was no coincidence. You know as well as I do about all the

weird stuff happening on the base. The Red
Rose Killer who killed those two trainers, Clinton Lockwood, and then all of the dogs getting
out."

Nick pursed his lips. Those dogs. Out of the
twenty-one still missing, he would have thought
they would have located a few by now. And
those four highly trained German shepherds
should have come back. But they hadn't. Which
probably meant someone had them.

Uncomfortable with his eavesdropping, he
knocked.

"Come in," Bobby called.

Nick stepped inside and found the trainer sitting up in the bed and Heidi in the chair next
to him. She raised a brow when she saw him.
"What are you doing here?"

"Me? What are you doing here?"

"I thought I'd stop by and check on Bobby."
She shot the man in the bed a warm smile and
something twisted inside Nick. Something he
could only identify as jealousy. But he knew that
couldn't possibly be true. His only explanation
for the unexpected—and unwelcome—feeling
was that he'd had far too little sleep last night.
And *every* night since the Red Rose Killer had
struck the base and set off a chain of events
with the murder of the two trainers as well as
of his former Basic Training Commander, Chief

Master Sergeant Clinton Lockwood. Since then Boyd Sullivan had continued his reign of terror over those who had any connection with him at all.

Nick cleared his throat. "Do you mind if I join you?"

Heidi shrugged, but Bobby shifted on the bed and wouldn't meet his eyes. Interesting.

"I thought I'd see how he was doing and ask him a few questions about the bombing," Heidi said. "Unfortunately, he doesn't remember much."

"I see. How are you feeling?" Nick asked Bobby.

"I'm all right." The young man seemed grateful for the distraction. "They tell me I should make a full recovery, so that's a relief."

"I'm sure." Nick settled himself in the window seat. "I've got a few questions for you myself, if you don't mind." Without giving the man a chance to answer, he said, "What was your shift at the training center yesterday?"

"Second."

"So, what do you think the man in the building wanted? The one Heidi saw run out?"

Bobby looked away again, over Nick's shoulder and out the window. "I was... I needed a break so I was going to step outside for a breath of fresh air and that's when I saw Heidi. She yelled at me to run." He shrugged and briefly met Nick's eyes. "She sounded really intense, so I ran." He turned his gaze back to Heidi. "You saved my life."

Heidi smiled. Nick ran a hand over his jaw. "So, no idea who the man was?"

"No. I've already said it several times. I've got no idea." The young man plucked at the sheet near his knee. Then he linked his hands and turned his gaze to the television, effectively dismissing them.

Nick frowned. Bobby was lying. He slid a glance over at Heidi and saw her eyes on the man. Her wrinkled forehead said she wasn't buying his story, either.

But why would he lie? Was he somehow involved in the explosion or did he know the identity of the bomber and was too scared to tell?

A knock on the door brought a flicker of relief to Bobby's pale features. A woman in her midfifties entered. The lab coat and blue lettering stitched on her shoulder identified her as the doctor. "What's going on in here?" she asked.

Nick stood. "We're just having a chat with your patient."

"Well, you're going to have to leave. In case you haven't noticed, he has a head injury and needs his rest."

"We've noticed." He turned to Bobby. "Thank

you for your time. If you remember anything else, will you give me a call?" He handed him his card.

"Ah…sure. Yes, of course." He stared at it, then set it on the table by the phone.

"Get better, Bobby. I'm glad you're going to be okay," Heidi said.

Bobby's gaze softened when he turned to look at her and, once again, Nick's blood pressure surged. He shook his head and told himself to get a grip. He was not attracted to her. *Liar.* Okay, fine, so he was, but that was neither here nor there. The only reason he was going to keep an eye on Heidi was to make sure she didn't wind up a victim of the bomber—and to make sure she didn't report anything she shouldn't.

Maybe if he told himself that enough times, he'd eventually believe it.

Once outside the hospital room, Heidi turned to Nick and crossed her arms. "What was that all about?"

"What do you mean?"

"I mean, I was in the middle of a conversation with Bobby and you showed up to interfere."

"You mean you were in the middle of pumping a poor, wounded man for information so you could get a scoop on a story."

"I already got the scoop. I was going for the follow-up," she said.

He blinked. Then laughed and held up a hand in surrender. "I can't believe I'm laughing. I should be really annoyed with you."

"So why aren't you?"

His blue eyes flashed with something she couldn't identify. "I don't really know," he said softly.

"That bothers you, doesn't it?"

"In more ways than I'd like."

She waited for him to explain, but he simply sighed and looked away.

"You don't trust me, do you?" she asked, then raised a hand. "Never mind. Don't answer that. It's as clear as the nose on your face what you think of me."

He gave a short laugh. "You're a reporter. That automatically puts you on the *Do Not Trust* list."

"What happened?"

His brow lifted. "What do you mean?"

"What made you not trust reporters?"

And just like that, his face closed up. "It doesn't matter. It doesn't have anything to do with you or this case, so—"

Her phone buzzed and he snapped his lips shut.

"Sorry," she said. She looked at the screen. "I've got to answer this. It's my boss."

"Of course." The coolness in his voice pierced her, but she swiped the screen and lifted the phone to her ear. "Hello?"

"Heidi, where are you?" Lou Sanders demanded.

"Still at the hospital. I just finished talking to Bobby Stevens, the man who was hurt in the training center explosion."

"Right. Well, forget about him for now. Three more homes were burglarized last night, medals were stolen and you're needed to conduct interviews and cover the story."

Heidi bit her lip on the complaint that wanted to slip out. Instead, she nodded. "All right. Text me the addresses, and I'll get on it."

"Good. I expect something on my desk by the end of the day tomorrow."

"Yes, sir."

She hung up and found Nick staring at his phone. He tucked it into the clip on his belt. "I've got to get to a meeting. Are you going to be all right?"

"I think so. Nothing's happened, and last night was peaceful."

"I hate leaving you alone."

His concern sent warmth coursing through her. He might not trust her simply because of her profession, but he obviously cared about her as a person. How long had it been since someone had been genuinely concerned about what happened to her? A man, anyway. She had friends on the base, of course, and she and her neighbor, Felicity, had gotten pretty close over the last month in spite of the fact that Westley, her new husband, didn't seem to like Heidi very much. Heidi was glad Felicity was willing to give her the benefit of the doubt.

Heidi waved off his worry. "I'll be fine. I'm going to be working on this story, so I'll be talking with people all day. The base is as busy as a hive. If I need something, someone is within yelling distance at all times."

Nick nodded. "Okay, just be careful."

"Of course."

He didn't move.

She raised a brow. "Now what's wrong?"

"What was your impression of Bobby?" he asked.

"He's in pain and he's lying through his teeth. He knows something, and he's scared to tell what it is. I'm not sure why he's scared, but he is."

"Yeah. That was my take on him, too. What makes you think so, though?"

With a shrug, she said, "He never actually said he didn't see the guy at the center. He never asked me to describe the man I saw. He just denied knowing who the guy was. Which makes me think he did see him and doesn't want to say."

"That's impressive, Heidi."

"Thanks?"

"No, I'm serious. You're perceptive. That's how a cop thinks."

She laughed. "Well, I'm no cop, that's for sure—and I have no desire to be one. Too dangerous."

Her wry statement and roll of her eyes seemed to amuse him.

"Right. Because being a reporter has kept you safe and sound thus far."

"I like my job and I like to do it well. Part of that entails being able to read people and to read in between the lines."

"Which tells me that OSI needs to dig a little deeper into Bobby's background."

"I'd say so."

"I'll give them the rundown on our visit with Airman Stevens." With a nod and one last look in her direction, he turned on his heel and headed down the hallway to the elevator.

Heidi sucked in a breath and told her feelings to settle down. Yes, Nick was a good-looking man. Yes, she was attracted to him. And no, nothing was going to come of that because…because he didn't respect her occupation, for one. He was bossy and demanding, for two. And he'd awakened long-dormant dreams of what could one day be. A family. A home with children and a husband who loved her—in spite of her job.

With a groan, she knew this was going to be a long day. But at least the interviews would distract her from thinking about the handsome lieutenant. Maybe.

Nick felt slightly better about leaving Heidi. She was right. The base was teeming with people during the day and she'd be with someone constantly on her interviews.

But still…he couldn't shake from his mind the fact that Heidi could be in danger and it was only a matter of time before someone showed up to do her harm.

The guy who'd run from them—and pulled a gun on them—was still out there.

Unable to just drive away, he waited until she came out of the building and watched as she set off on foot. He continued to observe, noting the others leaving at the same time. No one seemed to be following her and that allowed him to draw in a relieved breath and relax a fraction.

Nick then climbed into his vehicle. Annie welcomed him back with a "woof" and he gave her ears a scratch. He drove to the base command office and found a parking spot outside the building that housed the large auditorium-style conference room. Once he was inside, Annie at his side, the executive assistant to the base commander, Brenda Blakenship, met him in the reception area. After they exchanged salutes, she nodded to the nearest door. "Everyone's here. Captain Blackwood is ready."

"Thank you." This was a last-minute meeting on a Saturday. Obviously, something was important.

When he entered the conference room, the large oval table was full of those investigating the Boyd Sullivan case. He saluted and took his seat next to Security Forces Captain Justin Blackwood. Annie settled at his feet with a contented sigh while Nick studied Justin. The captain was a tall, imposing figure, his blond hair cut with military precision. His blue eyes could slice right through a person, but Nick liked the man. In fact, he liked and respected every person in the room. They made a good team. Which was why he knew they would have Boyd Sullivan in custody soon. They had to. This whole investigation had gone on too long.

Across from him sat First Lieutenant Vanessa Gomez, whose insight into Sullivan could be helpful. It was a long shot, but worth having her on the team. Sitting beside her was Captain Gretchen Hill, who had been temporarily transferred to the base to learn how the K-9 Unit and a large security force were run. She'd been assigned to work with Justin, whose former partner had been killed. Nick briefly wondered how that was going. They both looked slightly stressed whenever they were in the same room together. But it wasn't any of his business. They were professionals; they'd work through any problems. Tech Sergeant Linc Colson, a Security Forces investigator, First Lieutenant MP Ethan Webb, Westley James, Ava Esposito and Oliver Davison rounded out the team.

"Thank you all for coming in," base commander Lieutenant General Nathan Hall said. He stood to Nick's left. "I know it's Saturday, but I wanted us all together for an update. It's no secret that Boyd Sullivan is still out there causing grief. He's a killer who shows no mercy and it's up to us to stop him. Fast. First order of business, I think we need to focus a little closer on Yvette Crenville. I still think she's our link. It's well-known how crazy she was about Sullivan, and he seemed to return the feeling."

"True," Nick said. "But we've been looking into her. What else do you suggest?"

"Closer scrutiny. I want constant eyes on her. I want proof supporting our suspicions. I've done some checking and she's regular as clockwork to show up for work, so it should be easy enough to keep her under surveillance. Any volunteers to trail her and report back her routine, who she talks to, where she goes, et cetera?"

Several hands went up and the lieutenant general pointed to Vanessa. "Since you're at the hospital where Yvette works, you're the obvious choice, but are you sure you're up to it?"

"Yes, sir. I'll have to work around my schedule, of course, but I'm happy to do it when I'm not on the clock. Then again, she *is* the base nutritionist, so I may be able to catch up to her occasionally during the day, to see if she's up to anything suspicious."

"All right, you're on it. The only reason I'm asking is because when Ava and Oliver were searching for Turner Johnson last month, they spotted Sullivan in the woods." Seven-year-old Turner Johnson, the son of a base colonel, had been on a school field trip when he'd disappeared. Ava Esposito and Oliver Davison had brought the child home safely. "Turner talked about the 'bad guy and mean woman.' Unfortunately, he never got a look at her. She had on a black hoodie and stuff. But he was sure it was a woman. So, by process of elimination, we're down to Yvette. If it's her, she's going to be suspicious of anyone in law enforcement. But she wouldn't have any reason to connect you to the investigation," he told Vanessa.

"No, we've talked a couple of times, and she

knows I got a rose as well." Yvette had received one the same night as Vanessa.

"But I don't want you doing this alone. I think you're safe at the hospital, surrounded by people, but I'm going to find someone to partner with you. When I decide who it'll be, I'll let you know."

"That sounds good, sir. I do feel safe at the hospital." Vanessa shrugged. "It might be a false sense of security, but for now, I think I'm all right."

"Good, let me know if anything changes."

"Of course."

For the next thirty minutes, the team discussed the case in detail. With one glaring, depressing fact right in front of them. Boyd Sullivan was still on the loose and no one had any idea where he was or how to find him.

"One last thing," Lieutenant General Hall said. "Our anonymous blogger is still wreaking havoc. This time he—or she—has decided to smear the investigators all over the place."

"What do you mean, sir?" Nick asked.

Nathan tapped his phone's screen and read from the blog, "'Well, folks, it looks like the training center bombing wasn't just a random thing. There's speculation that the Red Rose Killer is somehow involved. That it's possible he's back on base. Lock your doors, folks. I know I'm going to.'" Nathan tossed his phone on the table. "I want this person stopped."

"Whoever it is has mad tech skills," Nick said. "But there's got to be more to it."

"What do you mean?"

"I'm just saying, it's like this person has a bug planted in our meetings. We've talked about everything the blogger's mentioned. As we've noted, these are confidential discussions that are being plastered in the posts. I think it's time to play our cards a little closer to our vests." He looked around. "I'm not saying it's one of us, but I do think it's someone we're trusting."

Justin scowled. "Then from this moment on, trust no one but the people in this room. Discuss nothing, and I mean nothing, about this case with anyone but the people here. Is that understood?"

A chorus of "Yes, sirs" echoed through the small room. "Good. That's it for now. Stay in touch."

Most everyone filed out, but Nathan reached out to Nick. "Hang back, will you? You, too, Justin, Gretchen."

With a raised brow, Nick glanced at Gretchen, who shrugged and shoved a strand of short dark hair behind her ear and then tucked it up under the blue beret.

After the others were gone, Nathan turned to them. "Gretchen, what do you think about pairing up with Vanessa in order to keep eyes on Yvette at all times?"

"I'm happy to do it," she said.

"I know that we had considered Vanessa might actually be Boyd's accomplice. I truly don't think she is, but I'd feel better knowing you were observing. And not only that, it's possible she's a target since she got a rose and a note. I'd like someone watching her back as well."

"Absolutely. I agree."

"What do you think, Nick?"

"I think that's a great idea. We don't need to take any unnecessary chances with anyone's life."

"Good, that's settled, then. Gretchen, why don't you catch up with Vanessa and let her in on the plan?"

"Of course, sir." She hurried off.

Once she was gone, Nick raked a hand over his crew cut. "I think we need eyes on Heidi Jenks as well."

"You think she's up to something?"

"No. I think she's in danger." He didn't bother explaining why he thought that. Nathan and Justin were both aware of everything that had happened last night.

Nathan pursed his lips, then nodded. "All right. Why don't you take on that responsibility?"

"Yes, sir. Happy to."

"Excellent. I still want you to be a part of the investigative team, but my gut's telling me Heidi needs to be a priority. Until we know for sure she's safe, you and Annie stay close to her."

"Yes, sir." He paused. "One more thing. I know OSI is investigating the bombing of the training center and is keeping you in the loop."

"Right."

"Heidi and I saw the trainer who was hurt in the blast, Bobby Stevens."

"How's he doing?"

"Recovering. But he's lying about something."

Justin raised a brow. "How's that?"

Nick told them about the visit. "I think he and Heidi have established some sort of bond, simply because she's the one who warned him to run in time and saved his life. But he's hiding something even from her."

"Hiding what? The identity of the person who set the explosion?"

"Maybe. He claims he doesn't know who it was. I think he does know, but is too scared to say anything. Maybe." He shook his head. "I don't know what it is, but there's something."

"You want to do some digging?" Justin asked.

"I can. I don't want to step on OSI's toes, though."

"I think as long as you agree to share whatever you find out, they'll be all right," the Lieutenant said.

"Of course."

Justin nodded. "See if Heidi will agree to continue to keep that bond with Stevens. Maybe at some point he'll tell her what he's hiding."

"That wasn't really what I was thinking, but I can do that."

"What were you thinking?"

"That someone needs to do an in-depth background check on him."

"They did that when he enlisted," Nathan said.

"I know, sir, but I still think he needs to be investigated. Finances, daily routine, the people he hangs out with and socializes with."

"So, a full-blown investigation," Justin said, rubbing his chin.

"Exactly, sir."

"I'll mention your concerns to Agent Steffen."

"Thank you."

Nick left, satisfied that everyone seemed to be in agreement that Heidi needed protection—and that he was the guy for the job. He told himself that his happiness had nothing to do with the fact that he wanted to see Heidi again and everything to do with the fact that he just wanted to make sure she stayed safe. He'd feel the same about anyone in her situation.

*Liar.*

He huffed a sigh and decided not to examine any of that too closely.

He'd keep Heidi safe and that would be that.

So, why was he wondering what her favorite flower was?

Nick put the mental brakes on once again.

*No flowers, no romance, no nothing.* Why did he have to keep reminding himself of that when it came to her? He hadn't had that problem until she kept crossing his path. Now, when he thought about the future, blue eyes and shoulder-length wavy blond hair kept intruding. It was ridiculous. She was a reporter. The one profession that filled him with disgust.

*No flowers, no romance, no nothing.*

But takeout wasn't included in that list. He'd grab some Chinese and stop by to check on her. Just to be sure she was safe. Chinese wasn't romantic.

Unless he included candles.

"No candles, Donovan," he muttered. "Get your mind off romance and on keeping her safe."

After all, he had a direct order to that effect.

# FOUR

"Thank you for seeing me, Mrs. Weingard." Heidi stood on the front porch of the house and smiled at the woman who'd answered her knock.

Children's voices echoed loudly behind her. The young mother nodded and swiped a stray hair from her eyes and turned. "Billy! Stop jumping on the couch and take your sisters upstairs."

"Can we play video games?"

"Yes, for a little while."

Screams of glee at the apparently unexpected treat trailed behind the youngsters as they raced up the steps. A door slammed. Silence descended. "Call me Kitty," the woman said. "And come in if you dare."

Heidi stepped into the chaos. And longing pierced her. Would she ever have a family to call her own? With children who would leave their toys strewn around the furniture and the floor in testament to a play-filled afternoon?

Heidi wasn't getting any younger, and she had to admit that as the months passed, the questions seemed to rear their heads more and more. First Lieutenant Nick Donovan's flashing blue eyes popped into her mind for a split second and she cleared her throat. "You look like you stay busy."

Kitty laughed. "Are you kidding me? I rarely get to sit down, that's for sure." She paused. "But I love them. They're high-energy, but have sweet dispositions. Do you have kids?"

"No, not yet. Hopefully, one day."

Kitty picked up a children's book, two toy trucks and a plastic tiara from the couch. Then waved a hand at it. "Have a seat."

Perched on the edge of the cushion, Heidi pulled her voice-activated recorder from her bag. "Do you mind if I record this? It makes it easier to just transcribe everything later." It also was proof if someone discounted her reporting.

"Sure, that's fine."

"So, can you start from the beginning?"

"Um…like I told the police, my husband was deployed a few weeks ago for his third tour to Afghanistan. He's earned a purple heart and other medals that we kept in a drawer in the bedroom. I'd gone grocery shopping while my kids were at school and when I got home, I found the house torn apart."

"So, this happened during broad daylight."

"Exactly."

"And no one noticed anything at all?"

She shrugged. "No, I think the MPs questioned the neighbors and looked at the security camera footage, but all they could see was a guy in a black hoodie strolling casually out my front door, with his hands tucked in his pockets."

"A black hoodie, huh?"

"Yes."

Like the guy who'd bombed the training center? Sounded like him.

Heidi continued to question the woman, but her mind was only halfway on the interview as she really wanted to know if the training center bomber, the guy who'd pulled the gun at her home, and the person stealing the medals were one and the same. Although it didn't make much sense to her. Why go from stealing medals to bombing an unused portion of the training center? What could be the purpose in that?

Soon, she wrapped up and tucked her recorder back into her purse.

Kitty stood. "Do you think my story will help?"

"I don't know. But it sure won't hurt. The more people who are aware of what is going on, the more likely they are to keep their eyes open."

"I suppose. You know, the thefts are sad and

it's infuriating that someone would do such a thing. I'm more angry about the disrespect to my husband and the other soldiers than the loss of the medals. They aren't worth much. Maybe a couple hundred dollars each. But what they represent…that's priceless. And stealing them just makes me mad."

"I agree completely," Heidi said. "Unfortunately, a few of the medals that have been stolen have been passed down through the generations and are worth quite a bit of money. I think the thief is just taking his chances with the value. He doesn't know who has what, but finds something worthwhile to keep stealing more. And, also, a few hundred dollars times a hundred-plus medals is some nice pocket change. In addition to the jewelry and money he finds on top of the medals."

"True. But it sure makes my blood boil."

"I understand. Hopefully, this person will be in custody soon and everyone can relax." On that score, anyway. With Sullivan still on the loose, no one would be relaxing anytime soon. Heidi walked to the door. "Thanks again for meeting with me. If you think of anything else, please give me a call." She held out her card.

"Of course."

"Mom! Can we have some popcorn?"

"In just a minute, hon," Kitty called over her shoulder to her son.

"Thanks! And some apple juice boxes?"

"Yes, I'll bring them in a minute if you won't interrupt again, please."

"Okay."

The door slammed again and Kitty rolled her eyes, but the smile curving her lips said she didn't really mind. She looked tired as most moms with multiple children were, but it was obvious she loved her brood. The longing hit Heidi again, and she had to push it away, yet again. It would happen for her. Someday. Maybe.

Heidi left and headed for the next interview, where she heard basically the same story as Mrs. Weingard's, except the break-in had occurred at night when the newly married couple had gone to dinner. The thief had taken the young man's great-grandfather's Medal of Valor, awarded to him by the President of the United States for his service in World War II. The young groom almost cried as he described the loss, and Heidi's heart ached for him.

Hours later, she decided to call it a day. It had been a long one and she was exhausted from the emotional roller coaster she'd ridden while doing the interviews. She'd done her best to offer comfort and sympathy, and now she needed some space to gather her notes and write the article.

Walking home, Heidi felt slightly guilty once again. While listening to Airman Keith Bull talk about his great-grandfather with pride gleaming in his gray eyes, it had occurred to her that she was doing the story—and the families—a disservice with her lack of focus. They deserved her full attention even if the stolen medals story hadn't been her first choice for an assignment.

So she didn't get the lead on the Red Rose Killer story.

So her boss couldn't seem to see past his own nose—or his obvious favorite, John Robinson—to see her potential.

So John Robinson drove her batty.

So what?

She was a good reporter and she needed to give this story her best. The families deserved that.

Decision made, guilt assuaged, she drew in a deep breath of the night air. As the sun dipped lower on the horizon, the temperature dropped. She loved being outside in the fall. It was time to open the windows and turn the air-conditioning off. And write.

She strode with a little more pep in her step, actually looking forward to transcribing her notes and sending this article to Lou.

Footsteps sounded behind her and she spun. The setting sun blinded her for a moment, but she thought she saw a shadow dart off to the right and slip down the sidewalk that led to more houses off the main Base Boulevard.

Chills swept through her. That was weird. And creepy. And secretive. For a moment, she considered searching for the shadow, but memories of icy blue eyes, exploding buildings and the man with the gun steered her steps toward home. Quick steps. Sure, she could just be paranoid, but that didn't mean someone wasn't following her. One blessing was that there were plenty of people out tonight enjoying the weather. She passed several officers and saluted, thankful for their presence on the sidewalk.

But the darting shadow still bothered her.

A hand on her shoulder spun her around and she let out a startled squeal. She raised a fist and swung it—only to have it caught.

"Heidi! It's just me, Nick."

He released her hand and she placed it over her racing heart. "Wow. You scared me. Seriously?"

"I called your name twice. You started walking faster."

"I didn't hear you. But a few minutes ago, I thought someone was following me." She frowned. "When I turned, he shot off down a side street."

"I must have crossed the street about then because I saw you turn around. Where are you headed?"

"Home."

"Do you mind if I walk with you?"

Was he kidding? "That would be great, thanks." She looked behind him. "Where's Annie?"

"Back at the kennel. She's finished her work for the day so she gets to take a break."

Once they were inside her home, she kicked off her shoes and turned on a lamp. And sniffed. The trash in the kitchen. Great. It wasn't horrible, but it wasn't great. She'd meant to take it out first thing that morning, but in all of the chaos of everything, she'd forgotten. Oh, well. Hopefully, he wouldn't judge her. "Want something to drink?" she asked him.

"Sure. Whatever you've got is fine."

She returned with two glasses of iced tea. He took his and settled on the couch. She turned her air conditioner off and opened the two windows in the den to let in the fresh air, then took the recliner. "Any progress on finding the man who blew up the center?" she asked.

"No. Unfortunately. And nothing on Sullivan, either. That man is as slippery as a snake."

"As scary as one, too." She shuddered.

"Depends on the snake," he said. "How's the story coming with the stolen medals?"

She shrugged. "I'm talking to the victims. The MPs are tight-lipped about the investigation so I have to get the details from the people who'll talk to me."

"People don't trust reporters. Especially law enforcement."

"No kidding. At least not until it suits their purposes, then they're the first ones to call."

He tilted his head. "How do you live with that? Doesn't it get frustrating?"

"Of course."

"So, why do it? Why pick a career that a lot of people don't have a lot of respect for?"

She sighed. "Because it's in my blood. My father was a reporter and a good one. He was killed while investigating a story and after the shock wore off, the anger set in. I was mad. Livid. It felt like if I could pick up where he left off, I would be carrying on his legacy." She shrugged "I don't know if that makes any sense or not."

"Strangely enough, it kind of does."

His soft words pierced the chunk of armor she'd had to wrap around her heart. "Thank you."

He cleared his throat and nodded.

"And besides," she said, "journalism is a very respectful career. It's just a few who give it a bad name. I'm trying to be one of the good ones."

"I'm starting to see that," he said softly.

"You are?"

"Yeah."

"Well, good. Thanks." They fell silent and she studied him for a moment.

"What is it? You're looking at me weirdly."

"I was wondering what happened to you."

"What do you mean?"

"You're very anti-media, anti-reporters. More so than what seems normal for the average person, I guess. I figure something must have happened to make you feel that way."

Nick looked away. She'd brought the subject up before and he'd managed to avoid answering. He didn't like to talk about his mother's death to anyone. Much less a reporter. Then again, she could easily research it and find out everything she wanted to know and more. Of course, most of it wouldn't be truth. And he wanted her to know the truth.

For a moment, he wondered why he cared. When he couldn't come up with an acceptable answer, he shook his head. "My mother was a Type 1 diabetic. She'd battled the disease from the age of eight. But she did well, got married and had me. My father was a political star and rising through the ranks in Washington when a reporter took pictures of him in a very compromising position with his young and very pretty political assistant."

Heidi's eyes widened. "Uh-oh."

"Exactly. Those pictures wound up in the newspapers and all the media outlets you can think of and his career was destroyed."

"I'm sorry."

His eyes frosted. "Are you? Are you saying you wouldn't have done the same thing had you been in that reporter's place?"

She bit her lip. "I'm sorry it happened. Would I have done the same thing?" She frowned. "I don't know."

"Right."

With narrowed eyes, she did her best to filter her response. "Look, until I'm walking in someone else's shoes, I can't tell you what I would or wouldn't do in that same situation. I *can* tell you that I do my best to act with integrity at all times. I get that not all reporters have the same code of honor, but I do." She paused. "Was the story fact or not?"

"Fact."

She huffed. "Then, yes. I might have done the same thing."

He stood and shoved his hands in his pockets as he checked the locks on her windows.

"Where's your father now?" she asked him.

"Married to that assistant and living in San Antonio. She's sixteen years younger than he is."

"Do you talk to him?"

"No. Not often. He doesn't seem to care."

She winced. "Nick, I'm sorry you had a rough time, I really am. It's no fun being in the spotlight, I get that. Trust me. Probably better than you think."

He turned to her. "You're talking about when your dad was killed?"

"Yes."

"Where's your mother?"

"Happily remarried to a pastor, living in Tennessee."

"Nice."

"It is." She sighed. "But if the story about your father was fact, why are you so antagonistic?"

"Because it led to my mother's death. Indirectly."

She blinked. "Oh. How?"

"The story led to her depression, which led to her not taking care of herself, which led to her insulin issues going out of control, which led to her passing out at the wheel and going over a cliff.

"Anyway, that was one story the papers got all wrong because a diabetic passing out at the wheel and driving over a cliff isn't nearly as sensational as saying she killed herself. And that's the conclusion they immediately came to when there were no skid marks indicating she tried to stop."

With a gasp, Heidi surged to her feet. "That's horrible, Nick."

She sounded like she meant it.

"Horrible is one way to describe it," he said.

"And completely unethical. I'm so sorry. I really am."

He raked a hand over his hair. "I am, too." And why was he telling her this?

"Did you confront the reporter?" she asked.

"I did, actually. He didn't care and there was nothing I could do to make him grow a conscience. There was no way to prove Mom didn't commit suicide—even though the autopsy later revealed that her blood sugar was so low that she probably passed out. But even with that evidence in hand, the paper wouldn't print a retraction or admit they might have jumped the gun and not done a thorough investigation before printing the story. But Mom wasn't suicidal. She was hurt and she was mad at my dad and aggravated with the media up to that point, but she'd just bought us tickets to go see the Rangers play at the stadium that weekend." He gave her a short smile. "We were big fans." He sighed. Enough. He didn't come over here to go down memory lane.

He turned away and once again examined her windows. Maybe just to give himself something to do. "Do you have an alarm system?" he asked.

"Um, no. Why?"

"Because I think you probably need one."

With a slow nod, she let her gaze sweep around her home. "I've never felt unsafe here. This place has been my sanctuary since I moved in. And now…" She rubbed her arms. "I feel like a sitting duck."

"We'll work on that. What are your plans tomorrow?"

She shrugged. "Church, then lunch. Sometimes Felicity and I see a movie if Westley is busy. Other times I ride out to the lake. I'll probably work some in the afternoon after I make my weekly call to Mom and take a nap. And then I have that last interview I need to do with the latest theft victim so I can get this article in to Lou."

"You don't have many friends, I gather," he said softly.

She gave him a sad smile. "Well, I had a few more, but when rumors of me being the anonymous blogger started gaining some traction, a lot of them kind of dropped off the radar."

His jaw tightened. He didn't want to feel sympathy for her. And yet, he did. "We go to the same church here on base. So...come to church with me tomorrow and let's grab lunch after."

Her eyes went wide, then narrowed. "Wait a minute. Is this pity company?"

He blinked. "What?"

"You know. You feel sorry for me, so you're trying to do something nice. Not because you really want to, but because you feel you should."

His jaw dropped and for a moment, he just stared at her. Then he stood and glared, jabbing a finger at her. "I don't do pity company. Sure, I feel bad that you're feeling the brunt of the gossip, but I don't spend time with people because I feel sorry for them." Much. Okay, maybe occasionally, but that didn't apply to this situation. "And if I do," he said, completely negating what he'd just claimed, "I don't volunteer to spend *that* much time with them." Her eyes sparkled, and he cleared his throat—something he found himself doing a lot around her. "Anyway, no. Definitely not pity company."

His glower didn't seem to faze her. She searched his eyes. "I think I believe you," she said. Then grinned.

Having her throw his words back at him sent his anger down the drain. A bark of laughter escaped him and he stepped back. "Well, thank you, ma'am. I appreciate that."

A small smile tugged at her lips. "You're welcome."

"So? Church and lunch?"

"Sure," she said. "Church and lunch."

"Good. I'll pick you up." With that, he left her standing in her den, staring after him, speechless.

The smile on his face died when he saw the Security Forces vehicle parked outside her home. Nope, not pity company. Protective company, yes. Because while he had no plans to fall for the pretty reporter, he was genuinely worried about her safety. He sighed and did a one-eighty. Back at her door, he knocked.

She opened it with a frown. "Are you okay?"

"Yes. I just need to know your favorite flower."

"Pink carnations. Why?"

"Just needed to know. See you tomorrow."

"But—"

"Good night, Heidi."

Her confused huff made him smile again. A tight smile that stayed with him all the way home.

When he stepped inside, he found his grandfather in the recliner, a football game playing on the television mounted over the fireplace. A retired colonel, the man had moved in with him after Nick's grandmother had died last year. He was able to function on his own, but Nick felt better with him there so he could keep an eye on him. And besides, he liked the company. "Hey, Gramps, how's it going?"

"It's going fine. Where've you been?"

"I went over to see Heidi." He'd told his grandfather about the explosion. As much as he could, anyway. Even though the man was retired military, there were still things Nick had to keep to himself. "I was worried about her."

"Uh-huh. You like her, don't you?"

"Did you miss the part where I said she's a reporter?"

"I didn't miss it. So why do you like her?"

"I didn't say I did."

Gramps harrumphed and let out a low laugh. "Okay, boy."

His grandfather could make him feel like a child of ten without even trying. "Gramps…"

"I picked up your shirts from the cleaners. You can wear the blue one tomorrow to church."

Church. Right. "Ah…about church. We have to swing by and pick up Heidi. She's going with us."

"That reporter you don't like?"

He sighed. "Yes, sir, that's the one."

"Gotta find me a woman I don't like as much as you don't like that one."

With a groan, Nick made his way back to his room and shut the door on his grandfather's chuckles.

"Just keeping her safe, that's it," he muttered to the quiet room. Because in spite of the light-hearted banter with his grandfather, Nick's pulse pounded a rhythm of fear every time he thought about her being a target of the man who bombed the training center.

Which meant nothing special, he told himself. He'd be concerned about anyone who'd caught the attention of a man who bombed a building.

But Heidi…

He did like Heidi. A lot.

And while his head argued that it was a bad idea, his heart was jumping all over it.

He had a feeling he was in big trouble.

# FIVE

Heidi had found sleep difficult to come by last night, but when nothing had happened by one o'clock, and she could see the MP was still parked outside, she'd been able to fall into a restless doze. By the time her alarm buzzed, she was already up and getting ready.

And questioning her sanity as she slicked pink gloss across her lips. "We go to the same church here on base. So…come to church with me tomorrow and let's grab lunch after."

She rolled her eyes at her reflection and decided she would do. She'd left her hair down and it rested against her shoulders, the strands straightened with the help of her flat iron. Light makeup enhanced her blue eyes and the lip gloss added a subtle sheen to her mouth.

In her day-to-day work life, she looked professional and neat, not made-up. It suited her. So why was she making more of an effort today?

She knew exactly why and his name was Nick Donovan. She might as well admit it.

With a grimace, she turned from the sink and headed for the kitchen for a bagel and a cup of coffee. Her nose reminded her she still needed to take the trash out, but she wasn't about to risk dirtying her nice clothes. She put that at the top of her after-church to-do list. A glance out the window revealed the Security Forces vehicle still parked on her street. She frowned. The man she'd seen running from the training center hadn't liked that she'd seen his face. In fact, he'd been so desperate to get away he'd pulled a gun on her and Nick. Then he'd managed to escape the base perimeter. Would he come back or was his work done? Or had he decided the smart thing to do was disappear? She hoped it was the latter.

While she was on her second cup, her phone rang, and she snagged it. "Hi, Mom."

"Hey, stranger."

Heidi grimaced. "Sorry, it's been crazy around here."

"I know. I've been keeping up with what's happening on the base. They haven't caught that serial killer yet. Boyd Sullivan."

"No, they haven't, but they don't think he's on the base anymore. He was last seen in central Texas."

"And what about the explosion at the training center?" her mother asked.

"Oh. You heard about that, huh?"

"Like I said, I keep up."

What could she say that would be the truth, but not send her mother running to the base?

"We're not sure, Mom. OSI is investigating so we hope we hear something soon. Until then, security is super tight."

"I would hope so. Do you need to take a leave of absence and come here?"

"No, ma'am. I need to stay here and do my job."

"In spite of the fact that it might get you killed?"

"I'm not planning on putting myself in any danger."

"Your father—"

"Dad knew exactly what he was walking into when he started working that story. Now that I'm older, I understand his thought processes. He didn't want to die, but he was doing what he believed in." She paused. "I'm not Dad, but I'm a lot like him. I don't plan to do anything that may put me in danger, but I believe in ferreting out the truth."

For a moment her mother didn't respond and Heidi wondered if she would hang up on her.

Then a watery sigh reached her. "On the contrary, my dear, you are just like your father."

"Well...okay."

"And I'm very proud of you."

Heidi snapped her mouth shut. Then let out a low sigh. "Thanks, Mom. I needed to hear that."

"Please let me know if there's anything I can do."

"I will."

"And someone needs to tell that blogger to quit posting. Whoever is writing that stuff is revealing things probably better kept under wraps."

A choked laugh escaped her. "I agree, Mom. They're working on silencing that person."

"Which means they don't know who it is."

"You're very astute."

Heidi could almost hear the smile her mother no doubt wore. "I love you, hon."

A knock on the door made her jump. "I love you, too, Mom. We'll talk later, okay? Give Kurt my best." She really did like her stepfather. Mostly because he adored her mother.

"Of course."

"Bye." Heidi hung up as another knock echoed through her small home. She rose and placed the cup in the sink, then grabbed her purse.

When she opened the door, she blinked.

Nick in his military fatigues was one thing, but dressed in civilian clothing, he plain looked *good*. Amazing. She'd seen him at church before in his civvies, of course, but to have him standing on her doorstep put a whole different kind of beat in her heart.

"Hi," she said. "Good morning."

"Morning." He blinked as his gaze swept over her. "Wow. You look different."

"Thanks?"

He shook his head and laughed. "Sorry. I mean different as in good."

Did a little makeup make that much of a difference? Apparently, it did, judging by how his eyes were focused on her. "Thank you. You look different, too. As in good."

She thought his cheeks might have gone a little pink. He cleared his throat. "I think I need to work on my manners. Let's start over." He turned his back to her, walked down the steps, then back up. When he stood in front of her once more, he offered her a slight bow. "Heidi, you look lovely this morning."

And there went her heart. "Thank you." She was sure her cheek color now matched his. And where did that breathlessness come from? She cleared her throat. "Is it okay if I don't say 'you do, too'?"

He laughed. "I'm more than fine with not being called lovely. Are you ready?"

"I am." She locked the door, then shut it behind her. Then she smiled up at him. "But you are handsome."

"Ah, thank you." More throat clearing. "I hope you don't mind that we have some company."

"Not at all. Who? Annie?"

"And my grandfather. Colonel Truman Hicks, retired. He lives with me and decided to come to church this morning."

"Sounds wonderful." She hoped it would be, anyway. "So, how does he feel about reporters after what happened to your mother? His daughter, I presume?"

His eyes narrowed. "Yes, he's my mother's father. Let's just say he's reserving judgment on any reporters, present company included."

"Uh-huh."

At the car, he introduced her to the man who sat in the back seat. He looked familiar, like she'd seen him in the church before, but she wouldn't have placed him if Nick hadn't introduced them. "Very nice to meet you, sir, but I'm happy to take the back."

"I've got better manners than that, young lady. Climb in."

"Yes, sir." She raised a brow at Nick and he

shrugged and opened the door for her. Oh, boy, this might just get interesting.

Annie rode in the very back. The colonel stayed quiet the entire ride while Nick did an excellent job with small talk. She figured the colonel was listening and observing, because while he didn't seem to resent her presence, she wasn't sure he approved of it.

So, Heidi focused on Nick and thought she managed to sound halfway intelligent. The sight of a handler walking his dog brought the missing animals to mind. "Any word on the dogs still missing from the kennel?" she asked.

"No."

"What about the four German shepherds? Felicity said Westley was especially concerned about them."

"They're definitely the more trained and special dogs, for sure, but there's been no word or sightings on them. It's frustrating."

"I'm sure."

They fell silent and she couldn't hold back the sigh of relief when the church came into view.

The jaunt from her home to the church had taken all of three minutes. It had felt like at least thirty.

Nick parked and everyone climbed out into the heat that was already starting to steal the oxygen from the air. She was definitely ready for cooler weather.

The colonel went on ahead, his steps confident and sure, his back straight and strong.

"Why'd he retire?" Heidi asked as Nick released Annie from her area. "He seems a little on the young side."

"He is. He'll only be sixty-eight on his next birthday, but a couple of years ago, my grandmother got sick," he said, "and he wanted to give her his full attention so he requested a leave and was granted it. She passed away. Losing my mom and then grandmother was hard for him. Grief knocked him for a loop. He had his forty-five years—and then some—in, so he was able to retire. Since it was just the two of us left in the family, I decided to ask him to move in with me. He didn't argue about it too much. I think he was lonely."

"I see." She walked with him up the steps and into the sanctuary. "You've had a lot of pain in your life."

"Hmm No more than anyone else, probably. Life comes with a guarantee of pain. It's how you deal with it that matters."

"Maybe." He was right, of course. She just didn't want to think about how she'd dealt with the pain life had served her. Avoiding it wasn't exactly dealing with it.

They found their seats. The colonel sat in the front row. Now she knew why he'd looked familiar. She saw the back of him most Sundays. Nick led her to a pew in the middle and slid in. She sat next to him, ignoring the suddenly speculative looks of some of the others around them. "You don't sit with your grandfather?"

"No. Sometimes I have to slip out and I prefer not to do that in front of the whole congregation. He's sat in that seat since he's been on base so he's not about to move. And see that empty space next to him?"

"Yes."

"He puts Gramma's Bible there in her place."

"He likes tradition."

"Thrives on it."

"And no one says anything? What if a new person sits there without knowing the history?"

He smiled. "Then Gramps finds another place to sit. But the nice thing is, most newcomers don't sit in the front row so it's not an issue."

"Cool." Nick came from a long line of love and an impressive family—at least on his mother's side.

Westley and Felicity slid in beside Nick, then looked around Nick to greet her. "How are you doing? Recovering from the blast, I hope?" Westley asked her.

"I still have sore knees, but other than that, I'm doing fine, thanks."

He nodded and started to say something else, then snapped his lips shut as John Robinson approached. Heidi's stomach turned sour, but she kept her face blank, not wanting the reporter to see her reaction.

"Good morning, all," John said. "Thought I'd catch you here. Master Sergeant James, can you give us an update on the Red Rose Killer?"

"I cannot. Have a nice day, Robinson."

The reporter flinched and narrowed his eyes at Heidi. "Lou isn't going to be happy to hear about this. This is my story."

Heidi crossed her arms and raised her chin. "Did I say it wasn't?"

"No, but everywhere I go, you're there." His gaze flicked to Nick. "With someone working the investigation. If you're hoping to scoop me on this—" The music started and he was forced to end his bickering. "We'll talk later."

"Not if I can help it," she muttered as John walked across the aisle and Nick placed a comforting hand at the small of her back. She shot him a tight smile and drew in a deep breath that was supposed to help lower her blood pressure.

It helped. A little.

Security Forces Captain Justin Blackwood and his sixteen-year-old daughter, Portia, entered and quickly found a seat. Portia carried her ever-present iPad and looked about as happy to be in church as she would being stuck in after-school detention. Not for the first time, Heidi wondered what her story was or what went through her head—the daughter of a high-ranking military official. But also the daughter of a single dad. From what Heidi had learned just from keeping her ears open around the base, Portia was the result of a high school romance. She'd lived with her mother until the woman had died about a year ago and then Justin had gotten custody. She'd been living with her father ever since and didn't seem at all happy about that fact.

Heidi couldn't remember seeing a smile on the girl's face and that made her sad.

She let her mind flip from the girl to what she needed to do on the Red Rose Killer. While she'd been honest about not working the story, it didn't mean she just had to ignore it, right? Of course, she had her priorities straight. First and foremost, she needed to figure out what was going on with the missing medals, but if she happened to come across something that could lead them to Boyd Sullivan, then so be it. John would stroke out if that happened, but there wasn't anything she could do about that. That was his problem.

When the second song ended and it was time to sit, she realized she hadn't even been aware of standing. However, she was very aware of Nick's hand still at the small of her back. Which made her wish they'd sing at least one more song.

But it wasn't to be.

She sat and continued her musing even as she tried to focus on the sermon and not on the man next to her. And then it hit home what Pastor Harmon was talking about. Something about loving one's enemies. She slid a glance at John Robinson across the aisle and clamped her lips together. *Lord, don't ask me to love him, please. That's going above and beyond, isn't it?* Then her gaze moved to the man on her right. *But Nick Donovan might be another thing altogether.* However, Nick wasn't her enemy, so she was pretty sure that wouldn't be the correct application of the sermon. Still...

"Are you all right?" Nick whispered.

She started. "Yes, why?"

"You're squirmy and distracted. Like a little kid."

Heat suffused her cheeks. "Sorry." For the rest of the service, she sat still as a rock and forced her mind to stay on the sermon.

Once the service ended, they made their way to the back of the church and stood in line to greet the pastor and exit. Annie stayed obediently beside Nick. "She's really an amazing dog, isn't she?" Heidi said.

Nick leaned down to scratch the hound's ears. "Truly amazing. Not very pretty and the slobber sometimes gets to me, but she's all heart and give. I couldn't ask for a better partner."

"I hate that the other dogs are still missing. I hope someone's taking care of them."

He frowned. "I do, too."

"It's been five months since Sullivan released them. Do you think there's still hope?"

"Of course there's hope, Heidi." But it wasn't Nick who answered. It was Pastor Harmon who'd no doubt heard her remark as they approached him. He reached for her hand and gave it a friendly squeeze. "There's always hope—even when the situation looks hopeless."

Heidi smiled at the friendly and wise man she'd come to enjoy speaking with on Sunday afternoons. "Hello, Pastor Harmon. I know God can use even this situation. Sometimes it's hard to focus on that, though."

"I know. I'm praying those dogs come home soon."

"Thank you," Nick said. "We appreciate that." They moved on and stepped out into the heat. "Lunch?" he asked.

"That sounds fabulous."

They found his grandfather talking to three officers and making a golf date. When Heidi and Nick approached, his brown eyes turned speculative. "I'm going to skip out on lunch with you two if that's all right. These three need a fourth."

"Of course, Gramps, just call me if you need a ride home."

"One of these guys can drop me off. Y'all mind?"

"No, sir, happy to do it," one of the officers said. Heidi tried to pull his name from the recesses of her memory, but couldn't find it.

Then Nick's hand was under her elbow and he was leading her to his car. "Is the Winged Java okay with you?"

"Sure. I love their potato soup and Caesar salad."

"Perfect."

They were stopped by Pastor Harmon, who called out Nick's name. He stood at the top of the steps, waving him over.

"Go on, I'll meet you at the car," she said.

The parking lot was almost empty. The car was twenty yards away.

He nodded and jogged over to the steps while she headed for the vehicle. The sound of an engine caught her attention and she turned to see a vehicle heading toward her. Black-tinted windows blocked her view of the driver. As he rode toward her, his window rolled down, his right arm lifted…

…and she saw the semiautomatic in his grasp aimed right at her.

Nick turned at the sound of the first crack from the gun, followed by a *rat-a-tat-tat* that spit up the asphalt near his SUV. "Heidi!" He ran toward her, pulling his weapon. She'd darted behind the vehicle as the weapon fired, but had she been fast enough? "Heidi! Are you hit?"

The silver sedan roared to the edge of the parking lot, then out into the street without stopping. Within seconds, it had sped around the corner.

He turned to see his grandfather on the phone, yelling orders. The MPs would be here soon, but there was no one here to follow the guy. No matter, someone would catch him soon enough. He was on a closed base and wouldn't get far. Nick rounded the side of the vehicle to find Heidi crouching behind a tire. When she saw him, she launched herself into his arms. He held her, his heart thudding with the knowledge that she didn't appear to be harmed.

He pushed her back to look her over. No blood in sight.

"He didn't hit me," she said. "Came close, but

I think trying to shoot me from a moving car threw off his aim."

The colonel hurried over, phone still pressed to his ear. "Do we need an ambulance?"

"No, sir," Heidi said, although Nick knew they'd send one anyway. "Let me sit for a minute, please," she said. "My knees are shaking."

He lowered her to the asphalt and knelt beside her. "You're sure you're okay?"

"Just shaken."

"Understandable."

Sirens were already screaming closer, racing down Canyon Drive. Nick tucked his weapon back into his holster as the first Security Forces vehicles turned into the church parking lot. "You'll need to give a statement," he told her.

"I know. I'm just trying to get it together. It's a story, right? I can do this. I can write this from my perspective."

Already she sounded stronger, but Nick was floored. "A story? You were almost killed!"

Her eyes met his as she stood. "I'm aware of that, thanks."

"Apparently not. It's not a story. It's your life!"

"Stop shouting, Nick, and let me handle this my way."

Belatedly, he realized what she was doing. Compartmentalizing. "You know you completely exasperate me, right?"

"Can't say I'm surprised. I think I have that effect on most people I meet."

At least she was responding with a bit of morbid humor. He got it. Most people in law enforcement used sarcasm or bad humor in order to deal with what they had to live with on a daily basis. Heidi had been around long enough to adopt the technique.

He groaned. "Fine."

A hand on his arm pulled his attention from her to his grandfather. "Gramps?"

"More trouble for the pretty reporter, huh?" While the older man looked steady as a rock, his brows were drawn tight and a muscle in his jaw pulsed, revealing his tight hold on his anger and fear.

"No kidding," Nick told him.

From the corner of his eye, Nick spotted John Robinson heading straight for Heidi. Knowing she was in no condition to deal with her colleague, he nudged his grandfather. "Can you head that guy off at the pass? He and Heidi don't get along, and she may deck him if he says something snarky."

With a gleam in his eyes, his grandfather nodded. "My pleasure."

Turning, Nick found Heidi staring at him. She blinked. "Thanks."

"You're welcome. Now, let's give your statement and get some food. I have a feeling we're going to need it."

# SIX

When Heidi was done giving her statement to the police, it was two o'clock in the afternoon.

She was conscious that Nick was right by her side through the whole thing. All of it. He held her hand while she spoke to the MPs. He kept his hand on her shoulder when he encouraged her to let the paramedic check her out. And, finally, he took her to the newspaper office and sat patiently in the corner of her cubicle while she typed up the story for Lou.

"Wow, you just can't stay out of trouble, can you?"

Heidi paused and then lifted her head to find John Robinson hovering just outside her cubicle. Nick looked up from the magazine he'd been reading and set it aside.

"Not in the mood, John," Heidi said and turned her attention back to her computer.

"A shoot-out is a pretty big deal. How did that guy get a semiautomatic on the base, anyway?"

"I think that the MPs are probably working on that," she said.

"Really? And you were the one who saw the guy run out of the training center, too. As well as get chased by a gun-wielding maniac outside your home."

"He didn't chase us. We chased him." She paused, looked up. "What are you implying?"

"I'm not implying anything. I'm just saying it's kind of odd, isn't it?"

"Spit it out, Robinson," Nick said.

"Fine." He jabbed a finger at Heidi. "I think you want to work on the Red Rose Killer so bad that you're setting up these little incidents to make Lou think you're the better reporter. Kind of like a daredevil reporter who'll go after any story no matter what."

Heidi stared at him for a good three seconds, then rose. "Get out."

"You're not going to deny it?"

"No, I'm not. You've made up your mind, and your blinders wouldn't allow you to see the truth if it bit you on the nose. Now, get out of my space and leave me alone."

Robinson's nostrils flared. "You're going to get knocked off that pedestal you've put yourself on. Real soon."

"Is that a threat?" Nick asked and stepped

casually in front of Heidi, partially blocking her view.

"No," Robinson said. "A promise." He spun on his heel and left.

Heidi's breath whooshed from her lungs. "What a jerk."

"Yeah. You better watch your back with that one."

She caught his gaze. "Guess I'll trust you to do that while you're watching for the other guy who's out to get me."

He huffed a short laugh. "Right." His phone rang. "I'm going to get this while you finish up."

When he returned a few minutes later, Heidi had just put the finishing touches on her piece and hit the send button. "I'm starving," she said.

"We'll grab some food on the way back to your place. That was Westley. He said they think they've figured out how the gunman got on base."

"How?"

"Looks like he hopped a ride on a delivery truck. Security footage showed him getting out of the back when no one was watching. The weapon was in his hand. Then he tried a few cars until he found one with the keys left in it. Piecing together the footage from different cameras, it's apparent that he drove around base for a few minutes—looking for you, they think—

before stopping at the church. And you know what happened after that."

"Did they catch him?"

"No. Unfortunately, he managed to get away. He ditched the car and slipped inside the Base Exchange. With the baseball cap and sunglasses, we weren't able to get a good picture of him off the security footage."

She sighed and nodded. Then stood. "All right. I think I'm ready to get out of here and get something to eat. Do you mind if we just hit the drive-through? I don't feel up to sitting in a café."

"Sure, we can do that. Let's go."

He loaded her and Annie into his SUV and they swung through a drive-through before he took her home. Once inside, he placed the food on the table.

In companionable silence, they worked together, grabbing plates and silverware, and soon, she found herself sitting across from him—albeit a bit tongue-tied. After several bites, she took a sip of soda and eyed him.

"What?" he asked before taking another bite out of his burger.

"Why are you being so nice to me?" she blurted.

He blinked. "Someone just tried to kill you. Should I be mean to you?"

She gave a low laugh. "Of course not. I don't think that would even be in your makeup. But you don't like reporters. That means you don't like me by default."

"Hmm. That's been the general feeling over the last few years."

She raised a brow. "And with me being fingered as the anonymous blogger, that should really make you think twice."

"But you're not the blogger."

"I know that, but I don't have any proof."

"I think you've proven you're not."

"Really? How's that?"

"I'm not blind, Heidi. I've been watching you, and you have integrity."

A lump gathered in her throat. "Thanks, I appreciate that. But you still don't like reporters."

"I have to admit, there's a certain reporter who might be changing my mind."

"Let me guess. John Robinson?"

He choked. Then went into coughing spasms while she pounded his back. "Are you okay?"

"I may take back my statement about liking a certain reporter. She may have integrity, but her wicked sense of humor can hurt a guy."

Heidi grinned. She couldn't help it. His expression set her heart racing. "You actually like a reporter?" She was proud of the calm, matter-of-fact tone she managed to use. "Judging by your reaction, I'm guessing it's not John."

"No, John is exactly the kind of reporter I don't like."

"So, who might it be?" Seriously? Was she *flirting* with him? The guy who hated reporters? Obviously, she was still traumatized from the day's events and was in desperate need of a good night's sleep.

Now that he had himself under control, his eyes narrowed, but a smile played around the corners of his mouth. "You really have to ask?"

Dropping her gaze to her food, she gave a small laugh even while heat crept into her cheeks. "No, I guess I don't." So. He was inclined to flirt back. Interesting.

And then the gunfire she'd escaped that morning echoed in her mind and she frowned.

His smile slipped away. "What is it?" he asked.

Swallowing the last bite of her burger, she shook her head. "This probably isn't a good idea."

"What?"

She met his eyes. "You know what. Us hanging out. Flirting a little. You being anywhere near me. That's what."

"Why not?"

"Because I might get you hurt. Someone shot at me today. Obviously, this guy is crazy and doesn't care who's in the path of his bullets."

"You were the only one in the path of those bullets. They didn't come close to anyone else."

"This time. What about next time?"

He ran a hand over his eyes. "I'm hoping there won't be a next time."

She bit her lip and nodded. "I appreciate that. But if the shooter and the bomber are one and the same, he's not going to stop."

"Then someone will have to stop *him*. Period."

The flat confidence he infused into his words gave her hope and terrified her at the same time. Because stopping him might mean putting Nick's life in danger. "Nick—"

"It's going to be okay," he said.

She shot to her feet. "Don't say that!"

His brows rose. "What? Why?"

"Because you don't know that it's going to be okay." She jabbed a finger at him. "It might *not* be okay. Sometimes, it's just *not* okay." She paced to the window and looked out through the blinds, hating that she thought to stay to the side so no one could see her. The afternoon sun shone bright—a direct contrast to her moody, overcast emotional state.

He gave a slow nod. "All right. That's true. Sometimes it's not okay."

Crossing her arms, she closed her eyes for a moment while she gathered her emotions tighter. Then she turned. "I'm sorry. It's just my dad used to tell my mom that every time he left to cover a story and she expressed concern or fear. Those were some of his last words. 'Don't worry, honey, it'll be okay,' he said. Well, trust me, it wasn't okay."

"Aw, Heidi, I'm so sorry." Nick rose and stepped over to her, the look of sheer compassion in his eyes making her want to cry all over again.

But she refused. That wouldn't help anything. She set her chin. "Don't worry about it. I shouldn't have reacted so strongly."

"But some things do turn out okay, right?"

She sniffed and offered him a small smile. "Yes, some things do. Specific things. Like the fact that I'm still alive. And I have you watching out for me. That's definitely okay."

"Good," he said softly. "Because I'm glad you're still alive and I'm for sure watching out for you."

"Thank you. I appreciate it." She sighed. "And now, I need to work."

"Anything I can help you with?"

"Not unless you want to give me the scoop on the evidence you found at the training center."

"Sorry, that's a negative."

Letting her shoulders droop, she nodded. "I kind of figured."

He sighed. "Heidi, it doesn't have anything to do with whether or not I trust you. It's an investigation. There are some things I simply can't talk about."

"I know." She smiled. "It's okay."

When his brow lifted at her use of the words, she shrugged. "You can say those words when it really is—or is going to be—okay. Just don't say them when you have no way of knowing if it's going to be okay or not. You can't predict the future."

"Got it." He cleared his throat, stepped back and started cleaning up the remains of their lunch. "I'll let you do what you need to do. Work, take a nap and recover, or whatever. Just do me a favor?"

"What?"

"Don't go anywhere alone. Don't make yourself a target. Stay inside and stay safe."

Her jaw tightened at the request. "I won't be a prisoner in my own home."

"Don't look at it as a prison. Look at it as a safe house."

She rolled her eyes. "Nick—"

"Please." He placed his hands on her shoulders. "I don't want to see you get hurt—or worse."

The look of compassion in his eyes had morphed into something entirely different. "Why do you care so much?" she whispered.

"I don't know." He gave a low laugh. "A few days ago, I would have said you were as irritating as a gnat."

"Well, thanks. And now?"

"Now that I'm getting to know you a bit more...well, let's just say I want to continue to be able to do that."

She swallowed. Hard. "Okay."

"So, are you going to be all right if I leave you here alone? And be honest with me. Today was really scary. It's only natural that you might not want to be alone."

"Are you a counselor now?" she teased half-heartedly.

His lips turned up in a sad-tinged smile. "Just a guy who's been through some scary stuff."

She nodded. "I think I'll be all right. I've got coverage on my home, remember?" With a sigh, he stepped over to her and wrapped her in a hug. "I like you, Heidi Jenks."

The thud-thud-thudding of her own heart said she liked him, too.

He pressed a kiss to her forehead and she blinked.

"Call me if you need anything," he said. "Promise?"

Still reeling from the feel of his lips on her skin, she simply nodded.

And then he was gone.

And she was alone...

...with the fact that someone wanted her dead. And she was falling in love with Nick Donovan. She wasn't sure which scared her more.

Nick gave himself a mental slap. He was doing it again. Letting his heart have a say in how he acted. He decided he needed some rules when it came to Heidi.

Rule number one: keep your distance. Emotionally and physically. Which led to rule number two.

Rule number two: stay at arm's length—i.e. not close enough to hug.

Rule number three: definitely no hugging.

New rule number four: no kissing of foreheads.

Seriously, he had to get it together.

He let himself into his home and found his grandfather in the recliner, watching football. "Gramps? What are you doing here? Thought you were golfing."

His grandfather muted the game. "After everything settled down, the others decided to postpone and try again next week. I'm on the schedule. How's your girl?"

"My girl?"

A raised eyebrow was the only response from Gramps.

Nick resisted rolling his eyes. "She's fine. For now."

"Why was someone shooting at her?"

"We think it's the person who bombed the training center. She was there when it happened and saw a guy in a ski mask and hoodie running from the place just before the explosion. The guy didn't realize she was there and took off his ski mask. Then saw Heidi."

"That would explain it."

"Only the hoodie hid his face enough that she was only able to give a partial description. Good enough for a detailed drawing of a guy wearing a hoodie, but nothing more than that."

"Frustrating."

"No kidding."

"So what are you doing back here? You should be watching out for her."

"She's got someone on her place."

"Then what are you going to do?"

"What do you mean?"

"You're standing there, with your keys in your hand and that look in your eyes."

"What look?"

Another raised brow. Nick huffed a short laugh. His grandfather could read him so well.

"I think I'm going to talk to Justin Blackwood and see if he thinks any of this is related to our ongoing investigation of Boyd Sullivan."

"It's Sunday. Supposed to be a day of rest."

"Unfortunately, killers don't seem to care about that. Which makes it hard for the good guys to take the day off."

"I know, boy. I've been there. Just don't like to see you working so hard."

"Wish I didn't have to, but at least I like what I do." He did like his job. He might wish it wasn't necessary, but as long as there were bad guys with bombs, he would do his best to stop them.

He shot a text to Justin, who answered that he was in the conference room of the base command office. The captain agreed to meet and Nick headed back out the door. "Sorry I can't stay and watch the game with you."

"Trust me, you're not missing anything. The Cowboys are playing like they've never seen a football. It's maddening."

Nick gave a low laugh and headed for his truck.

When he pulled into the parking lot of the

base command building, he noted several other vehicles he recognized.

Inside, he made his way to the conference room, where he found Justin with Westley, Oliver and Ava. Files were spread across the table and yellow legal pads held copious notes. "Did my invitation get lost in the mail?"

Justin waved him to a seat. "You didn't miss anything. I knew you were with Heidi." He met Nick's gaze. "Is she all right?"

"She is. She's at home resting. Or working. Probably the latter. There's an officer on her house, watching out for her."

"Okay, good." Justin caught him up on what the quartet had been discussing. "Vanessa's been keeping an eye on Yvette but hasn't seen any indication that Yvette is hiding anything or is in contact with Sullivan, but it's only been twenty-four hours. We're going to keep up with the surveillance."

"That sounds wise. If Boyd had anything to do with that explosion, he could be lying low for a bit until the investigation slows."

Justin nodded. "The good thing is, Sullivan's targets have received no more threats. We've got those who've received roses under protection and there've been no movements against them. Heidi still needs protection, though, so we'll keep someone on her."

"Which brings me to a question," Nick said. "Do you think Sullivan is behind the threats to Heidi?"

"I don't know. If Sullivan had a hand in blowing up the training center, then I'd say it's possible. But until we find the bomber, I don't think we can make that assumption."

"So, in the case of the others, Sullivan's biding his time," Nick said. "Waiting."

"That's what I think. He sure hasn't decided to stop."

Nick shook his head. "This shouldn't be taking so long. Why is it so hard to catch him?"

"We've all been asking ourselves that question," Oliver said.

Ava shrugged. "He's smart."

"And rubbing our faces in the fact that he's smarter," Westley muttered.

"He'll mess up," Justin said.

"Right," Nick said, "hopefully before someone else dies."

His phone rang, and Heidi's number flashed at him. "Excuse me while I get this." He slipped into the hallway. "Heidi? Everything okay?"

"I need a favor, if you don't mind."

"What's that?"

"I'm going to do a couple of interviews. MP Evan Hendrix is going with me so I should be fine, but could you pick me up when I'm finished?"

"Yes, of course. Wait a minute. What interviews?"

"For the medals, Nick."

"And you have to leave your house? Can't you just do phone interviews?"

A sigh reached him. "I could, I suppose, but it's really hard to read body language over the phone."

"FaceTime? Skype?"

"Nick, this is my job. I promise to be careful. I'll take every precaution and I'll have Evan with me."

"I still don't like it."

"Sorry. Talk to you later. I'll text you my location, if you can come get me."

"I'll be there." Oh, yes, he'd be there. Because while Evan was very likely a good soldier, there was no way he'd watch out for Heidi like Nick would. And he was going to make sure this type of situation didn't crop up in the future.

Heidi glanced at her watch and pressed a hand against her rumbling stomach as she left the last interview for the day. She'd texted Nick her location and told him Evan needed to leave but would wait with her until Nick arrived.

And true to his word, he stayed as close as a burr.

They walked down the steps of the latest theft victim's home and Heidi placed the recorder in her pocket.

"You're good at that," Evan said.

"Thanks."

"Seriously. You asked great questions, were compassionate about her loss, and didn't lead her to answers that you wanted her to have. You let her come up with her own. I've seen a lot of reporters, even answered some of their questions, but I've never seen one do it the way you do."

Heidi gave him a smile. "That's really kind of you to say so. Unfortunately, not everyone in the business acts with integrity." Understatement of the year? "But my dad taught me that integrity comes before the story. And that if I act in such a way, I'll always be the better reporter—and others will trust me." A flash of grief speared her. "And while it takes years to build relationships and gain the trust of others, lies can destroy that in seconds."

"You're referring to the fact that people think you're the anonymous blogger."

"Yes."

"Do you know why they think that?"

"I suspect because John Robinson spread that

rumor." She sighed. "You know, I get that he's ambitious. This job is very competitive and cut-throat and it can bring out the worst in people." She met his gaze. "But it doesn't have to be that way. I want to help catch the bad guys, not tell them what's going on in an investigation by leaking stuff that will help them." She shook her head. "But I don't know how to prove to everyone that I'm not the blogger. Other than to continue doing my job with integrity and honesty." She shrugged. "And hope, in the end, that pays off and people see it."

"After hanging out with you and watching you work, I don't believe you're the blogger."

She squeezed his hand. "Thank you, I appreciate that. Now, pass the word, will you?"

He laughed. "Sure."

Nick pulled to the curb and stepped out. "Sorry it took me so long." He walked around and opened the door for her, a scowl on his face.

"No problem. Evan kept me company." She said her goodbyes to the MP and climbed into the passenger seat of Nick's work truck. She buckled her seat belt and scratched Annie's head while watching her ill-tempered chauffeur settle into the driver's seat. "Are you okay, Nick?"

He shot her a frown. "I'm fine."

"Then why are your eyes narrowed, brow furrowed and smoke curling from your nose?"

"Smoke?"

"Might as well be. What's the problem? Did something happen with the case?"

A sigh slipped from him and the frown faded a bit. "Nothing."

"Nothing's wrong or there's nothing more with the case?"

"Both."

"Liar. Maybe not about the case, but something's definitely wrong about you. What is it?"

"I didn't—" The scowl deepened. "Never mind. It's not important."

She let it slide while a fragment of hurt lodged in her heart. "Fine." Once thing she'd learned about Nick—if he wasn't going to talk, he wasn't going to talk.

Silence dropped between them.

"What are you going to do now?" he finally said as he turned onto Canyon Boulevard.

"Go home and write this story."

"What did the victim have to say about the robbery?"

"The same as all the others. She was out to dinner with her family. When she came home, her house had been ransacked and the medals were missing from a box in the top of her closet. Along with three hundred dollars in cash."

"Doesn't anyone use safes anymore?"

She huffed a laugh. "Guess not."

He pulled to a stop in her driveway. "Thanks for being smart."

Hand on the door handle, she paused. "What do you mean?"

"You called me. You took precautions."

With a sigh she turned back to him. "Of course. I'm not stupid."

"I didn't mean to imply you were. It's just that I guess I didn't expect that. I would have thought you were the type to get a lead on a story and just take off regardless of the consequences. That if you needed to conduct an interview you would just do it without thinking things through."

"Remember the fact that someone tried to kill me today?" She stepped out of the vehicle. "Thanks, Nick. I really appreciate that you think so highly of me. Go home. And don't come back until you can get over your preconceived notions of who I am and are willing to take the time to find out." She stared at him, fighting tears. "Because you really don't have a clue." She slammed the car door.

And then she ran for her home. Once inside, she leaned against the door and placed a hand over her pounding heart. A heart that was more and more drawn to the man who'd just hurt her feelings in a major way. She was so on the emotional roller coaster when she was in

Nick's presence. The thought that they might never really get along or move forward into some kind of romantic relationship because of her job pained her.

She sighed and moved into the den. And stopped. Wait a minute. Something was off. She took in the sofa, the recliner, the end tables. What was it? Everything looked fine… except for the throw on the back of the chair by the fireplace. When had she put that there? She kept it on the couch.

Had Nick moved it when he'd been here last? Pressing a hand against her forehead, she couldn't remember. Uneasiness settled in her gut. Had someone been in her home?

Nick slammed a fist on the wheel and Annie whined. He glanced at the animal, and her sad eyes drilled him. If he didn't know better, he'd almost believe she was chastising him for being a jerk.

He sighed. He *had* been a jerk. A colossal one. What had compelled him to say such a thing to her?

Fear.

The answer leaped into his mind. He shoved it away before snatching it back. Fear? Yes. Because if he gave her the power, she could hurt him.

Not to mention the fact that someone was out to kill her.

What if that person actually succeeded?

And he'd pushed her away. Made her run from him.

Jerk.

His phone rang and instead of opening the door and going after Heidi, he lifted the device to his ear. "What?"

"Having a good day, I see?"

Justin's voice made him wince and clear his throat. "Sorry."

"Have you seen the latest blog post?"

"No. Why?"

"It claims the bombing of the training center is being linked back to Boyd Sullivan."

"What? We haven't said that officially. It's just been speculated about. How would they know that?" He slapped the wheel again.

"Just like all the other information this person is managing to get her hands on."

"It's not Heidi."

The line fell quiet. Then Justin cleared his throat. "Are you sure about that?"

Was he? Completely one hundred percent sure? "Yes, I'm sure. As sure as a gut feeling can be."

"Sometimes a gut feeling is better than any evidence," Justin said. "All right. We'll keep looking. Not that Heidi won't still be in the pool of suspects, but—"

The explosion rocked his car, throwing him into the passenger seat. The windshield shattered, raining shards of hard glass down on him.

Ears ringing, he lifted himself up to squint against the flames shooting from Heidi's front window.

# SEVEN

Nick pulled himself out of his SUV and let a barking Annie out of her area. Keeping the leash around his wrist, he stumbled toward the house only to fall back when the heat scorched him. "Heidi!"

Sirens were already screaming. Westley and Felicity hurried down their front porch. Westley reached him first and gripped his forearm. "Nick! Are you okay? You're bleeding."

"Heidi's in there!" Horror clawed at him. His lungs tightened against the smoke and the fear. There was no way she could have survived that.

Westley went white and Felicity cried out, covering her mouth with her hand. "No," she whispered. "I don't believe it."

There had to be a way in, a way to save her. Nick raced through the narrow pathway between her house and Felicity's, rounded the corner and stopped. The fence. He'd forgotten about the fence. Scrambling for a way to climb over, he paused.

A noise caught his attention even over the sirens and the roar of the burning home. A cry? A cough?

He followed the fence line and turned to see Heidi sitting outside the fence, staring at her home.

"Heidi!"

She looked up at his call, her face streaked with tears and dirt. He raced over to her and dropped to his knees. Gripping her upper arms, he took in the sight of her, looking for any outward signs of trauma. "Are you all right?"

"No!" She swiped a hand across her cheek, smearing the dirt. She pointed. "Look what he did! Just look! It's gone. All of it." He pulled her to him and she buried her forehead against his chest. Annie whined and tried to shove her face between them. Then she licked Heidi's ear. Sobs broke through and Heidi hugged him tighter and let him hold her.

"Heidi! Nick!"

Westley's harsh cry pulled Nick's attention to the man who'd followed the same path Nick had taken just minutes before. He hurried over to them. "Heidi! Boy, am I glad to see you."

She sniffed and hiccupped, but didn't move from Nick's hold.

"What were you doing out here? Because whatever it was, it saved your life."

She giggled, and Nick frowned. Was she going to get hysterical on him? She said something and he missed it. "What?" She pointed and he followed her finger to a white trash bag lying on the ground. "Heidi?"

"The trash," she said. "I was taking the trash out." Another slightly hysterical giggle. "Taking out the trash—a chore I hate with everything in me and put off until the last possible moment— saved my life. I'll never complain about *that* again." She dissolved into another fit of giggles, followed quickly by gasping sobs. Nick simply held her while her home burned.

His gaze met Westley's. "We have to stop this guy."

"I pulled security footage from the night of the training center explosion and saw the man she saw, but there's no way to tell who he was. By the time Heidi said he pulled the ski mask off and turned, he was out of range of the camera. So far, we've gotten no leads on the sketch Carl worked up."

Heidi had stopped crying and he figured by her stillness she was listening. "He pulled the mask off because he knew it was safe to do so.

He knows this base. First we need to investigate every single person who lives on this base."

Westley sighed, but nodded. "That's what I was thinking. I'm also thinking it's going to take a while."

"Then we might as well get started."

Heidi sat in the back of the ambulance next to Nick, who hadn't let her out of his sight. The paramedic had checked her out, then cleaned and bandaged several cuts on his face, arms and hands.

"They're not deep, but your face didn't like the force the glass came with," the medic said.

"I know. It's fine."

"No head trauma that I can see on either of you, so you can count your blessings for that."

"I'm alive," Heidi said, "I'm grateful." But the loss hurt. She wouldn't put on a brave face and pretend it didn't. Her notes, her laptop, her files. Everything. Gone. Either to the explosion and fire or water damage. The only reason she wasn't in a puddle on the floor of the ambulance was because she had almost everything backed up to the cloud. The only thing she might not be able to access was the latest piece she'd been writing. Unable to remember if she'd saved it to her online backup, Heidi gave a mental shrug. She could rewrite it.

A flash to her right cause her to recoil. She blinked and finally focused her gaze on John Robinson lowering his camera. "Really?" she demanded.

He shrugged. "I just follow the stories."

"Right." She wouldn't get into it with him. One, it seemed to spur him to be even more obnoxious, and two, she simply didn't have the energy.

Nick stepped out of the ambulance and stood in front of the doorway so Robinson couldn't see into the back where Heidi was. "Get away from here. Now."

His low command sent Robinson stumbling backward. Heidi leaned to the right to see fear flash in the man's eyes, but his chin was raised. "You have no right to stop me from getting my story."

"You have no right to impede medical treatment."

With a roll of his eyes, Robinson left. "I got my picture. I guess that's all I need. I'd love a statement from the victim, but I'm assuming that's not going to happen."

He had that right. "Thanks, John. I appreciate your concern." She couldn't help it. His lack of professionalism infuriated her. No story was worth sacrificing the human touch, expressing sympathy to one's fellow man. Reporters like him made reporters like her look bad. And she just plain didn't like it.

"I can see the smoke coming out of your ears," Nick said to her when Robinson left, "and it has nothing to do with your house blowing up."

She scowled. "That man gets under my skin. Way under. I've got to find a way to let him and his actions roll off my back."

"Be a duck."

"What?"

"Your new mantra when it comes to Robinson."

"Oh. Be a duck. Meaning let the irritation I feel for the man roll off?"

"Exactly. Come on," he said. "Forget about Robinson. We've got to get you settled somewhere."

"I guess I'll have to find a hotel."

He frowned. "No way. Not when you have friends."

"I do have a few friends, but I'm not going to put any of them in danger. Not when this guy is going around blowing up houses."

Felicity pushed her way through the gathering crowd. "Heidi!" She rushed forward and hugged her, forcing Nick to drop her hand and step back. "I'm so glad you're okay," Felicity

said. "At first, I thought you'd…that you'd…
that you were—"

"That I was in the house when it blew?"

"Yes." Another tight hug. "I'm so glad you're
all right."

"Thank you." Heidi looked back at the smol-
dering structure. "At least it was just mostly
the front of the house that took the brunt of the
blast. It wasn't big enough to take the whole
thing down. Or cause damage to yours."

"I'm just glad you weren't hurt." Felicity
squeezed her hands, then let her go. "What can
I do to help?" She bit her lip. "You'll need a
place to stay."

"She can stay with me and my grandfather,"
Nick said.

Heidi blinked and her mouth rounded as she
processed his words. "What?"

"We have a guest bedroom, and the colonel is
there most of the time. And he obviously knows
how to use a gun so you'd have built-in protection."

"But I—"

"That sounds like the perfect solution," Felicity said. "I'll run back to my place and grab
you some clothes to wear. I'm going to assume
all your uniforms are gone?"

"Except the two at the cleaners, yes."

Annie whined at his side and Nick stroked her

ears. "We'll get to work on this one soon, girl."
He looked up at Heidi. "We've got to wait for
clearance from the fire department, then we'll
go in."

Justin Blackwood climbed out of his official
vehicle and approached. "Anyone hurt?"

"No, but not because someone wasn't trying," Nick answered for her. Surprisingly, Heidi
didn't care. The two of them talked while she
rubbed her still-ringing ears. She just wanted
to leave, to be alone and process all that had
happened.

After some questions, she finally got her wish
and Nick led her and Annie to his vehicle. "Stay
here for now. I'm going to get the colonel to
come take us to my house." He squeezed her
hand and called his grandfather. From the quick-
ness of the call, she assumed the man hadn't
asked any questions. "He'll be right here." He
glanced at his vehicle. "Thankfully, I was in my
work truck. It'll be impounded for evidence. I'll
be back with Annie to see if we can determine
what caused the blast. Meanwhile I'm sure Justin will check out each camera within a mile of
your home and see if there's anyone suspicious."

Three minutes later the colonel pulled to a
stop just beyond the scene. He stepped out of
his sedan and took in the sight with a shake of

his head and concern in his eyes. "Are you two all right?" he asked as he approached them.

"We're fine, Gramps. Just need a ride home."

"Come on, then."

Once at the men's home, Colonel Hicks led the way up the front porch steps and into the foyer. Nick shut the door behind them.

"You're welcome to stay here as long as you need," the colonel told her.

"Thank you, sir."

"Nick can show you where to stow your gear. I'll get the bathroom ready for you."

She followed Nick to the guest room and stepped inside to see a twin bed against the far wall, a dresser next to the door and a comfortable chair under the window.

"The bathroom is just outside the room, off the hall," Nick said. "In the second drawer, you'll find toiletries. We keep them for visiting family and friends. Help yourself to anything you need."

"Towels and washcloths are by the sink," the colonel said from behind Nick.

"Thank you very much."

The colonel led the way back to the kitchen, where he gestured for her to sit. "Coffee?"

"Decaf?"

He laughed. "Of course. Even that keeps me up at night sometimes, though."

With the mug in front of her, she wrapped her hands around the warm porcelain and took a deep breath. Someone had just tried to kill her. And almost succeeded. The thought almost didn't compute. "How did someone get a bomb in my house?" she asked.

"Probably picked a time when no one was watching it," Nick said with a sigh. "If you weren't there, there was no reason to have someone on your home—or so we thought."

"Of course."

His phone buzzed and he glanced at the screen. "Looks like it's time for Annie and me to go to work." He called for the dog and she rose from her spot by the fireplace to pad into the kitchen. "You ready to go catch some bad guys, girl?"

Her tail wagged, and he slipped her into the harness hanging near the door. Then he added booties to protect her paws. He looked over his shoulder at Heidi and his grandfather as he slung his pack over his back. "You two lie low. I'll be back soon."

Nick arrived at Heidi's home to find the place roped off and the crime scene unit working in an organized grid. He showed his ID to the officer in charge and was allowed to pass under the tape.

Annie trotted at his side. Justin was still on the scene and Nick made his way over to him and Westley.

"Glad you're here," Justin said. "Let us know what you and Annie find."

Even though firefighters had put the fire out, just like with the training center, he and Annie started examining the debris farther away from the hot areas. While they worked, Nick thought. What was the best way to catch the guy who wanted to wipe Heidi off the planet? Because failing to do so wasn't an option.

Footsteps behind him caught his attention and he turned to see Westley.

"Find anything, Nick?"

"Some scraps that Annie found interesting. She was most interested in the den area. Looks like he hid a bomb, possibly dynamite or C-4, in the den area. We'll see what the lab says."

"ATF is here once again. Didn't even have to use the GPS this time. We've got to stop this guy."

Probably hadn't had to use it the last time, either. But Nick got the point. Two explosions on base were two too many. "My thoughts exactly."

"Security Forces are going crazy scanning video footage of the training center explosion. And now this." He gave a disgusted sigh and shook his head. "I'll leave you to it. Let me know what you find."

"Of course."

The man left and Nick and Annie went back to work. Once the place cooled down, he and Annie and the ATF investigators would go inside and see if they could find what triggered the explosion. When they had some of the materials, they would be able to compare it to the training center evidence.

However, Nick was pretty sure he knew exactly who the bomber was. It had to be the guy from the training center. He was scared Heidi could ID him and he was going all out to make sure she didn't. He was a guy who wanted Heidi dead and he had to be stopped before he succeeded in getting what he wanted.

# EIGHT

Heidi sat curled up in the large chair next to the fireplace and sipped her second cup of decaf coffee. Her eyes had grown heavy as the hours passed. The colonel had finally declared he was headed to bed. The weapon in his hand made her wonder, but she hadn't argued. She wanted the time alone to think. And she'd had that. Now she was tired of thinking and just wanted to go to bed.

But her mind wouldn't let her.

The fact that Nick wasn't back kept her glued to the chair.

Minutes later she heard footsteps on the front porch, followed by voices. She walked to the window to look out.

"...might be back on base," Justin said.

"When did you learn that?"

"Just now. When we were finishing up at Heidi's house, Vanessa Gomez reported that someone was watching her house. When MPs arrived, the person ran."

"Vanessa got a rose from Sullivan. You think he's back to make good on his threat?"

"I do. I don't have proof, though, so keep this under your hat."

"Of course."

"I was on the way home and figured I'd stop by and let you know. Anyway, get some rest. I'll see you tomorrow."

"Thanks."

The door opened and Heidi stumbled back. Nick raised a brow, then frowned. He stepped inside and narrowed his eyes. "Guess you heard that?"

"Um…yes. I guess I did. But I wasn't eavesdropping on purpose. I heard voices and looked out the window."

He sighed. "That's not to go in the paper, understand? We don't need to cause a panic on base until we have more information."

"But you think Sullivan's back."

"There's evidence to indicate he is. Yes."

"Nick, people have to know. They have to be on guard."

"And we're going to let them know. As soon as we're positive. So, please. Nothing in the paper about it until we're sure."

"But you'll let me have the exclusive?"

"Sure."

She nodded. "Okay."

"You wouldn't have printed it, anyway, would you?"

"No, but I figure it doesn't hurt to weasel the exclusive." She took a sip from the mug. "So, how did it go at my house? What's left of it, anyway."

He sighed. "Annie did a good job as always. There weren't any other explosives to be found and we scooped up some evidence that the lab will examine. Now she's back at the kennel getting some much-deserved rest."

"Good, I'm glad." She stood and began to pace.

"Heidi, what's going through that head of yours?"

She stopped and faced him. "Who am I, Nick?"

"What do you mean?"

"I mean, tonight, just about everything I've worked for has been destroyed. Sure, all my files are safe, but I've been thinking. What if they weren't?"

He took her hand and pulled her over to sit on the sofa, then planted himself opposite her. "I'm not following."

Palming her eyes, she fell silent, then lowered her hands and looked up. "I guess what

I'm trying to say is, if I can't do my job—and right now, that's looking pretty iffy—then who am I?"

"You're still you. First Lieutenant Heidi Jenks. And not being able to do your job is just a temporary problem. As soon as we catch this guy, you're back to being a star reporter."

She sighed. "I've never been a star reporter." She shrugged at his frown. "Yes, I'm good at my job. Yes, I can write an excellent article. And yes, I can be like a bulldog with a bone. But I'm not cutthroat. I won't step on someone else to get to that next rung on the reporting ladder. So...what does that make me?"

"Admirable," he whispered.

"But John Robinson," she said as though he hadn't spoken, "now, there's a man who'll go behind your back and do whatever it takes to get a story. No matter the consequences or the fallout."

"He's a jerk."

"Yes, he is. But he also gets the job done. So, is that what I need to be? A jerk?"

"No." He clasped her hand. "Please don't even go there."

She sighed and blinked. "I'm sorry. I'm thinking out loud." She paused. "You don't think Robinson hates me enough to blow up my house, do you? You don't think he would be so desperate to keep me out of the loop on not only the training center bombing, but the Red Rose Killer story, that he'd do something like this to throw me off?"

Nick threaded his fingers around hers. "I don't know, but you shouldn't jump to conclusions until you talk to him. Does he even have any experience handling explosives?"

His touch grounded her. Centered her. Made her very aware of him. "As far as I know, he doesn't have any background dealing with explosives. Then again, I guess if someone's desperate enough, it's not hard to find out what you need to know. He's been awfully territorial. I mean, you saw him at church—and then after my house blew up. He'll do anything to get a story. I think I need to talk to him."

"Look, Heidi, you're a good reporter with good instincts. But don't let your emotions start getting in the way. Get the facts before you act."

Heidi drew in a deep breath. "Of course. You're right."

"Why don't you get a good night's sleep and we'll take care of whatever needs to be taken care of in the morning? For now, I think you need to relax and take some time to regroup."

She nodded. "I think that's a good idea."

He stood and pulled her up. For a moment, she simply stared into his eyes, thought he might say something else, but then he cleared his throat and took a step back. "Good night, Heidi."

"Good night, Nick."

In her bedroom, she drew in a deep breath. Somehow she'd ignored the spark of attraction that had flared when she'd stood in front of him in the living room. She had other things that needed her focus. Not chasing a romance with a man who was so gun-shy around reporters. She pulled her small recorder from her pocket and spoke in detail the conversation she'd overheard. Then with more reluctance than bravado, she grabbed her phone and dialed John's number.

"Hello? Robinson here."

"Did you blow up my house?"

"Did I what? Heidi? What are you talking about?"

"Did you blow up my house? Are you so threatened by me that you want to get rid of me? To kill me?"

For a moment silence echoed back at her. "You're a piece of work, Heidi. I know we're rivals, but for you to accuse me of that is really low. Especially for you."

He sounded so sincere that guilt immediately flooded her. She swallowed. "I'm… I'm sorry, John. I didn't want to ask. I just figure I need to cover all my bases."

"Well, you don't have to worry about me being the one trying to kill you." He gave a short huff. "I'll admit to being willing to profit from all the trouble you're having, but I'm not the one instigating it."

"Wow. Thanks."

"Hey, it's just the way it is." He paused. "But no, I'm not trying to kill you."

"Well, I appreciate that. I'm…sorry I practically accused you of doing so. I know how false accusations can hurt."

"Exactly." He paused. "You wouldn't want to give me an interview, would you?"

She laughed. "Good night, Robinson. I'll see you around."

So, if it wasn't John, it had to be the guy she'd seen at the training center. She picked up the recorder and worked out her thoughts on the machine. It always helped to go back and listen and make sure she hadn't forgotten anything when she worked on a piece.

A light knock interrupted her. She opened the door to find Nick standing there, a speculative gleam in his eyes. She raised a brow. "What?"

He set a glass of water and some ibuprofen on her dresser. "Just in case."

"Ah. Yes, that's a good idea. Thanks."

"Night again."

"Night."

He turned, paused and turned back. "Heidi?"

"Yes?"

"I couldn't help overhearing your apology to Robinson."

She flushed. "I suppose you think I should have waited to confront him in person."

"I don't think it matters. Were you wrong? You don't think he was involved in blowing up your home?"

"It sure sounded like that on the phone. I wouldn't mind having concrete proof, but if I were to go with my gut, I'd say he wasn't involved."

"And you apologized."

"Of course. I try to do that when I make a mistake."

He shook his head. "If I hadn't seen it, I don't know that I would have believed it."

She rolled her eyes. "Thanks."

"No, I need to be thanking you. It was refreshing. I needed to see that—as a reminder that everyone is different and deserves to be judged based on who they are, not based on preconceived notions. Like you said in the car before you slammed the door in my face." She winced and he smiled. "I deserved it."

"Sorry about that. I kind of lost my temper a bit."

"I understand." He drew in a deep breath.

"Anyway, thanks. Say, I figure you have tomorrow off since I doubt anyone is going to expect you to work after losing your home. Would you like me to take you into town to shop for some things?"

"I was going to ask Felicity if she wanted to go with me, but I know she has to work tomorrow."

"So, is that a yes?"

She nodded. "It is if it won't inconvenience you any."

"It won't. Maybe getting off the base will help."

She frowned. "Do you think it's safe?"

"As safe as staying here."

"That's not a very good argument."

"True. I'll watch out for you. We can watch each other's backs."

"All right, sounds good."

"Perfect. Good night."

He left and she carried the water and medicine to the end table. She shut the door and got ready for bed, feeling safe in the home of the man who seemed to want to hold her at arm's length and pull her close—all at the same time. She sighed and decided not to get too comfortable. As she'd learned the hard way, feeling safe didn't mean she was.

\* \* \*

Nick took a sip of the coffee his grandfather had made and thought about what he'd accidentally overheard. Heidi had actually apologized to Robinson. Since when did reporters apologize? Especially ones who were as competitive as those two. He had a feeling if the shoe was on the other foot, Robinson wouldn't have had the gumption to do the same as Heidi. The reporter who'd covered his mother's death sure hadn't. But Heidi had. To someone she didn't even like, no less.

Nick had to admit, it said a lot about her character. She hadn't known he was listening—albeit unintentionally. When he'd realized she was on the phone, he'd started to walk away, but stopped when he heard her say Robinson's name. He'd been ready to offer his comfort if Robinson lit into her, but it had sounded as if they'd had a civil conversation. Not exactly friendly, but at least she hadn't become upset and hadn't needed his intervention. A strong woman, she could take care of herself.

Except when someone was blowing up her house.

"You okay, son?"

His grandfather stood in the doorway, dressed

in his pajamas and long robe with matching slippers. "I'm okay. You look dapper."

"Have to dress a little better when we have company."

"We don't have company often."

"Exactly. Now, what's eating at you?"

Nick raised a brow. "What do you think?"

Gramps laughed. "Yeah, I thought so."

"I don't know what to do about her."

"Take it one day at a time."

"Hmm." He sighed. "I have to admit that I'm worried someone's going to succeed in killing her before I find who it is."

His grandfather slipped into the chair next to him. "I would say that's a real problem."

He met the older man's eyes. "How do I take care of her, Gramps?"

"Don't know what else you can do short of taking her off base and hiding her away somewhere."

"An idea I've thought of, but doubt she'll go for." He paused. "She's getting to me."

"I know."

Of course he did. "I overheard her apologize to someone just now. A reporter. Apologizing. It struck me."

"Right in the heart?"

"Something like that."

"You've wanted an apology from a reporter

ever since your mother died and they printed that ridiculous story."

"I guess you're right. And hearing hers...well, I think it just healed something deep inside me."

"You need to tell her that."

Nick smiled. "I will."

His grandfather stood and bid him good-night, then disappeared down the hall to his bedroom.

Sitting at the table in the quiet with only a soft glow coming from the light over the sink, Nick considered the next steps in the investigation. They'd confirmed the training center explosion was deliberate. Residue identified it as C-4. Easily set off with a timer.

"Which explains why he was in such a hurry to get away from the training center," he muttered.

It was obvious the man in the hoodie was after Heidi and pretty determined to shut her up for good. Although, Nick had to wonder what purpose it would serve to kill her now. She'd already talked to OSI and Security Forces and told them everything.

Then again, he supposed it would help if Heidi weren't on the base to accidentally run into the man she could identify. Which, if that was the concern, meant he was on the base frequently. Or lived on it.

There'd been no word from Justin on the progress being made in checking the visitor logs, but Nick knew that was like looking for the proverbial needle in the haystack. He sighed. And running it around in his head all night wasn't going to help matters. But one thing did concern him. Did the person who wanted Heidi dead know she was staying with him and his grandfather? He couldn't help thinking about that possibility.

Nick rose and glanced out the window to see a Security Forces vehicle stationed in front of his home. He knew there was another one at the back.

He took a weapon from his safe, then stepped out onto the front porch. With a wave to the airman in the car, he started his trek around the perimeter of his home.

Nothing caught his attention. There were no moving shadows that made him jump, no mysterious sounds that he needed to investigate. All was still.

Back inside his home, he locked up, then checked all the windows. Still unable to relax—and knowing he wouldn't sleep if he tried—he kept the gun with him and stretched out on the couch, ready to defend his home and protect the woman he was growing to care about way too much.

# NINE

Shopping with Nick had seemed like a good idea last night. Unfortunately, in the light of day, Heidi's indecision weighed on her, leaving her embarrassed that Nick had to see her at her worst. Indecisive and incredibly picky.

She finally stomped out of the last store, crossed the street and found a booth in the small café. He followed at a brisk trot and handed her the two bags he'd so chivalrously carried for her. "Hold on to these. I'll be right back."

Fortunately, since it was two in the afternoon, the café's busy lunchtime rush was over and only a few stragglers remained. When he returned, he set in front of her a steaming mug of hot chocolate topped with whipped cream and a caramel drizzle. He'd gotten himself the same, along with a cinnamon roll that he set in between them. "Let's eat."

She blew out a breath and couldn't help the smile that wanted to curve her lips. "Thanks.

I'm sorry I'm such a lunatic when it comes to shopping. I'm just so particular and I loved my wardrobe. Before it was incinerated, anyway."

"It's okay. Shopping for clothes can be hard."

"And I don't really need that much. Not with wearing a uniform every day."

"I get it."

"And I'm not used to shopping with a guy. You make me nervous."

He slid around to sit beside her. She'd chosen a corner booth for a multitude of reasons. The most important one being it was away from windows and doors and she didn't have to worry about someone shooting her in the back. "I don't want to make you nervous," he said as he scooted closer.

She cleared her throat. "Ah. Well, that's not helping."

"Why?"

"Because you're a little close." And he smelled really, really good.

"I like being close to you," he said softly.

"You do?" The squeak those words came out on could not belong to her.

"I do. You've gotten under my skin, Heidi Jenks, and I'm really not sure what to do about it."

"I…um…hope you're not asking me for advice, because I'm really not sure what to—"

His lips cut off her words. She froze, unsure what to do. Then instinct took over and she closed her eyes, lifted her hand to cup his cheek and let the lovely sensation of being kissed by Nick Donovan wash over her.

When he lifted his head, the tender expression in his eyes was nearly her undoing. "Well, I suppose that's one thing to do when someone's under your skin," she whispered.

He grinned. Then shook his head. "Like I said, I like you, Heidi. A lot. And I'm not sure it's a good idea."

"Why? Because I'm a reporter?"

"No, you pretty much opened my eyes on that one. I'm not worried about your motives or that you're only out for a story. I've seen your heart. You're very good at what you do and you put others first. It's obvious you care and that's why people respond so well to you."

Tears welled before she could stop them. One dripped down onto her cheek and he swiped it away with a thumb. "Thank you for that," she whispered. "I needed to hear it. I need someone to believe that I'm not the anonymous blogger and that I have integrity. I mean, *I* know it, and usually, that's enough. But this time, I think I just need others to see it, too, I guess. Which is probably stupid."

"It's not stupid," he said. "It's human."

She smiled. "I'm definitely human. With all of the shortcomings and failures that come with it, but I'm trying to rise above those, you know?"

"I know. I'm right there with you."

"You? You seem pretty perfect to me."

He let out a low chuckle. "Trust me, I'm far from perfect."

"Oh, that's right. You do have that whole distrust of reporters thing." She sighed. "But you definitely have a reason to feel that way."

"I told you. I don't feel that way about you." He leaned over and kissed her again. A light, sweet, comforting kiss that she wished could go on forever. It made her forget about the troubles surrounding her, the fear and anxiety, the despair about her lost home…everything.

When he pulled back, he enveloped her in a hug that took away what breath she had left. "I trust *you*, Heidi."

Nick listened to the words coming out of his mouth with something resembling shock. Had he just told Heidi, a reporter, that he trusted her?

Apparently. And the funny thing was, he did. He'd seen her in action. She was a go-getter and good at what she did, but she didn't step on other people or lie to get her story.

He looked down at her. "Are you all right now?"

"Yes. I'm much better. Thank you."

"Ready to do more shopping?"

She groaned and he laughed. They finished the cinnamon roll and the hot chocolate, making small talk, and Nick realized not for the first time that he could fall for this woman.

And he really shouldn't.

Why not?

Because she was a reporter.

But he trusted her, right?

Until he didn't.

"You ready to go?"

She wiped her mouth with a napkin. "Sure. I guess so."

For the next hour, they continued their shopping, with Heidi a little more relaxed and Nick a lot more conflicted. He liked Heidi. A lot. He'd been honest with that statement. And while he trusted her in the moment he told her he did, he wondered if that would last. Then he was disgusted with himself for his wishy-washy feelings. He should be able to give her the benefit of the doubt.

His gaze followed her reflection in the storefront glass as they passed a shop advertising fresh fudge. He grabbed her hand and pulled her inside.

"Whoa." She lifted her head and inhaled deeply. "Mmm. The smells in here are intoxicating."

"I have a really hard time resisting fudge—and strawberry shortcake. What's your favorite dessert?"

"Besides chocolate turtle cheesecake? Chocolate turtle fudge."

"Give me a pound of the chocolate turtle and the peanut butter cookie crunch," he told the woman behind the counter.

When he turned back to Heidi, he caught sight of a man in a hoodie just outside the shop window. He was just standing there, his face shadowed by the hood, his hands shoved into the front pockets of his jeans. Nick frowned as he pulled out his debit card and passed it to the clerk. She swiped it and handed it back to him.

He took a second to scrawl a tip and signature. When he looked back, the man was gone.

He sighed. Paranoia was not a good thing. Then again...

Picking up the bags, he nodded to the door. "Ready?"

"Sure." She unwrapped a piece of the fudge and took a bite. Then gave a piece to him.

He chewed and smiled, but his attention was on the window. "Stay behind me, okay?"

Her eyes sharpened and she frowned. "What is it?"

"I'm not sure. Maybe nothing."

"Maybe something. What?"

"A guy watching through the window. Could have been nothing, but it's making me nervous."

"You think someone followed us here?"

He shook his head. "I don't know. I was watching and didn't see anyone, but that doesn't mean someone couldn't have trailed us."

They stepped out of the shop and Nick made sure to angle himself in front of her. People walked on the sidewalk to his right and to his left. Across the street, a family sat outside at one of the tables belonging to the little café.

But he saw no man in a dark hoodie.

While he knew he hadn't imagined seeing the man, maybe he was overreacting. Nevertheless, he gripped the bags tighter with one hand and slipped his other under her elbow as they walked.

"You're making me really nervous, Nick."

"Sorry."

They made it to his car with no incident, but the whole way he felt like he had a target on his back. Or Heidi did. Once they were on the way back to the base, Nick watched the rearview mirror.

"Do you see someone?" Heidi asked him.

"Maybe. A car pulled out of the parking lot behind us." He flexed his fingers on the wheel. Then relaxed. "And it just turned off."

"I'm sorry you've gotten all caught up in this," she said softly.

"Not your fault."

"Maybe not, but I still feel bad about it. When do you think you'll hear something about the explosions? Like whether or not they're related?"

He shrugged. "Probably in the next day or so."

She fell silent and he continued to watch the road, the mirrors, the surrounding area. The shopping center wasn't too far from the base, and soon, he was turning into the entrance.

Back at his house, he helped her unload the bags and led the way inside.

He found his grandfather talking to Felicity James. She stood. "Hello, Heidi, I just stopped by to check on you."

Heidi set her bags on the end of the sofa and gave her friend a hug. "Thank you. I'm doing all right. I'm just in the process of replacing my wardrobe. I'll be sure to get your clothes washed and back to you soon."

"There's no hurry on that. Any news on who was responsible for the explosion?"

"No, not yet."

She nodded. "Well, I brought a casserole and pie for you guys for dinner. I won't stay. I just wanted to check on you."

"Thanks, Felicity, I appreciate it."

"And…"

"And what?"

"Have you seen the latest blog post?"

Heidi groaned. "Seriously? There's more?"

"Yes. Westley and Justin are fit to be tied. This anonymous blogger is causing everyone on the investigative team a lot of grief. Are you sure you don't know who it is?"

Heidi froze. "What are you saying?"

"Nothing. And I'm not accusing. I just thought maybe a name might have occurred to you, or—"

"Westley told you to come over here and ask me this, didn't he?"

A flush crept up her friend's neck and into her cheeks. She groaned. "Yes. I'm sorry."

"It's not Heidi," Nick said from behind her.

Felicity stilled, then looked past Heidi to meet Nick's eyes. "I don't think so, either."

"Then convince your husband and tell him to leave her alone. Please."

Biting her lip, Felicity gave a slow nod. "All right. I'll do my best."

"Thank you."

She rose. "Well, I guess I'll take off. Heidi, if you need anything, you'll call, right?"

"Of course. Thank you."

"No hard feelings?"

"None toward you." She scowled.

Felicity gave her a small smile, then left. Heidi's shoulders wilted. An arm slid around them. "She means well."

"I know." She sniffed. And then she followed her nose into the kitchen. "That smells amazing."

"Guess we know what we're having for dinner."

"So," the colonel said, "who's up for a game of Scrabble?"

Heidi grinned. "I love that game. And I'm good at it, too."

Nick raised a brow. "Hmm. We'll see about that."

"Is that a challenge, First Lieutenant?"

"It is, First Lieutenant."

"You're on."

It was a fun evening. They played two games and ate half the casserole and the entire apple pie before calling it a night.

On his way to his room, Nick cupped her cheek. "I'm glad you're here, Heidi." He paused. "Let me clarify. I'm not glad for the reason you needed a roof over your head, but I'm glad Gramps and I were able to provide this one."

"Thanks, Nick." He smiled, and she watched him disappear into his room before slipping into hers.

She lay in bed and stared at the ceiling. She'd enjoyed today. She'd actually had fun in a way she hadn't had in a very long time. Scrabble had been her dad's favorite game and playing tonight had resurrected memories she'd thought she'd tucked away forever. Good memories, but still painful because they brought home how much she missed her father.

But Nick's grandfather was clever and smart. He'd won the first game before Heidi had trounced them in the second. Nick had simply shaken his head and declared the tiles had been against him. "How am I supposed to come up with a word with six vowels and a *Z*? No one can win with that."

His good-natured grumbling had endeared him to her even more, and she'd been astonished at how fast the time had flown.

While she'd been granted more time off due to the explosion, Heidi planned to get back to work on the story of the stolen medals first thing in the morning.

Fatigue pulled at her and she gave in to it. Feeling safe and well guarded, Heidi let her eyes close.

Only to have them fly open after what seemed like seconds, but according to the clock, was two hours. One in the morning. What had awakened her?

She sat up and listened.

Voices.

Nothing that sounded alarming, but the reporter in her perked up. She rolled out of bed and pulled on a new pair of jeans and a lightweight sweater she'd purchased on the shopping trip with Nick.

She opened the window and the voices sharpened. "…just sitting here. I say you need to call the trainer. It's probably one of the still-missing dogs. Call Westley James. He can be here in no time."

Heidi shoved her feet into the tennis shoes next to her bed, grabbed her recorder and notebook, and hurried into the living area, where she found Nick standing in the foyer, hand on the doorknob. "I'm just going to see what's going on," he said. "You can go on back to bed."

Heidi laughed. "Right. Let's go."

"Heid—"

She slipped around him, turned the knob and was on the porch before he could blink. She thought he might have emitted a low growl, but she was more interested in what was happening over near the entrance gate. Since Nick and his grandfather lived in the end unit of the row of houses, they were closest to the gate entrance.

Which explained why she heard the commotion. With her voice-activated recorder in her pocket, notebook in hand and a protesting Nick right behind her, she hurried to see what was going on.

Nick pulled up beside her when she stopped near the growing crowd of onlookers. "What is it?" she asked the airman nearest her.

"A dog showed up."

"One of the working dogs that are still missing?" Heidi asked.

"That's what they're trying to figure out. Master Sergeant James should be here soon as well as Rusty Morton." Rusty was one of the trainers from the K-9 center.

Rusty arrived first, followed by Westley and Felicity. "What do we have here?" Westley asked.

A young airman stepped forward. He was one of the guards who monitored the base entrance gate. "Sir, I was on duty when I noticed this dog just outside the gate. He simply walked up and sat down as though waiting for someone to let him inside."

"Does he have a collar?"

"I didn't get close enough to check, sir."

Westley nodded and approached the open gate. "That looks like Patriot." The German shepherd watched him, ears up, tail wagging. "He's friendly like Patriot." Westley murmured, "Stay."

He reached for the tag and Heidi moved so

she could see while describing the scene into her voice recorder. Nick stayed by her side and she thought he was looking everywhere but at the action in front of them. It hit her that he was nervous about her being out in the open.

But she was surrounded by people.

"His tag says Poco." Westley looked back at Rusty. "Call him."

"Poco! Come!" The dog's ears twitched, but he didn't move.

"Try Patriot," Westley said.

"Patriot, come!" The dog bounded over to the trainer, who scratched his ears. Rusty looked up. "This is Patriot, all right."

Other than his coat needing a good brushing, he looked healthy enough to her.

Rusty looked up. "Someone's been feeding him. Or he's found a well-stocked trash can. Not sure what made him come home, but I'm glad he's here." Westley nodded. "This gives me hope. Patriot's one of the best. One of our superstar dogs. If he found his way home, then maybe the other three will, too." He spotted Nick in the crowd and waved him over. Heidi stayed on his heels. Westley's brows rose at her presence, but she simply shot him a smile. He turned his attention to Nick. "I want to meet with the investigative team as soon as possible. We need to go house to house and see if anyone has noticed who's been taking care of this dog. Tell them his name is Poco since that's what the person would have called him."

Heidi's jaw dropped. "It's one in the morning. You're going to wake people up?"

"We do what we have to do in an investigation. You know that."

"Of course."

*Zip it, Heidi.*

Heidi stepped up to Westley. "Where do you think he came from?"

"I don't know. We're working on finding out."

"So, if Patriot got off the base, then did the other dogs get off, too?"

"Working on that, too. Wish I had the answers to those questions."

"And why is he wearing a different collar?" Nick asked. "Someone changed it."

"So, this guy has been missing for months and now he shows up out of the blue," Westley said. "He's on the skinny side, but not starving so he's getting food from somewhere." He ran a hand over the dog's coat. "Needs a good brushing."

"Someone's been taking care of him," Heidi said.

Westley examined the dog's paws. "And probably someone who's fairly close to the base.

He didn't walk too far to get here. Paws are in fine shape."

"What's being done to find the other twenty dogs, sir? Especially the three others that Nick said were so special?" Heidi held her pen over her notebook.

"We've got people looking for them."

Heidi wasn't going to be deterred by his vague answer. "Looking where, sir?"

"Off base." He quirked a smile at her, not at all fazed by her persistence. "Is this going to be the headline in the morning?"

She shrugged. "Of course. It's news."

"Yep, I guess it is."

"Are you planning to offer a reward for the safe return of the other dogs now that you know it's possible they could be nearby?" she asked.

"We were hoping it wouldn't come to that, but it's possible we're going to have to do that. That's enough questions for now."

He started to walk away, but she kept up with him. "Just a couple more, if you don't mind." She didn't give him a chance to answer. "Has anyone discovered Sullivan's motive in releasing the dogs a few months ago? Have you figured out what reason he could possibly have?"

Westley sighed. "Come on, Heidi, you've already asked me these questions. I didn't have answers then, and I still don't. I wish I did.

Now, that's enough. I've got a case to work."
He turned to the young man who'd clipped a
leash on the collar. "All right, Rusty, get him
to the vet and have him checked out, will you?
The rest of you fan out and let's see if anyone's
going to admit to missing a dog named Poco.
Someone put that collar on him, and I want to
know who it was. Don't let on that he's a base
dog. Just act like he's a stray."

Rusty left with Patriot, while several members of the investigative team who'd been called
in left to begin knocking on doors.

Westley nodded to Nick and Annie. "Are you
still on Heidi duty?"

"I am."

*Heidi duty?* She grimaced, but let it go. Already, she was forming the article in her head
while she continued to watch everything play
out.

She finally nudged Nick. "Come on, let's go.
I want to get the reaction of the neighbors being
questioned at one in the morning."

He frowned. "I don't like that we're out in the
open like this."

"I don't like it, either, but honestly, I'm not
going to let this guy keep me from doing my
job. I've got a story to write and I need something to put in it." She scanned the area and,
across the street, spotted two MPs on the front

porch of the closest house. She headed that way and heard Nick's exasperated sigh. "Fine, I'll go and watch your back."

"Thanks." Although, she knew he might not spot a sniper. That worried her, but what was she going to do? Put her life on hold until whoever was after her was caught?

She grimaced. It might be the smart thing to do, but…" My dad wouldn't let this stop him," she said softly. "He'd go right into the fray and get the story."

"But—"

She cut off his words and shot him a sad smile. "I know. But he ended up dead. That's what you're thinking, aren't you?"

He shrugged. "Thinking, yes. Saying, no." He absently scratched Annie's ears and the dog leaned into him.

"It's okay. I can say it." She sighed and shook her head. "I just can't sit back and do nothing."

"I know. Let's just be careful."

"You're still sticking with me?"

"Those are the orders."

"Right." She looked at the ground. "Of course."

He tilted her chin to look her in the eye. "And if they weren't orders, I'd request them."

"You would?"

"I would."

"Why?"

"Because."

With another roll of her eyes, she did her best to hold back the smile that wanted to spread across her face. "All right, then. Let's go."

They approached the nearest MP speaking to the sleepy-looking woman who'd opened the screen door. She shook her head. "I don't know anyone who owns a dog named Poco. Sorry. Can't believe you woke me up for that." She slammed the door.

Heidi shook her head.

They walked to the next home and for the next hour they got the same response—and several more slammed doors.

Nick cupped her elbow and brought her to a stop. "Are you ready to head back yet?"

With a sigh, she nodded. "I guess so. This is looking pretty pointless."

Nick turned her back toward his house. "What would you think of leaving the base? Going into hiding until all of this is resolved?"

"What do you think I think about that?"

"Right. I kind of figured that would be what you thought."

She bit her lip. "I can't hide, Nick. Even though that's my first instinct, I just can't do it. This guy wants me scared and cowering."

"No, I don't think he does."

"What do you mean?"

"I think he just wants you dead, Heidi, and that's what scares me."

# TEN

"Come on, Heidi," Nick said. "There's nothing more to do here tonight."

She looked up from the little black notebook, then tucked it into her pocket with a sigh. "I guess you're right, but I've got some good stuff to work with."

"I suppose you're going to write this up for tomorrow," a voice said from behind Nick. He turned to see John Robinson looking at Heidi. That man was as annoying as a sandstorm.

"No, John, I'm going to ignore it—and my job. What do you think?"

The man's eyes flashed and he stepped closer to Heidi. "I think you'd better watch your step or I may have to go to Lou."

Nick ventured forward. "Hey, Robinson, you're out of line. Watch your space."

John looked back over his shoulder at Nick, then brushed past Heidi. She stumbled back a couple of steps and Nick reached forward to grasp her forearm. "You're dangerously close to assault, Robinson."

"Sorry, sorry." He held a hand up. "I stumbled." He smirked and stalked off.

Heidi stood glaring after the man and Nick turned her toward his house. "Forget him for tonight. Let's go home."

"Yeah. I've got a story to write."

Nick's heart rate finally returned to normal after he shut the door on the outside world. And whoever wanted her dead. He'd been blunt with her a few minutes ago, but the truth was, he was scared for her. His immediate attraction to her the first time he'd met her months ago had sent him scurrying. There'd been no way he'd allow himself to be drawn to a reporter.

But now that he'd gotten to know her, all he wanted to do was protect her.

"You know you're not making this easy," he said, keeping his voice low so as not to wake his grandfather. Nick had sent the man a text just in case he woke up and wondered where they were. No return text said he'd probably slept through everything.

"Making what easy?"

"Keeping you safe."

"Oh." Her brows drew together. She went to sit on the couch and he followed her.

"Someone has shot at you and blown up your house, Heidi."

"I'm aware, thanks. But you know what I've noticed?"

"What's that?"

"Everything he's done has been so that he had a way to escape. The bombing of the training center? He had his escape plan in place. The shooting at the church? He was in a speeding car that got away. The bombing of my home? Same thing. He had it rigged to blow either at a certain time or when he could set off the explosion with a remote. A cell phone or something."

Nick frowned. She was right.

Heidi continued, "And he always seems to target me when there aren't many people around."

"So, you think if you're surrounded by people, you'll be all right?" he asked.

"It seems to look that way. Tonight, I was around a ton of people and he didn't try anything."

"I'm not sure that logic works."

She raked a hand through her hair. "I don't know. I just know that I can't hide." She stood and paced the room till she stopped by the mantel. "I'm taking precautions, I'm being careful. I'm not stupid and I don't have a death wish, but I won't hide."

He nodded. "I can't say I don't understand because I'd probably feel the same way if I were in your shoes."

"Really?"

"Yes. Didn't say I liked it, but I do understand."

"Thank you."

Standing, he held out a hand to her. She took it and stepped forward. "I'm headed for bed. You should do the same."

"I know. But I still have to write the story about Patriot's return. I'll see you in the morning?"

"I have an early meeting with Westley and Justin about the Red Rose Killer. What are your plans?"

"I have a meeting with Lou at eight thirty. Then I have to write up my latest personality piece." She smiled. "You wouldn't want to volunteer for a spot, would you?"

"Me? No, thanks."

"I figured, but I had to try."

"Go to bed, Heidi. We'll catch up tomorrow." Instead of letting her go, he pulled her close and slanted his lips across hers. It was an impromptu action that surprised him. And yet, he didn't regret it. The kiss lasted a few seconds before he ended it with a hug.

When he finally let go of her, she looked... bemused. "I hope that was okay."

"Oh, it was more than okay," she replied. "Confusing, but a good kiss."

He chuckled, then sighed. "I don't mean to be confusing. The more I'm around you, the more I like you. The more I like you, the more I question my sanity."

"Well… Thanks?"

Grimacing, he raked a hand through his short hair. "That didn't come out right. I'm conflicted about you, but not enough to stay away from you. How's that for honesty?"

Her eyes glittered up at him. "I like honesty. And I like you, too." She patted his cheek. "Good night, Nick."

And then she was walking away from him. He waited until he heard her door close before he went to bed. "Lord, don't let me mess this up. Protect Heidi from whoever is after her. And, Lord? Please, protect me from myself."

Morning came faster than Heidi would have liked and she found herself scrambling to beat the clock. Fatigue pulled at her as she got ready, and for the first time since taking the job at the base, she considered calling in sick. After everything that had happened, she didn't think Lou would give her any grief about it, but the thought of John Robinson had her pushing forward. Which was silly. Why did she even care what he thought?

She didn't, really. But she did care about her job and what her boss thought. Once she was dressed for the day, she reached for her recorder and the little black notebook and frowned when she couldn't find the recorder. She'd used both last night and had them in her jeans pocket. She'd only used her notebook last night to write the story about Patriot's return because she had everything she'd needed. She hadn't bothered to check the recording.

Where had she put it?

A glance at the clock sent her scurrying. No matter, she'd have to find it later. She stopped. But what if it was just lying around somewhere and someone picked it up? *No, please no.* She'd recorded her thoughts on just about everything she'd written in her little black notebook. If someone found it…

She scoured her room once more and when she came up empty, she gave a groan of frustration. She'd *really* have to find it later. But for now, being late wasn't an option. She slipped out the door and climbed into the rental her insurance company had delivered late last night.

Her own car had been parked in the driveway and had taken a hard hit when the house had exploded. Most likely, it would be declared a total loss. She tried not to be too depressed about the fact that her house, her car and all of her belongings were gone, but kept reminding herself that she had survived and no one else had been hurt. Doing her best to be grateful for that, she parked and made her way inside the newspaper office. She called out greetings to the few coworkers she passed as she headed to Lou's office.

He looked up at her knock. "Heidi! I didn't expect to see you this morning."

She frowned. "I emailed and told you I would be here."

"I got it, then saw John this morning and he said he wasn't sure you'd make it."

Anger seethed inside her. "John has no idea of my schedule. Please don't rely on his word."

Her boss gave her a shrewd look. "Everything okay between you two?"

Heidi gave him a tight smile. "Just fine, sir."

"Hmm." Heidi thought that sound held a world of skepticism but didn't bother to address it. She would handle John Robinson without dragging her boss into the fray. Only as a last resort would she bring her troubles to him.

"I'm here, sir," she said.

"Just wanted to say great job on the piece you sent last night. That was some mighty interesting stuff."

"Well, thanks, I appreciate that. I just happened to hear the commotion outside and joined in."

"I liked the dog story, too. We'll run that one tomorrow."

She frowned. "Wait a minute. Isn't the dog story what we were just talking about?"

He eyed her. "Are you losing it, Jenks?"

"I didn't think so until right now. Exactly what story are you talking about, sir?"

"I'm talking about the one you sent on how you overheard a conversation between two high-ranking investigative officials and their speculation that the serial killer is back on base. And how he was targeting everyone on the base now. I can't believe the guy actually called in and gave them a heads-up that he was going to start killing again and officials have covered it up." He leaned back and crossed his arms. "You're a sneaky one, aren't you?"

"Sneaky? Overheard?" She sputtered. "Wait a minute, I didn't write anything like that."

"I don't know where you got the information from, but it's good. Just the kind of investigative reporting I like to see. Funny, I figured Robinson would explode when I told him I was printing it, but it didn't seem to faze him."

Panic rose within her. She leaned forward. "I

didn't do a piece on the Red Rose Killer. Or the fact that he was back on base."

It was his turn to frown. "What are *you* talking about? You sent it about five hours ago. It went out in this morning's paper—and let me tell you, it was a chore to get it out on time. I know it's not a huge paper, but it's still a lot of work."

He picked up the paper sitting on the desk beside him and handed it to her. Heidi stared at the front-page headline—and her byline—in horror. SERIAL KILLER BACK ON BASE.

"I didn't send this! I didn't even write this. And it's not even true! No one said Sullivan called in with more threats. No one's covering anything up. Those are lies." She didn't have to read the article to know she didn't write it. "Lou, please tell me this isn't happening." She couldn't help reading a few lines, and her heart dipped into her shoes. "No, no, no, no, no. Oh, no. No one on this investigative team will talk to me ever again. I've got their trust now and this piece is going to kill it." Not to mention Nick. Oh, Nick…he would think… "How did you get this? From my email account?"

"Yep."

Heidi stood and paced in front of his desk. "I don't understand. How can this be?"

"Heidi, calm down. Are you telling me that you didn't send it?"

How many times did she have to say it? Placing her palms on his desk, she leaned forward and looked him in the eye. "That's *exactly* what I'm telling you."

"Then you're telling me I just printed an article that can get me sued?"

She paused and bit her lip. "Yes. Maybe. The information is mostly accurate, but it wasn't supposed to be announced in the paper. I wasn't even supposed to know it. But the other parts are pure fiction." She slumped into the chair and covered her eyes. She was so done. No, she wasn't. She hadn't done this. How had this happened?

"How did this come from your email account, then?"

She narrowed her eyes. "John Robinson. He did this. Somehow, someway, he got that information and used it. He wants me off this paper and thinks he's found a way to make that happen. If no one will talk to me, what kind of reporter will I be?"

Lou scoffed. "What? Even if Robinson is inclined to do so, how would he get into your email?"

"I don't know, but he's resented me from day one. He was the only reporter on staff before the paper expanded to include me. All of a sudden, he had to share stories. I guess he doesn't like that." She picked up the paper again and settled back into the chair to read, ignoring the feel of his eyes boring into her.

The more she read, the sicker she came. "You have to do something," she finally whispered. "Print a retraction, something."

"But you said most of the information is accurate?"

"Yes, but some of it's not. It's going to cause panic on the base. The true elements are part of an ongoing investigation. As soon as Nick reads this, he's—" She bit her lip and fought the tears as she pictured his reaction. His feeling of betrayal.

"We'll fix the parts that are false, but the rest of the story stays."

"You realize this is just going to be fuel for the fire. Everyone is *really* going to think I'm the anonymous blogger now. They'll believe that not only am I releasing confidential information, I'm making stuff up. And I'm not! I only came by that information by accident and—"

Lou's tight jaw said he wasn't happy. At all. "All right, I'll talk to Robinson, but unless you have proof…"

"The proof is right there in front of you," she snapped. "I have to find Nick."

"Heidi—"

Her phone rang. She snagged it and lifted it to her ear. "Nick, I'm so sor—"

"This isn't Nick," the voice said. "This is Mark Hanson. You interviewed me about the stolen medals."

"Oh! I'm sorry, I thought you were someone else. How can I help you?" She was only half listening as her mind raced with how to explain this to Nick when she couldn't even explain it to herself. She'd jumped to the conclusion that John was behind the article, but could it be someone else? She couldn't imagine who.

"I've thought of something else you can add to the story," Hanson was saying. "I think I may know who the thief is."

He now had her attention. "Who?"

"No," he said, his voice now a whisper. "I think he's following me. I've got to go. Meet me in the alley behind the Winged Java in fifteen minutes and I'll tell you everything."

"No. Let's meet inside the cafe."

"I can't. He might see me! If you want the information, be there." He hung up.

She looked at her boss. "We're not done. I want a meeting with you and John Robinson as soon as possible."

"I'll talk to him. Where are you going?"

"To find out who the medal thief is and then to find Nick to explain that I didn't write that article and have no idea how John got that information—" She stopped. Yes, she did know. When he'd bumped into her last night. He'd lifted her recorder from her jeans pocket and listened to it. And wrote that piece.

She spun on her heel and raced out the door.

Nick set the paper aside and pinched the bridge of his nose. Betrayal, hot and swift, flowed through him. He stood and threw his mug across his office. The ceramic shattered and spilled coffee to the floor.

Annie jumped to her feet and barked. He settled a hand on her head. "Sorry, girl. Didn't mean to scare you."

Justin appeared in the doorway. "Nick?"

"I can't believe she would do this." He tossed the paper onto his desk as though it might bite him.

"I saw the article this morning," Justin said. "Before the meeting."

"And you didn't say anything?"

"Wasn't sure what to say, to be honest. I know the blogger posted that we suspected Sullivan was back on base, but that was just conjecture on her part. That article, though, is about a direct conversation people will be more inclined to believe. But the other stuff...that's just not true. I figured you may have told her some of the facts she got right, and she made up the rest."

"I didn't tell her. She overheard Westley and me discussing it." Nick pressed his palms to his burning eyes and let out a humorless laugh. "She promised not to write it." His gaze met Justin's. "And I actually believed she wouldn't. And the stuff that's not true?" He shook his head. "I'm an idiot." He stood. "I'm supposed to be protecting her." That was going to be interesting. How he would manage to do that and keep his anger at her under control at the same time, he wasn't sure. It would be a huge test of his will.

"I put someone on her so you could be here for the meeting." Justin cleared his throat.

"I know. That's not what I meant. I'm supposed to be protecting her and right now, I don't even want to be around her." He glanced at the man leaning against the doorjamb. "I thought she was different."

"I did, too. I've never seen an article by her that wasn't well researched and well written. This one, though? It's like a different person wrote that piece."

"Well, it wasn't. Her name's right there under the headline."

"Yeah. Doesn't make sense."

"Oh, it makes sense all right." Bitterness, so potent he could taste it, rose within him. "I made a huge mistake trusting her. A reporter!" He slammed a hand on his desk and Annie woofed again. "Apparently, I'm as dim-witted as they come. I guess I just have to learn things the hard way."

"Ask her about it before you take her apart. She may have an explanation."

Nick reached for the phone. "Oh, you better believe I'm going to ask her. I'm going to find her right now." If anyone would know where she was, it would be her boss.

When Heidi pulled into the parking lot of the Winged Java, she noted it was busy and crowded. Probably why Mark wanted to meet her in the alleyway behind it. She pulled around the side of the building, down the sidewalk and around back. Putting the car in Park, she looked around trying to spot the man. When she'd interviewed him two weeks ago, he'd been eager to tell his story and hadn't seemed like he was holding anything back. But if he'd decided he knew the thief, then she was going to find out.

She sat in her car for the next several minutes,

watching, noting that it was a pretty deserted area. Which made her feel a little nervous. She hesitated. Was she doing the right thing? Her dad would have gone after the story. He would have met anyone, anytime, anywhere. But she wasn't her dad. She'd promised to be careful. This wasn't being careful.

She cranked the car and backed away from the alley. A shadow to her left made her jerk. Then her window shattered and glass rained down over her.

With a scream, Heidi hit the gas. The vehicle lurched forward and slammed into the side of the building.

A hard hand grabbed her ponytail. Pain shot through her head and down the base of her neck when her attacker yanked her from her car. She let out another scream and threw an elbow back. She connected and her attacker let out a harsh grunt.

His grip relaxed a fraction and Heidi lashed out with a foot, connecting with a hard knee. In a dark hoodie, the man cried out and went to the asphalt.

And she was free.

Until he lunged forward to wrap a hand around her ankle.

"Hey!"

The voice registered in her mind. Nick. Relief flowed through her, but she was still in the attacker's grip.

"Let her go!" Nick yelled.

The attacker's other hand reached inside his zippered hoodie, causing Heidi to scream. "He's going for a gun!"

In the next instant, somehow she was free.

The release of her ankle threw her off balance and she fell hard to her knees. Pain shot through her. She'd probably reopened the healing wounds, but at the moment that was the least of her worries.

Nick had his grip locked around her attacker's wrist and was wrestling him for the weapon.

# ELEVEN

Nick's grip slipped and he clenched the muscles in his hand while he brought a knee up to the man's midsection. It was a glancing blow and did little damage other than to distract him a fraction. But it allowed Nick to get him on the ground.

In his peripheral vision, Nick saw a boot lash out. It connected with the side of the man's head and he went still, those icy blue eyes glazing over. The weapon fell from his hand and Nick scooped it up to aim it at him, then glanced up to see Isaac and Oliver. "Thanks. Can one of you check and see if he has any more weapons on him?"

A quick but thorough frisk by Oliver found him weapon-free. And glaring. Nick glanced at Heidi, noting her pale face, but set chin. "You okay?"

"Yes. Thanks."

He turned his attention back to the man on the ground. "Well, it's good to finally meet you," Nick said. Unfortunately, he didn't recognize him. Without taking his eyes from his captive, Nick asked, "The MPs on the way?"

"They are," Oliver said.

"Thanks for your help."

"Glad to do it," Isaac said. "What's the deal with this guy?"

Heidi stepped forward and looked at her attacker. "I recognize him. He's the one who blew up the training center—and probably my home."

"And shot at you in the parking lot of the church?" Nick asked.

"Possibly that, too."

The man on the ground moved as though to get up. "Stay put." Nick gestured with the gun.

The man stilled.

Two Security Forces vehicles pulled into the parking lot, lights flashing. The MPs approached, hands on their weapons. One covered the man and cuffed him while the other took the perp's weapon from Nick.

"What happened here?" that officer said.

"He attacked me," Heidi said, pointing to the blue-eyed man. She explained that he was the one she'd seen running from the training center just before it exploded.

"So, you're the one," one of the MPs said. "Let's go."

"Wait a minute," Nick said, stepping forward. "I'm part of the investigative team looking for Boyd Sullivan. We're not sure the bombing has anything to do with him, but do you mind if I ask this guy a couple of questions?"

"Go ahead."

Nick faced the cuffed assailant. "Why did you blow up the training center?"

"I didn't."

"Yes, you did," Heidi said.

"And if you don't cooperate, you're going away for attempted murder," Nick added.

The ice in those blue eyes melted a tad and a flicker of fear darkened them. "Murder! I didn't murder anyone."

"But you tried." At first, Nick didn't think the guy was going to talk. "Look, we've got you dead to rights here. We've got witnesses who saw your attack on Heidi. And she saw you come out of the training center just before it exploded. We've even got security footage of you." He snagged a handful of the hoodie and gave it a not-so-gentle yank before he dropped his hand. "This will match up to what's on video. You're going to go down for that. If you cooperate, you might get off with a lighter sentence. What's your name?"

The guy licked his lips and his shoulders dropped. "Airman Lance Gentry. And I really didn't mean for anyone to get hurt. The place was supposed to be empty."

"Right," Heidi said. "You didn't mean for anyone to get hurt. That's why you shot at me in the church parking lot."

He scowled. "Once I knew you could identify me…" He looked away. "I got scared," he said. "I had to get rid of you because I can't go anywhere on base without fear of being recognized. I can't live like that. If you were out of the picture, even if someone thought I was the guy, you wouldn't be around to confirm it." His eyes darted to the MPs listening to the exchange. "Guess I'm done now."

"Why are you doing all this?" Nick asked. "We know you went after Heidi because she could identify you. But why blow up the training center? That was the catalyst for all of this."

"Money. Why else?"

Nick exchanged a confused glance with Isaac and Oliver.

"Someone paid you to set the bomb?" Isaac asked.

"Yeah."

"Who?"

"I don't know his name, he didn't say. But he

knew I needed money so he'd obviously done his homework on me."

"How did he contact you?"

"Knocked on the door at my house."

"Do you live on base?"

"Yeah." He looked down and scuffed his foot.

"But why stay here? Why take the risk of being caught? Especially since you knew Heidi could identify you if she saw you?"

Gentry lifted his head, nostrils flared. "He still owes me the other half of my money. I had to stay until he paid me. I've been looking for him, but haven't come across him yet. But he'll be back. I was just waiting for him to put in an appearance, then I was going to grab my money and get out of here."

"You could have lain low."

"Can't find a guy when you're not looking for him. I had to be out and about on the base. But every time I set foot outside my house, I was afraid someone was going to spot me."

Nick pulled his phone from the clip on his belt and tapped the screen. He pulled up the picture he kept on hand and showed it to the prisoner. "Is that the guy who came knocking?"

Gentry's brows knit and he frowned as he studied the picture. "That's Boyd Sullivan."

"No kidding."

"No, that's not him." Nick sighed and lowered

the phone. "Wait. Let me see that again." Nick obliged. "You know, it's possible that could be him. The eyes look the same, but his hair was red and he had a beard."

"That doesn't surprise me. The man is a master of disguises."

"Whoa. Seriously?"

"Seriously," Nick said. "What else can you tell us? Did he say why he wanted the training center blown up?"

"When I asked, he just said he needed a distraction. He needed attention focused on something other than him."

Isaac gave a light snort. "Is he really that stupid to think that we would turn our attention to the explosion and off of him?"

Nick shrugged. "Well, it was one more thing to deal with. And it used resources and cost money. Sullivan is angry. He's out for revenge on those he feels have wronged him in some way. If he can cause us grief or inconvenience us in any way, he's going to do it."

Oliver nodded. "You've got a good read on him."

"I do."

"We done here?" The MPs were ready to get their prisoner to booking.

"We're done for now," Nick said. He turned to Heidi. "Done with him, anyway."

* * *

Heidi swallowed at the pure ice in Nick's eyes. She'd thought Gentry had a cold stare. He had nothing on Nick. "Can we talk?"

"We can," he answered in a clipped tone.

"Where?"

"Where we won't be overheard."

"Are you going to yell?" she asked him.

"Probably."

"Then let's go back to your place."

He eyed her with a flicker of confusion before his gaze hardened once more into unreadable chips of blue. "Fine. My grandfather is out today volunteering at the food bank."

She started for the rental, then stopped. "I guess they'll need my car for evidence."

"They will. You can ride with me."

Not sure she wanted to, she nevertheless didn't argue and climbed in. The ride to his home was made in silence. Heidi almost broke it but decided against it.

When he still didn't speak as he led the way inside, Heidi got an inkling of just how livid he really was. Once in the den, he didn't sit. He simply crossed his arms and faced her, his jaw like granite.

"How did you know I was in trouble?"

"I didn't. I called your boss and asked him to tell me where you were."

"I'm sure glad of that." His glare hadn't lessened with the small talk. "I didn't write that article," she said.

He scoffed and shook his head. "And now you're going to lie to my face?"

Heidi bit her lip and sighed. "I have a feeling who did, but it wasn't me."

His frown deepened to the point she wondered if he'd ever be able to smile again. "How is that even possible? It's in the paper. With your byline."

"John Robinson is how it's possible," she spat. Just saying his name made her want to gag.

"Really? You're going to blame this on him? Your editor published it!"

"Because he thought it was from me! He didn't know I didn't write it."

Nick paced in front of the mantel and raked a hand over his head.

Heidi sighed. "I'm sorry, Nick. I—"

"How?"

"How what?"

"How did he get that information? That was a conversation between you and me and I asked you to keep it quiet. I didn't share that with anyone else who could have passed it on to Robinson."

"My recorder is missing. I think when John bumped into me last night after Patriot was found, he lifted the recorder from my pocket. I haven't had a chance to confront him, but I'm going to do that right now." She headed toward the door and stopped. "But I don't have a car."

"That's okay. I'm not planning to let you face him alone. You almost decked him one time. I think this time I need to come along to keep you from killing him."

Nostrils flaring, she gave him a tight nod. "I think that might be a good idea."

# TWELVE

Nick didn't think he'd ever seen her so mad. Actually, the last person he'd seen this angry had been his grandfather when the story about his mother ran. When a person was this angry, it was hard to think straight.

That was why he was going along.

To make sure she didn't do anything that would get her court-martialed.

It didn't take long to track down Robinson. He was at his desk at the newspaper office. When he looked up and saw Heidi bearing down on him, Nick thought he saw a flash of fear in the man's eyes before he lifted his chin in defiance.

Heidi stopped at his desk. "I'd like to speak with you, if that's all right."

Admiring her calmness, Nick decided to stay back and let her handle it. At least until she decided to do him bodily harm.

John cleared his throat and rose. He grabbed his jacket and slipped into it. "Actually, I was just on my way out the door. I just got word that someone was arrested for the training center bombing—and that it's somehow related to the Red Rose Killer."

"Right. I was there."

Robinson froze. "What do you mean you were there? How were *you* there? How many times do I have to tell you that this is *my* story?"

"Then why do you have to steal my notes to get a story printed? Why are you trying so hard to discredit me?"

He flinched. "I don't have to stand here and listen to this garbage." He reached for his car keys and Heidi moved fast, swiping them from the desk. They hit the floor and skidded under the chair. "Hey!"

"You're not going anywhere until you tell Lou what you did." She crossed her arms.

"Are you nuts? You can't just come in here and act like this."

"Like what, John? Like a woman who is confronting a man who is not only a liar, but is willing to do just about anything to ruin her career?"

"I'm not—"

She stepped forward and Nick tensed. His phone rang and he shut it off, unwilling to have any distractions at the moment. He might have to intervene.

But Heidi didn't lift a hand, she simply thrust out her chin. "Yes, you are. You stole my recorder, listened to my notes and picked the one thing that would be sure to bring the hammer down on my head—and possibly my career. All you had to do was make sure those working the investigation wouldn't talk to me. How did you get into my email account?"

"Heidi, you're delusional. I don't know where you're getting all of this, but I've got to go."

"It should be easy enough to prove," Nick said.

Robinson stilled. "What are you talking about?"

"I'm talking about getting one of our IT people over here and letting them examine your computer. If you hacked into Heidi's account, it can be found. If you didn't, then no worries."

Robinson's face went bright red. "This is ridiculous! Get out of my space!"

"Have someone come over and check it out," a voice from behind Nick said.

Heidi spun. "Lou?"

Her boss shrugged and met Nick's gaze. "I don't want to think one of my reporters would do such a thing. Have someone come over and prove he didn't do it. That way, we'll shut everyone up."

"Lou." John rubbed his hand across his lips. "Really? You know I wouldn't—"

"Right. I do. But she doesn't. I'm doing this for her, too."

"Thanks, Lou," Heidi said.

"Don't thank me. You're going to feel pretty foolish when we prove you wrong."

She huffed. "I'll take that chance."

John's jaw got tighter. "Fine!" he exploded. "I did it."

Heidi blinked, her shock holding her silent for a moment. Had John actually admitted it? Nick nudged her and she snapped her mouth shut. Her shoulders slumped. "Why?" she whispered.

John groaned and dropped back into his chair. "Because I'm afraid I'm doing a lousy job on this story and just last week, I overheard Lou saying what a great reporter you were and I thought if I offered some kind of proof that you could possibly be the anonymous blogger—and were reporting false information on top of that—then Lou would get rid of you."

"So you were jealous?" She gaped, then shot a look at her boss, who looked ready to stroke out at any moment. Her gaze swung back to Robinson.

He shrugged.

Heidi turned again to Lou, who gave a disgusted grunt and shook his head. "I'm disappointed in you, Robinson."

"I know, sir. I'm disappointed in myself."

"I should fire you."

Robinson flinched. "Sir…" He lifted a hand as though to argue his case. Then he dropped it. "Whatever you decide, sir."

"Don't fire him," Heidi said.

All eyes turned to her. "What?" Lou asked.

"You don't have to fire him."

"I can't let him get away with this."

"I agree. But…can you just take appropriate disciplinary action and let that be it?"

Lou stared at her for a few seconds before shaking his head. And Nick watched her, his expression a cross between pride and disbelief—and what she thought might be a smidge of admiration mixed in.

She shrugged. "Don't ask me to explain. I can't. I just know I don't want him fired."

"I'll print a retraction, then—or something," Lou said. "Actually, Robinson will. He'll print a confession."

"No," Nick said. "We don't want the paper's reputation to suffer."

"Then how are we going to fix this?" The man looked ready to explode.

"I think," Nick said, "you could have Heidi write a piece about how her email was compromised by someone she trusted, someone who's had a grudge against her and wanted to smear her name and the readers will buy it. Not only is it true, but with everything that's been happening to her—and the fact that she's been reporting on it—the readers will also be sympathetic that she's being targeted. Of course, she will talk about grateful she is for her boss's support and the support of the paper overall."

"I like that," Lou said.

"She can also point out how the paper holds to the highest standards of professionalism."

"Because that's true, too," Lou grunted. He turned his glare on John. "Get out of here until I can calm down long enough to think straight. I'll call you later and let you know what I've decided."

"Yes, sir." He shot a look at Heidi. "I'm sorry. That was lower than low and completely unprofessional. I'm sorry and, if I get to stay, it won't happen again, I promise."

Heidi nodded. As John left, she let out a low, slow breath and ran a hand over her hair. "Wow. I did *not* expect that."

"I don't think any of us did," Lou said.

She looked at Nick. "Can someone really tell if he hacked my email?"

"Probably. Truthfully, I have no idea. Are you

ready to go or do you have something else you need to do here?"

She raised a brow at Lou and he waved a hand at her. "Go find a story." He headed for his office. "Preferably who the thief on this base is," he shot over his shoulder. "And I'm not talking about a recorder and story thief, I mean the guy stealing the medals!" His door slammed and Heidi flinched.

Then she cleared her throat. "What now?" she asked Nick.

"I think we should go back to my place and you should rest."

"Or write up my article you just assigned me."

He shot her a wry glance. "Sorry."

"No. It's brilliant. Thank you."

"Of course."

He took her hand and led her out of the building. She took a deep breath and looked around. "It's nice not to be looking over my shoulder and wondering if someone's going to try and kill me."

A low laugh escaped him. "I'm sure." Then he frowned. "But Sullivan is still on the loose. And if Gentry is to be believed, Sullivan had him blow up the center as a distraction, which means Sullivan still has plans. Evil plans, no doubt."

"So, what do we do?"

"We do what we can to find out who's stealing the medals." He looked away, then back at her. "Heidi, I—I apologize."

"To who? For what?"

"To you. For jumping down your throat about the article."

She shook her head. "You don't have to apologize for that. Your reaction was completely understandable."

"No. I knew better. Deep down, I really didn't think you'd do that, but when I couldn't find a better explanation…"

Heidi squeezed his hand. "Really, Nick. It's okay."

"Let me make it up to you."

"Hmm. Okay. How?"

"You feel like Mexican tonight?"

"That sounds good."

"So, I'll pick you up at six?"

She smiled. "How about we just meet at the front door?"

He laughed. "That works."

His phone rang, and he raised it to his ear. After a moment a dark look spread across his face. "I understand," he said into the phone. "Thanks." He hung up.

Dread curled through her. "What is it?"

"Lance Gentry just escaped custody."

"What? How?"

"He attacked one of the MPs escorting him, got his weapon and took off on foot. They chased him and lost him in the woods. They're bringing the dogs out, but if he manages to get off base, he's as good as gone."

"He lives on base. He knows how to come and go without detection."

"Yeah. Which means we're back to looking over your shoulder."

# THIRTEEN

Nick tugged at his collar and studied himself in the mirror. He couldn't believe how nervous he was. They'd decided to go ahead with dinner—and keep looking over their shoulders.

Gramps appeared in the bedroom doorway. "You look good, boy."

"Thanks."

"So why do you keep fidgeting with that collar?"

Nick dropped his hands. "Because I don't know what else to do with myself."

"She's come to mean a lot to you in a short time."

"She has. It scares me."

"Because she's a reporter?"

"Partly. I'm having second thoughts about this. I keep second-guessing myself. And her."

"It's your nature."

He huffed a short laugh. "I come by it honestly. When that story came out in the paper, I can't tell you how betrayed I felt. That feeling was not a good one and it never once occurred to me that she didn't write it."

"I can see why you're struggling, but you just have to talk through those times. But there has to be trust. If you can't trust her, you can't build a life with her."

"I know, Gramps."

"I know you do." He paused. "Your mother would like her."

A lump started to grow in the back of his throat and Nick cleared it away. He rubbed a hand over his eyes. "I think so, too. That's part of the struggle. I want to marry a girl Mom would approve of."

"I know, son. But truly, you can't go wrong with a girl who likes Mexican food."

Nick laughed, appreciating his grandfather's attempt to lighten the moment. "Maybe not."

His grandfather's expression sobered and his eyes narrowed. "She has a kind heart, Nick. Be gentle with it. But don't date her if you don't think you can work through the angst you still have about her."

Nick shook his head. "I think I'll talk to her, see what she's thinking. See if I learn anything new. I don't want to get hurt, but I don't want to hurt her, either. Maybe spending some time alone will help."

"Aw, you'll be all right. Now, let me get this for you." Gramps reached up and adjusted the collar, then patted Nick on the shoulder. "You look great, kid. She won't know what hit her."

Together, they walked out of the bedroom and into the foyer.

Heidi was pulling her coat off the rack. Nick stopped dead in his tracks when she turned and smiled. He gulped, wondering what happened to all the oxygen in the room.

His grandfather slapped him on the back. "I may have been wrong in my assessment."

"What do you mean?" he asked.

"I think it's you who doesn't know what hit him." He hugged a startled Heidi. "Go easy on him, honey. He's out of practice with this dating stuff."

"Gramps!"

The old man laughed and strode into the den to turn the television on.

Nick blinked at her. "You look amazing."

"Thanks. So do you."

"So...uh...are you ready to go?"

"Whenever you are."

He helped her on with her coat and opened the door. Her light vanilla-scented fragrance followed her outside and he breathed deeply—only to stop when he came face-to-face with

Justin Blackwood. Nick saluted, as did Heidi. "Sir?" Nick asked.

"Sorry to interrupt your evening, but we just got word that Bobby Stevens was attacked in the hospital."

Heidi gasped. "Oh, no! Is he all right?"

"He's wounded and under sedation right now, as well as heavy guard, but the doctor says he should be able to talk first thing in the morning. He's not to have visitors until then." He paused, his gaze on Heidi. "Because I want you there, I'm going to read you in on something that I need to stay out of the papers."

"Yes, sir."

"OSI Agent Steffen has been digging into Stevens's background, financial records, et cetera. At first, he couldn't find anything that set off any alarm bells."

"At first?" Heidi asked.

"As they kept digging, they expanded their search and found some interesting deposits into his mother's savings account. His name isn't on the account so it took some convincing to get a warrant for his mother's banking. Which is why it's taken this long to get back to you on Stevens."

"His mother has MS," Heidi said. "She's in a wheelchair." She cleared her throat. "I guess that has nothing to do with what you're saying. Sorry."

"It has everything to do with it. He told you about her?"

"He did."

Justin nodded. "That's exactly what I'm talking about. You saved his life and you have a rapport with him. I'm guessing he's being paid to keep his mouth shut about something and I want to know what. Between the two of you, I want you to drag every scrap of information you can out of him. He knows something and it's time we knew it, too."

"Yes, sir," Heidi said. "I'm happy to talk to him. I'm glad he's going to be okay."

"Me, too."

"Captain?" Nick asked.

"Yes?"

"Why didn't you just call?"

"I did. You didn't answer your phone."

Nick sighed and pulled it from the clip. "Sorry, sir. I'd turned it off during a meeting. It's back on ring now. If you need anything else, I'll hear it."

Justin nodded, climbed into his vehicle and left.

"Poor Bobby," Heidi said. "I have a feeling he was up to no good at the training center the night it exploded, but he doesn't deserve this."

"I'm not sure I have quite as much sympathy." Nick took her hand. "Let's grab dinner and then get a good night's sleep. Tomorrow's going to be a long one."

By eight thirty in the morning, the hospital was a beehive of activity. And so was Heidi's brain. Determined to get some answers, she led the way to Bobby's room even while her mind relived the dinner from the night before. It had been nice—and weird. Nick had seemed a bit distant, as though he wanted to be there, but wasn't sure if he should be. She chalked it up to distraction due to the news about Bobby and the fact that Gentry had escaped. But they'd kept the conversation light, touching on a variety of topics before finally landing on the case of the stolen medals.

"Why do you think the thief's doing it?" Nick had asked. "They can't be worth that much."

"Some aren't, but there are a few that are. I think this guy doesn't know who has the ones worth money so he's having to break into every home and just grab the ones he can—along with any jewelry and cash he can find—and get out."

"I suppose."

"A lot of these families are multigenerational military. Some World War II medals are going for hundreds of thousands of dollars."

"That's crazy. It's not the piece of metal that should be worth anything, but the heroism behind them."

"I agree. Unfortunately, our thief doesn't."

"And he might be able to pass one or two off as worth more than they are. There's no telling."

"Right."

Now Heidi stood in front of the door that would lead her to the man who could possibly help them figure out who the thief was. And she wasn't leaving until he told them.

The security officer at the door stood and eyed them until Nick flashed his badge. He nodded and returned to his chair, his posture alert, eyes moving over each person in the hall. Heidi was glad to see him taking his responsibilities seriously.

"Hi there, may I help you?"

Heidi and Nick turned. A nurse in her early forties stood next to a cart with an open laptop.

"We're here to see Bobby Stevens," Nick said.

"I'm sorry, he's still pretty weak. I just came out of his room. The doctor upped his pain medication and he dropped back off to sleep. You might want to give him a few hours or come back after lunch."

Heidi frowned. "We were told he'd be able to talk this morning."

"Well, that person was wrong. Sorry."

Heidi sighed and exchanged a shrug with Nick. "All right, thanks. Guess we'll come back later. If I give you my number, will you let me know when he can talk?"

"Sure." Heidi gave it to her and the nurse moved to the next room.

Nick blew out a low breath. "Great."

"I have my laptop with me," Heidi said. "I guess I could head down to the cafeteria and get some work done on a couple of articles."

"We have a team meeting at eleven that I could make. Justin excused me from it so we could be here, but if we're not going to be able to talk to Stevens until after lunch, then I guess I'll head over there."

"All right. Go get caught up and come back and fill me in."

He quirked a smile. "A lot of it will be classified, sorry."

"I understand. I'll take whatever information you can give me and try to be happy with that. I'll let you know you when the nurse calls."

"Sounds good. I'll catch up with you later."

Nick arrived at the meeting ten minutes early. He slipped into the room and took a seat near the door, hoping Heidi would be safe while working in the hospital. If her attacker was smart, he'd be long gone by now, but the fact that Sullivan still owed him money meant he might still be hanging around. And that worried him. Only the fact that the hospital had security would allow him to focus his full attention on the forthcoming discussion.

Justin entered the conference room and set his briefcase on the table. "Nick, I'm surprised to see you here. Weren't you going to speak with Bobby Stevens?"

"Yes." Nick explained and Justin nodded.

"All right, you can head back over that way after the meeting."

Gretchen and Vanessa entered and took their seats at the table. Once everyone was accounted for, Justin opened by bringing everyone up to speed on the arrest and escape of Lance Gentry. "We managed to ask him some questions before he escaped. Not that I'm happy he's still out there, but I think he's given us everything he knows about Sullivan. There's no security footage at his home, so we're just going to have to believe that Sullivan showed up there. I believe it happened the way he described it." He looked at Vanessa. "Why don't you give us an update on Yvette Crenville?"

Vanessa shook her head. "We've been watching. Tag-teaming it, so to speak. So far, there's nothing. She's gone to work, shopped for ridiculously priced health foods at the base market and spent any spare time doing yoga at the base gym. If she's an accomplice, we can't find any evidence of it."

Gretchen nodded her agreement.

"All right. I'm not ready to give up on her just yet. Keep up what you're doing and give us another report at the next meeting."

"Yes, sir." Gretchen nodded.

Vanessa also agreed.

"Let's move on to our next steps in finding Boyd Sullivan."

For the next two hours, they went over the case files, reviewing notes, interviews, and making more plans to track the man down.

Nick's phone rang just as they were wrapping things up and he motioned to Justin that he needed to take the call.

In the hall, he swiped the screen. "Hey, Heidi, everything okay?"

"That's sad."

"What?"

"The first question out of your mouth is asking if everything's okay."

He gave a low laugh. "Sorry, I guess it's become a habit at this point."

"I guess."

"What can I do for you?"

"The nurse just called me and said we should

be able to talk to him in the next few minutes. I'm going to head to his room."

"Perfect, I'm headed that way."

Heidi tossed the remains of her snack into the trash and headed for the elevator. Once on the floor, she went straight to Bobby's room and showed her ID to the officer on duty.

"You might want to wait a minute before going in," the officer said. "The doctor's in there."

"What? The nurse just called and told me to come on up."

"Oh, well, he'll probably be done in a few minutes."

"I'll just stick my head in and let him know I'm here."

With a frown, she shoved open the door. To find a man in a white lab coat standing over Bobby Stevens, holding a pillow over his face.

She screamed and launched herself at the man, slamming into him. Heidi went to the floor while he stumbled back into the IV pole, cursed and landed beside her. Then he was on his feet. Heidi tried to get up, but at the last second, saw the hard fist swing at her. She rolled and his knuckles grazed her jaw. A flash of pain shot through her face and she lost her balance, falling to the floor once more. She landed on her backside with a grunt.

The door swung open and the officer ran in. "What's going—"

The attacker slammed a fist into the officer's face. His head snapped back and he crumpled to the floor. As the officer rolled, the man jerked the door open and bolted into the hall.

"Bobby?" Heidi gasped. Once again, she surged to her feet, ignoring the throbbing in her jaw. She hurried to Bobby's side. When she got a good look at him, she flinched at the sight of his new wounds. He had a puffy right cheek and a bruised eye. She went to him and grasped his hand. "Are you all right?"

Bobby nodded, breathing hard. "Yes. I'd just dozed off when I felt the pillow over my face. But yes, I'm okay."

Hospital personnel swarmed the room. A nurse was kneeling next to the fallen officer. She looked up. "We've alerted security."

Nick stepped inside. "Heidi? What's going on?"

It didn't take long to fill him in. He touched her chin and she pulled back with a wince. "That's gotta hurt," he said.

"Yes, but, thankfully, it was just a glancing blow. I'll have a bruise, but nothing's broken."

"Did you see who it was?"

"No, not really. He was dressed like a doctor in a white coat but had on a baseball cap and sunglasses when he turned around. And before you ask, it could have been Lance Gentry, but I can't say for certain."

Once the officer was removed to receive more care and the doctor had checked out Bobby, he nodded to them. "You can have ten minutes. Then I want him resting again."

"Yes, sir," Nick said. The doctor left and Nick placed a hand on her shoulder. "Let me talk to him first, okay?"

"But the captain said…"

"I know what he said. Just go with me on this, will you? For now?"

She huffed and eyed him. He was up to something. "Fine. For now."

"Thanks." Nick opened the door and she followed him inside. Nick stepped up to the man's bed. "Bobby, who did this to you?"

"I—I don't know. It's all a little foggy."

"Maybe the attack is foggy, but I doubt the name of your attacker is," Nick said. "Who was it? Was it Lance Gentry?"

He flinched and then his expression shut down.

"Come on," Heidi said. "Without naming who it was, what happened with the previous attack?

We know what happened this time." She rubbed a hand across her still-throbbing jaw.

"The previous attack?"

"Yes. When you got the bruises to your eye and cheek."

"I was asleep," Bobby said, his eyes locking on Heidi's. "When I woke up, I couldn't breathe. Someone was holding a pillow over my face—just like this time. I started flailing, trying to grab something, anything, to make him let go. My hand landed on my mug of ice and I managed to crack him in the head with it. He let go long enough for me to push the pillow off. Then he punched me. A nurse heard the commotion and ran in. The other guy bolted out and down the hall. This time was like an instant replay."

"Let me guess," Nick said. "He was wearing a hoodie."

"No, but a hat and sunglasses," Bobby muttered.

Leaning against the sink area, Nick hooked his thumbs into his pockets. "Why are you protecting someone who tried to kill you?" he asked.

Bobby huffed and crossed his arms. He looked away while his teeth worked his lower lip.

"Because he's scared," Heidi said softly. She stepped forward and took the young man's hand. He was probably just a few years younger than she, but she felt a lot older. Almost maternal in the way she wanted to not only help him, but smack him upside his head and demand he cooperate.

She controlled the second compulsion and squeezed his fingers. "Come on, Bobby. You're not helping yourself here. You're a victim of the bomber. Someone tried to kill you. Twice. Why won't you tell us what we need to know? What was Lance Gentry doing there?"

His fingers trembled in her grasp and a tear slid down his cheek. He quickly swiped it away and Heidi pretended she hadn't noticed. "It's… I…if I tell, he'll kill me."

"Looks like that's his goal anyway," Nick said. "Let me just share something with you. We know Lance Gentry set off the explosion in the training center. He's been trying to kill Heidi because he knows she can identify him. Guess what? He knows you can identify him, too. We had him in custody, but he escaped. So, if he's the one after you, he's still around to come back and finish the job. And it looks like he's pretty determined. What are you going to do when you get out of here? Run?"

"If I have to. Look, Lance Gentry isn't trying to kill me. He never knew that I saw him at the training center."

"Then why protect him?"

"It doesn't matter," Bobby said. "Don't you understand? I can't tell you anything."

Nick's nostrils flared. "Are you really that stupid?"

He all but shouted the question and Bobby sank into the pillows even while his eyes flashed a defiance that hadn't been there a few moments earlier.

Heidi rose. "Excuse us, Bobby, I need to have a word with First Lieutenant Donovan." She raised a brow at Nick. "Outside, please?"

"Heidi—"

She gripped his forearm and all but shoved him from the room. Once the door shut behind them, Nick frowned down at her. "What are you doing?"

"Trying to get the name of his attacker, but if you keep shouting at him, he's just going to close up tighter and tighter."

"I'm not shouting."

"You are. And you act like you've never questioned someone before. Can't you read his body language?"

He smiled. "Yes, ma'am."

"Ah." She gave him an assessing look. "I thought you were up to something. You planned this, didn't you?"

"And you played the good cop perfectly." He paced three steps down the hall, then back. "But

I'm getting impatient. Go see if your more gentle approach works better. We know that Lance Gentry is the guy who attacked him. He knows we know. I want to know why he's protecting him."

"He seemed sincere when he said Lance never saw him."

"He's lying."

Heidi shook her head. "I don't think so. He has this tell when he lies. He rolls his eyes away from you, then looks down."

"Okay. Then if it wasn't Lance trying to kill him all this time, who is it?"

"I don't know."

"Then use those investigative skills and go find out."

She grinned. "Stay tuned."

"I'm going to have hospital security come cover the door while I grab some coffee. You want one?"

"I'd love one," she said.

He stopped at the nurses' station to arrange the security and she reentered the room. Bobby had shut his eyes, but opened them when she sat next to him. "Look, Bobby, I know this isn't easy. I get it. I do. You say Lance Gentry isn't the one who attacked you, that he never knew you were there. Then where is all this coming from? You might as well tell us because we're not going to stop asking. What are you hiding? You were there at the training center before the explosion."

"Of course I was. I was taking care of the dogs."

"That's what you said before. But there weren't any dogs in that part of the building, Bobby. Your story makes no sense."

He looked down and pleated the blanket with his fingers, then smoothed it out over his thighs.

Heidi sighed. "They found the money in your mother's bank account."

He froze. "What money?"

"Really?" She stared at him and his face crumbled. "What did someone pay you for? To keep quiet about the bombing?"

"No." His swift denial—and the fact that he met her gaze when he said it—had her believing him. Almost.

"Then what?" He sighed and rubbed his eyes. She pushed a little harder. "It's all going to come out in the long run," she said. "You might as well tell us what you know and catch a break legally."

"Do I need a lawyer?"

"Depends on what you were taking the money for."

Bobby hesitated only a moment before he

said, "You were right. I was taking it to keep my mouth shut."

"About what?"

"About who was stealing the medals."

Finally. "I kind of thought so."

"I know who's stealing the medals, and he paid me to keep quiet."

"Then how does Lance Gentry fit into this and why would you protect him?"

"Because I saw him at the training center, and he saw me. He has a certain reputation and if he knew I blabbed about him, he'd come after me."

Heidi wanted to do a facepalm right there. "If you had told the MPs who he was, they could have caught him and you wouldn't have had to worry about him."

He laughed. "Right. Like he wouldn't have been released on bail or something." He shook his head. "I couldn't take the chance. But if you caught him and he escaped, then he's probably a long way away by now."

She was done with the Lance Gentry subject. "Who's the guy stealing the medals?"

"Roger Cooper. He's a senior airman. He's stealing the medals and hiding them in the kennel. The empty areas. I walked in early for my shift one afternoon because I needed an extra cage and we store some in that unused portion of the training center. He was there. When he saw me, he pulled a gun and said he'd pay me to keep my mouth shut. I agreed because I needed the money. Sometimes, he'd pass the medals off to me and I'd hide them for him when I went in to work."

"Where?"

"Different areas of the training center. Always away from the dogs, though, because you never know when someone's going to be around."

Heidi nodded. "Anything else you want to add?"

"No."

"So it was definitely Cooper who tried to kill you?"

"It was him. I saw him."

"Then you're going to press charges."

Fear flashed. "I don't know—"

"If you don't, he'll go free. And then he really will kill you. You do understand that, right?"

The man wilted against the pillow and gave a short nod followed by a wince. He lifted a hand to his head. "I understand. I just want all this to go away."

"Good. I'm sure OSI Special Agent Steffen will be by to take your statement." And conduct an arrest, but she kept that to herself. "You need to tell him everything you told me, okay? It needs to be officially on record."

"I get it. I will."

"Good." She stood and walked to the door. "I'm sorry it's ending this way for you, Bobby. I don't think you're a bad guy. I think you just got caught up in something a lot bigger than you. But you have the opportunity to turn this around and do the right thing. I suggest you take it."

A deep sigh filtered from him. "I know. I will. I actually feel better already now that it's off my chest."

When Nick returned with her coffee, she patted Bobby on the arm and they said their goodbyes. Two officers now stood guard outside the airman's room. She filled Nick in on the conversation with Bobby and he shook his head. "You're amazing."

"No, I just connected with Bobby when I saved his life. And he's really not a bad guy. I hope he can get his life straightened out at this point."

"His air force career is finished."

"I know. And so does he. He's just afraid. He's been afraid for a long time, but I think he feels better now that he's manned up and told the truth." She drew in a deep breath. "How's the officer who was hurt?" she asked. "Did you hear?"

"I checked on him. He has a fractured jaw, but he'll be all right."

"Wow, he really took a hard hit."

"He did."

She cleared her throat. "Okay, so what's next?"

"We look for this Roger Cooper character and see what we can shake loose from him."

"No, *I* look for Roger Cooper," Heidi said. "This is my story, Nick. Roger doesn't have anything to do with Boyd Sullivan."

His eyes narrowed. "Why don't we fill Justin in on what we know and see what he says? Although, if you think about it, my orders are to protect you. So if you're going looking for Cooper, that means I am, too."

# FOURTEEN

Nick returned to the car after searching for Cooper and slammed the door. "Another negative." Annie nudged the back of his head from her spot behind him and he reached back to scratch her ears.

"Great." Heidi sighed and rubbed her eyes. "And nothing from Justin?"

"Nope. They've got the MPs out in force looking for him and Gentry, but so far they don't have any solid leads as to where either could be."

"I get that Lance Gentry might be hard to find since he knows if he shows his face on base, he'll be caught, but how is it that no one has seen Roger Cooper lately? It's like he's dropped off the face of the planet."

They'd been tracking down Roger Cooper's known associates, asking information. Nick figured the easiest way to keep Heidi safe was to go along with the hunt. He had hopes that Justin and the Security Forces would find the man first, but it looked like none of them were going to find him.

Now they had only a couple of hours of daylight left. Nick really wanted them to locate the man before the sun went down, but he wasn't holding his breath.

"What did Captain Blackwood find after looking into Cooper's background? Has he said when he'd have something?" she asked.

"Shortly."

"Okay, what now, then?"

"Let's grab something to eat. A drive-through." The longer he could keep her in the car, the easier it was to keep her out of danger. Between Gentry and Cooper, things could get deadly fast. He shuddered at the thought.

His phone buzzed. "Hold on. Justin just texted. He said Senior Airman Cooper has a spotless record. Which is why no one's thought twice about him being out with the flu the last four days."

"Does he live on base?"

Nick texted the question to Justin. "No. And the officers sent to his home said he wasn't there."

"Then he's hiding somewhere," Heidi said. "Close by if he's the one attacking Bobby at the hospital."

Nick nodded. "I'd be inclined to agree with that statement."

"Any local relatives?"

"No." He scrolled the text. "According to Justin, he has a sister in El Paso and a brother who's married with three kids, living in New Mexico."

"So he's not with them."

"Nope. Local authorities have already checked just as a way to cover their bases. He's here—somewhere. Justin's put a BOLO out on him." He stood. "I want to head to the kennels."

"Why? Aren't they already searching them?"

He shook his head. "I asked Justin if we could do it. With officers tied up searching for Gentry and Cooper, until I know for sure that Stevens is being straight with us, I'm not causing a scene or going on a wild-goose chase."

"Yeah. I see what you mean."

"So, let's go see what we can find."

With Annie in the back, Nick drove to the training center and parked close to the door.

He climbed out of the SUV and put on his backpack, then got Annie from her area and put her protective gear on. She sat and let him do what he needed to do with no protest. She knew she was going to work and her body quivered with excitement. Once they were ready, he scratched her ears, then looked at Heidi. "Stay behind us, okay? I don't know how safe this place is."

"Okay."

With Heidi behind him and Annie beside him, he pushed aside the yellow crime scene tape and led the way to the warped steel door. "I think the opening is big enough to get through. I don't know if you know the layout, but the door is higher than the ground floor. Once you're inside, you have to walk down three steps, okay?"

"I've been in there before. I know what you're talking about."

"Good. Let me go in first, then Annie, then I'll help you in if you need it."

Placing one foot carefully on the door, Nick had to climb over it and stop. The steps down had been destroyed and lay in crumbles two feet below. He hopped down. "Annie, come. Jump."

The dog scampered over the door and into his arms. He gave a grunt when she landed. "I think you've gained a few pounds, girl." She swiped a tongue across his face.

As always, her absolute trust in him never ceased to send a pang through his heart. Nick set the sixty-pound animal on the dirty, sooty floor and wiped the slobber from his cheek. He then turned back to warn Heidi. "Watch it, the steps are gone."

"Got it."

With his hands holding her waist, he helped her through the opening. She placed her hand on his shoulders and he lowered her to the floor beside Annie.

"Thanks," she said.

"No problem." Even in the dim light of the broken building, she took his breath away. He didn't remove his hands from her waist immediately.

And she didn't step away from him.

"Heidi…"

"Yes?"

"I…uh…" What was he going to say? That he must be going crazy because he was crazy about *her*?

"Nick?"

"Yes, sorry." He dropped his hands and stepped back. He took his flashlight from his belt and clicked it on. The small windows lining the top edge of the wall just beneath the ceiling let in the waning natural light, but they needed the flashlight to illuminate the damage.

"Wow," she whispered as she looked around. "This is awful."

"No kidding."

"Why blow up this part of the kennel?" she asked. "I'm assuming Sullivan chose the location to bomb. Odd, I wouldn't think he'd care if he set off a bomb that killed people. It's almost like he picked an area that would cause damage, but wouldn't kill anyone. Human or animal."

"I don't think he cared whether he killed anyone or not. He probably picked this area because it's easy to get in and out of without being noticed and he could get the distraction he wanted."

"True."

They walked through the lobby and into the hall that would lead them to the large kennel area. "Where would you hide a bunch of medals if you were going to do so?" Nick asked.

"Someplace inconspicuous. Where no one would think to look—or accidentally stumble upon."

"That sounds about right. So, where is a nice inconspicuous place in a training center? The kennel?" He flashed the beam over the walls and then along the floor, looking for a path. There were large pieces of concrete and rubble that made the going slow down the hallway, but they kept at it until they reached the kennels. The outer door stood open. "It's not that bad back here. The bomb must have been set to go off near the entrance. It took the brunt of the blast. This is just soot from the smoke, and lots of standing water."

"Did they say what the bomb was made from?"

"C-4," he told her. "Annie found RDX, which is a common ingredient in the explosive."

"Where do you think he got it?"

"No telling. It's used with construction projects or demolition." He shrugged. "Could be from anywhere. And it's fairly stable. Like you have to set it off with a detonator."

"But you can attach a timer to that detonator, right?"

"Sure."

"Or use a remote to set it off?"

"Yes."

A noise behind them stopped him. "Did you hear that?" he asked her.

"I did. You think someone else is in here, too?"

"Shouldn't be," he said. "Unless one of the other investigators decided to come check it out, too."

"Or Roger Cooper's been hiding out here the whole time."

He nodded. "That was my next thought. Then again, it could just be the building shifting. It might not be safe. Hang back while I check it out, will you?"

"Not a chance."

"Heidi—"

"Nope."

He sighed. "Then at least stay behind me."

"I can do that."

\* \* \*

Heidi did as he'd asked, but noted that Annie resisted the change in direction, pulling on her lead, wanting to go ahead.

"What is it, girl?" Nick muttered. "Go on. Show me what's got your attention."

A good handler always paid attention to his dog and Heidi realized that Nick wasn't just good, he was incredible, always completely in tune with Annie when they were working. The animal darted ahead to the end of the leash, sniffed around a pile of crates and then sat. Nick froze.

"What is it?" Heidi asked.

"Head for the entrance where we came in."

"Nick—"

"Just go! Now! Get out of here!"

One of the crates flew off and a figure rose from beneath it. "Don't move," he said.

Heidi stepped back and her heel caught against a piece of broken concrete. She fell back, landing hard on the debris, her phone skittering behind her. Her back protested the sudden stop and her palms scraped the floor, stinging. Gasping, she stared up at the man who held a weapon in one hand and something else in the other. A cardboard box sat beside his feet.

"Roger Cooper, I presume?" she asked, blindly reaching for her phone. She couldn't find it.

Nick stepped in front of her, hands raised in the surrender position. "Put it down, Cooper. It's all over for you."

"It's not over yet. At least not for me. But looks like you two showed up at the wrong time."

"Or the exact right time," Heidi said, ignoring the fear thrumming through her. Her fingers searched blindly for the phone, but she couldn't land on it. "We've been looking for you."

"I know. Everyone's looking for me."

"So you decided to hide out here?" Nick asked.

"Not exactly hiding."

"You're getting the medals so you can run, aren't you?" Heidi asked.

"Smart girl." His eyes flicked to Nick and Annie, then back to Heidi. "Only now, I've got to come up with a plan to get rid of you two."

"What are you doing with the bombs?"

"Insurance. Looks like that's going to pay off."

"So you're going to blow us up?" Heidi asked, hating the quiver in her voice.

"Not if you cooperate."

Nick shifted more fully in front of her. "What do you want us to do?"

"Walk. That way." Roger Cooper pointed with the hand he had clamped around the firing button, thumb hovering, ready to press it. Nick shuddered, his mind spinning for a way to get it away from the man. Tackling him might cause him to press the button.

Heidi moved, her foot catching on the rubble, and she stumbled against Nick. He caught her and pushed her behind him. Her hands landed on the small of his back, just under the Kevlar vest.

Her touch stirred his protective instincts in a way he didn't think he'd be able to explain if he had to. But one thing was for sure. Cooper was going to have to go through him to get to Heidi.

Nick eyed the man. "Is that the button that'll set that explosive off back there?"

"Yes, so don't try anything funny."

"Wouldn't think of it. What is it? C-4?"

"Like you don't know."

"So, what's the plan now?"

"I'm going to blow the place up. Some of those medals are worth a fortune, but it's obvious things are heating up and the investigation is getting too close. It's time for me to make my exit." He waved the firing button device. "Thanks to the guy who blew this place up the first time, I can now blow it again and everyone will think the original bomber did it."

"No, they won't," Heidi said.

Cooper frowned. "Why not?"

"Because the other bomber used a timer, not a firing button."

"It doesn't matter. It'll confuse the issue for a while and I'll be long gone."

Heidi's fingers trembled against his back and Nick couldn't help wondering where his backup was. He'd give anything to use his radio. Thankfully, Cooper hadn't told him to lose it yet.

"All right. New plan." Cooper licked his lips and his eyes darted over the training center. They hardened when they landed back on Nick. "Go to the kennels."

"What?"

"To the cages! Now!"

Annie gave a low growl and took a step forward. The man lowered the weapon to the dog and Nick placed a hand on her head. Annie calmed, but her fur still bristled. Nick took a step back and grasped Heidi's upper arm. "Go on," he said.

Heidi moved toward the kennels, making her way through the rubble once more. Nick stayed behind her, between her and the gunman. Would Cooper really do as he threatened? Maybe. He didn't seem to have any hesitation when it came to trying to kill Stevens. He didn't think the man wanted to die, but the uncertainty kept Nick from jumping him.

Once in the room with the kennel cages lining the walls, Cooper motioned to Nick. "Throw me your radio."

When Nick hesitated, he lifted the weapon and aimed it at Heidi. Nick tossed him the radio. Cooper gave it a hard kick and it skittered across the floor and out of the room. "Now your phone."

Nick complied.

Roger waved his hand with the firing button. "Get in."

The doors hung open, the locks swinging from the hooks.

"What's the plan once you lock us in the cage?" Nick asked, stopping just short of entering the chain-link kennel.

"I get out of here."

"And blow us up," Heidi whispered.

The sound of sirens caught Nick's attention. And it caught Roger Cooper's as well. He paused and flicked a glance over his shoulder. That was the distraction Nick needed. He struck, launching himself at the man's hand and knocking the firing button to the floor.

# FIFTEEN

Heidi bolted for the device while Nick and Cooper wrestled for control of his weapon, but Cooper's foot caught the small box and swept it from her reach.

The men rolled into her path and Heidi jumped back to avoid being hit. Only she moved a fraction too late. A boot landed on her calf and knocked her feet out from under her. She went down hard for the second time.

"Give it up, Cooper," Nick ordered.

The man didn't stop his desperate quest to escape. Over her shoulder she could see his hand reach for the firing button and then he screamed. Heidi flinched and rolled to her side to see Annie's jaws clamped down on the man's leg. He thrashed and kicked with his other leg, but Annie held fast—and Cooper didn't give up his attempts to gain control of the device.

Heidi scrambled toward it just as his hand landed on it and Nick's fist smashed into Cooper's face. He screamed again, but managed to clamp his fingers around the device.

And his thumb came down on the red button.

The explosion rocked the area. Nick rolled, covering Heidi with his body while the ceiling tiles fell. When the building settled, smoke and dust filled the room. Coughing, gagging, Heidi tried to drag in a breath. She shoved at the heavy weight pinning her to the floor. "Nick. Move," she gasped.

He groaned and rolled. Pain engulfed her left arm and blood flowed from the wound. She clamped a hand over it, wondering how bad it was. "Nick, are you okay?"

He'd taken the brunt of the falling tiles. His vest had protected him some, but one had caught the back of his head and a river of blood trickled from his scalp. He coughed. "Yeah." He winced and lifted a hand to the back of his head. When he saw the blood on his fingers, he grimaced, then wiped his hand on his pants. "What about you?"

"I think so. Other than you crushing my lungs, I think I'm mostly unhurt." She looked around for Cooper. "He's gone."

"Annie!" Nick hauled himself to his feet and stumbled to the animal, who lay on her side. She whined and Nick settled down beside her, running his hands over her. "I think she's all right. Stunned, like us, a few cuts and scrapes, but okay." Annie proved him right by lurching to her feet. She shook herself and Nick gave her one more check before he turned to Heidi. "I'm going after him."

"I think he went toward the exit."

"He'd have to." He helped her to her feet and his expression changed when he saw her arm and her hand covered in blood. "You said you weren't hurt."

"I said *mostly* unhurt." She looked at the wound. "Looks like I can use a stitch or two, but I'm not worried about that right now. Let's go. We have a thief to catch."

Without questioning her further, he looped Annie's leash over his wrist and held his weapon in that hand. "Let's try this again. Stay behind me, all right?"

"I'm here."

She stayed with him as he led the way toward the exit. The bomb had been more in the back this time, not the front, so there was no added rubble to trap them.

Until another explosion rocked the training center.

Once again, Nick pulled her to the ground while the ceiling fell down around them, along with part of the flooring above.

"Nick! What's going on?"

"Unbelievable," he muttered into the side of her neck. "He set that one off to trap us. To give him time to get out."

"But I heard the sirens. Law enforcement's here. He can't get away." She pushed herself to her feet, coughing, wheezing. "It's hard to breathe in here."

"I know. Pull your shirt up over your mouth and nose. It might help filter some of the dust." She did so while he pulled a bandanna from his pocket. "Here, use this."

"No, you use it. My shirt's working fine."

He wrapped the piece of cloth around the lower part of his face, then checked on Annie. She was panting and probably could use some fresh air and water just like he and Heidi. He rummaged through his pack and pulled out two bottles of water. And Annie's bowl. He handed a bottle to Heidi, who drank half of it. When Annie had her fill of the second bottle, Nick finished it off and tossed it aside. Then he reached into his pack and pulled out a mask that he fit over Annie's muzzle. It would filter some of the dust for her. "All right, let's figure out how to get out—or at least let someone know we're in here." He scrambled over the added debris and made his way to the huge pile blocking their exit.

"I don't have my phone," Heidi said. "I lost it when I fell. Do you think we could find your radio?"

He hated the fear in her voice. "I don't know. I think it was probably buried in the first blast. My phone, too."

"What are we going to do?" she whispered.

Nick gripped her fingers. "We're going to stay calm and get out of this, okay?"

She gave him a slow nod. "All right. Tell me what I need to do."

"Let's take care of your arm, and then we'll have to assess the situation." Using supplies from his first aid kit he carried in the pack, he bandaged her arm. "That should hold you for now."

"It's fine. Thank you."

Together, they approached the pile of debris and Nick ran his hands over the mixture of tile and cement. He grabbed a piece and pulled. It slid loose and he tossed it aside. "I think we can try to dig our way out."

"They know we're in here, right?"

"They know. They'll be looking for us."

"They might think we're dead."

"Possibly. But they'll bring in search-and-rescue dogs and they'll alert we're here."

She grabbed a rock and shifted it. Debris tumbled, kicking up more dust. Choking, she shoved the rock aside and lifted her shirt to breathe through it. "Is that true or are you just saying that to make me feel better?"

"It's true." Nick stopped what he was doing and tore her shirt to make a mask. He tied it around her nose and mouth and went back to working.

Then she stopped. "Wait a minute. We can get out through the kennel. We can crawl out the little doggie door and into the dog run."

Nick shook his head. "It's a good idea, but won't work. They keep those doggie doors locked as a security measure and only open them when there are dogs in the cages."

Her shoulders slumped. "Oh." Then she shrugged. "Okay, then. Back to digging."

For the next several minutes, they moved more of the debris, working quickly. Nick's head pounded a fierce rhythm, but the fact that they seemed to be making a little progress helped him push through the pain. Until nausea sent him to his knees.

Heidi dropped beside him. "Nick?"

"I'm okay. I just have to rest a second."

She pulled the water bottle from her pocket and held it out to him. "Drink."

"I'm fine."

"Quit being stubborn and drink it."

He did and then handed it back to her with

a grunt. "I only agreed because I have another bottle in my pack. That one's yours, okay?"

"We'll split it if we have to," she said.

"We'll see." He paused. "I owe you an apology."

"What? No, you don't."

"Actually I do. I want to apologize for getting you into this. I should have left you outside the building while I investigated."

She huffed a short laugh. "You really think you could have talked me into that?"

"I should have tried, anyway."

"Rest easy, Nick. You would have failed."

He laughed. "You're very stubborn."

"I know. How are you feeling?"

"Better, thanks." He rose and spotted a steel rod about five feet long. "Let's see if this does anything."

Nick started to insert the rod in between two rocks, then stopped to grab Heidi's arm. "You hear that?"

"No. What?"

The distinct sound of barking.

Annie's ears perked up and she rose from her spot on the floor. She gave a low woof through the mask and stepped over the debris. Nick worked the rod like a crowbar and managed to send more tile and concrete falling from the pile to the floor. Then he pressed it into the small opening and sent the same rolling down on the other side. A whoosh of stale air hit him in the face and relief flowed through him. "Hey! Back here!" he yelled.

The barking intensified and Annie answered with three short barks of her own.

"At least she'll lead them this way," Heidi said.

Nick continued to roll the remnants of the ceiling from the pile. Workers started in on the other side and soon, there was a hole large enough for Heidi to crawl through. He helped her scramble through it and then picked up Annie. "Got a dog coming through. Someone needs to catch her. She's got on her boots so she can walk."

"Hand her through," a voice called. He thought it might be Isaac Goddard. Ignoring his throbbing, swimming head, Nick passed Annie through the opening, then crawled up to shove his head and arms through.

Hands grasped his wrists and pulled.

And he was finally on the other side. Isaac greeted him with a slap on the back. Justin and Westley were checking Annie out. A paramedic was trying to get Heidi to go with him. Only she shook her head. "Not until Nick's free."

"I'm here, Heidi."

She spun and ran over to throw herself in his arms. He grasped her tight. "We made it," she whispered.

"I know." He glanced at Justin, whose brows rose at the sight of Heidi in Nick's arms. Nick ignored the look and instead asked, "Did you happen to catch the guy responsible for this? Roger Cooper."

"He's outside," Justin replied. "Wrapped up nice and tight, with his rights read to him and everything."

"How did you know it was him?"

"He tried to run with a big ole box of medals. We figure he's the one who's been breaking into houses and stealing them along with whatever cash and jewelry he could find."

"You figure right."

"He set off the explosions, too," Heidi said.

"And we found more on him," Justin explained. "C-4 and firing buttons. The bomb squad is here and is going to search the building for more."

"Do you need Annie and me?" Nick asked.

"No." Justin clapped him on the shoulder. "You and Heidi are going to the hospital to get checked out, Annie's going to the vet, and then you've got a couple of days off to recuperate. Annie might the best bomb dog on base, but she's not the only one."

"I don't need a hospital, sir," Heidi said.

"Doesn't matter, you're getting one."

"Yes, sir."

Nick knew he'd get the same answer if he protested the hospital so he simply kept his mouth shut.

"Anyone find Lance Gentry yet?"

"Not yet," Justin said. "But we got a lead he stole a car. We've got a BOLO out on it. I'll let you know as soon as he's in custody."

"Thanks. You'll have to leave a message. My phone and radio are buried in there somewhere."

"I'll have a phone delivered to the hospital. Until Gentry's caught, you don't need to be without one. Now, we need statements."

It didn't take long to finish up their statements. Annie headed for the base veterinarian and Nick and Heidi were transported to the hospital. A young airman met them there. "I was told to deliver this to you." He handed Nick a phone.

"Thanks."

"You're welcome."

He left and Nick watched Heidi as they rolled her into the adjoining examination room, suppressing the urge to race after her.

"All right, sir, let's get you transferred to the bed and take a look at that head."

His attention only slightly diverted by the

nurse, Nick decided to do his best to cooperate and hurry this whole unnecessary checkup along so he could rejoin Heidi and—what?

What would he say when he saw her? While the nurse shaved a small patch at the back of his head for the two stitches deemed necessary, Nick silently planned the words he'd say to Heidi—if he could gather his nerve. When his phone rang, he grabbed it, grateful for the interruption. Ignoring the glare from the nurse, he answered it.

When the doctor removed the bandage Nick had applied at the kennels, Heidi got her first look at the wound on her arm and grimaced. It wasn't pretty. But once it was cleaned and re-bandaged, she was ready to go. "I have a couple of articles to write," she told the nurse. "I need to get going."

"You'll be out of here soon enough," she said and left the room.

Heidi leaned back with a groan and closed her eyes. She was exhausted, but couldn't shut her mind off. All she could think about was Nick—and ceilings caving in.

Being trapped with him had been scary enough. If he hadn't been there with her—

She shuddered.

The door opened. "That was fast," she said,

not bothering to open her eyes since she assumed it was the nurse.

Tender fingers on her cheek brought her eyes open. Nick stood there, gazing at her with a look on his face that made her pulse pick up speed. "Nick?"

"I don't know how it happened," he said.

She swallowed. "What?"

"You got under my skin."

"Oh. I think you mentioned that once upon a time."

"In a good way."

"I like you, too, Nick."

He laughed and leaned over to kiss her. His lips on hers sent her pulse into overdrive. Warmth infused her and she realized she could get used to this on a daily basis. He pulled away with a pained groan and lifted a hand to his head.

She sat up. "Nick? You okay?"

"Yeah, I just can't kiss you bending over like that. Makes my head pound."

"Hmm. Makes my *heart* pound."

"Ha. Mine, too." He sighed and hugged her to him. "What am I going to do with you?"

"Oh, I don't know. Maybe take me out on a date?"

His laughter rumbled beneath her ear. "I think that can be arranged."

"Just not a shopping date. No shopping."

More laughter. "I like shopping with you."

"Hmm. Well, it wasn't too bad, I suppose. The fudge part was great."

"Wow. Thanks."

"Okay, how about this?" she said. "No bullets or bombs allowed on the date. Just fudge."

"Definitely. That's one rule I think we can follow now that Lance Gentry, Roger Cooper and Bobby Stevens are all under lock and key."

"They found Lance?"

"Justin called while I was getting looked at. They caught Gentry at the airport trying to board a plane. Someone recognized the car he'd stolen and called it in."

"Well, that was stupid of him."

"It was only a matter of time before he messed up."

She sighed. "Good. I'm glad he's no longer a threat to anyone. I still feel kind of sorry for Bobby, though. I think he just got mixed up with the wrong people and couldn't find a way out without disappointing his mother."

"I think you may be right, but unfortunately, there are consequences for our choices."

"True."

The door opened and the doctor entered. "Oh, hey, Nick."

"Porter Davenport, good to see you." The two men shook hands. "How's my girl here?"

*My girl?*

"Your girl?" the doctor asked. "I see a lot has happened in the two weeks since we last had lunch," he said as he turned toward Heidi.

She bit her lip, intrigued by Nick's sudden and interesting shade of red even as happiness suffused her. "Um, Heidi, this is Porter Davenport. He and I have been friends for a while now."

"Nice to meet you," she said. She liked being referred to as Nick's girl. A lot. And it looked like he wasn't going to be shy about letting others know he'd staked his claim. Wow. That was a lot to think about. And she would. Later. In the privacy of her room, where she could ponder what the future might hold.

Right now, she was ready to get out of here. She had articles to write. She could think about her feelings toward Nick later. Like whether or not she loved him. The thought made her mouth go dry and her throat constrict. Oh, boy. Love? Maybe.

"Let's find out."

She gasped. "Find out? Find out what?"

The doctor stepped over. "Find out how you are."

"Oh. Right. Thank you."

He checked her eyes, her breathing and her

pulse one more time. When he straightened, he nodded. "Pulse is a little fast."

No doubt. Heidi's flush deepened and she met Nick's wicked gaze. "Well, it's been an interesting few hours," she murmured.

"I heard what happened at the training center," Porter said. "Another blast. Unbelievable."

"No kidding," Heidi said. "And technically, it was two more blasts, but who's counting at this point? Fortunately, everything took place in that area that's deserted. It'll have to be completely razed and rebuilt, but at least no one was hurt this time."

He smiled. "Well, it looks like you two were incredibly fortunate. A few bumps and bruises, but no lasting damage. I'd say you definitely had someone watching over you."

"God just wasn't ready to take us yet, I guess," Heidi said.

Porter raised a brow and nodded. "I guess not." He turned and shook hands with Nick again. "And I, for one, am very glad of that fact." He backed toward the door. "Nice to meet you, Heidi. Take care of that arm and get some rest."

"I will. Thank you."

He left, and the nurse returned with her discharge papers—and Nick's. By the time they walked out of the hospital, the sun was creeping up over the horizon.

Nick wrapped an arm around her shoulders. "Are you hungry?"

"Starved."

"Feel like going on that date now?"

She laughed. "What? Now? No way. I'm a mess. I need a shower and a nap."

"All right, how does pizza sound?"

"For breakfast?" She shrugged. "As long as it's delivered."

"Of course."

"Then that sounds amazing."

He pulled out his new phone and placed the order at the twenty-four-hour pizza place while they walked.

The cool morning air was refreshing and Heidi breathed in. "I'll never take being able to breathe clean air for granted again," she said when he hung up.

"I know what you mean."

It didn't take long to reach his home. "Is your grandfather here?"

"No, playing golf." He glanced at his watch. "His tee time is in fifteen minutes, I think. He texted me a little while ago."

"You didn't tell him what was going on?"

"No, just that we were working. I'm sure he heard about the explosions at the training center.

Again. But he's used to my hours and doesn't get stressed about it when I'm gone."

"That's nice. And he's really gotten into the whole golf thing, hasn't he?"

He smiled. "It's good for him. The first few months after my grandmother died, he didn't really know what to do with himself, but he's adjusting—and learning to enjoy life again."

Once inside Nick's home, they both took the time to clean up and change before meeting back in the kitchen. Nick started to pull plates and glasses from the cupboard when the door-bell rang. "That was fast."

"Not fast enough." She darted for the door and Nick laughed. "Why don't you get that?"

She returned with the pizza box in one hand, a slice missing a bite in the other. Chewing, she set the box on the table. "Mmm…so good."

Nick laughed. And laughed again.

# SIXTEEN

*One week later*

Heidi walked into Lou's office and took a seat in the chair opposite her boss. "What's up?"

Lou pursed his lips and set aside his reading glasses. "It's been a long few months with this serial killer on the loose."

"I know. The whole base is still on pins and needles." They both knew this, so where was this going?

"I've come to a decision, and Robinson isn't going to like it."

She frowned. "Okay." Since when did Lou run his decisions by her?

"You've really proven yourself over the last few weeks. Your personality pieces are really popular, you caught the person stealing medals from the homes, helped catch the person who bombed the training center and almost died for your efforts."

So, he'd noticed. "Well, I didn't catch the person all by myself. I had a little help there."

"Whatever. I think it's time you were rewarded for your efforts," he said.

"Rewarded?"

"Yep. I'm making you senior reporter. I may be gruff, but I'm honest and I want this paper to reflect integrity. If our readers don't trust us, they're not going to read us."

"True." She managed to get the word out, but "senior reporter" kept echoing in her mind.

"And Robinson messed up in a big way. Thankfully, because of your and Donovan's willingness not to bring to light Robinson's deception, the people are none the wiser. But I can't risk it happening again. I trust you, Heidi. Unfortunately, I don't trust Robinson. He's going to have to work his way back to that."

"Sir—" Heidi's mouth opened, then closed. What did she say? Stunned, she couldn't find any words.

"So, do you want the job or not?"

"Or course, but John's not going to be happy about this. Working with him may be…uncomfortable." To put it mildly.

"Robinson will do what I tell him or he'll be looking for another job. He should be on his face with gratitude that I didn't fire him."

"I agree with that."

"Good. Now get out of here and go find me that serial killer."

Nerves tingling, excitement growing by the second, Heidi stood and rubbed her palms down her uniform pants. "Yes, sir."

She paused and Lou looked up. "What is it?" he barked.

"Thank you, sir. I really appreciate this opportunity."

"I know you do. Now scram."

Heidi did so, her heart light. And the first person she wanted to tell was Nick. She texted him. Can you talk?

Sure. His immediate response made her smile.

A second later, her phone rang. "I got promoted," she blurted on answering, and told him everything.

"No way. Heidi, that's amazing!"

"I know!"

"Let's celebrate."

"Okay, when and where?"

Once they had it set up, Heidi checked her schedule. "I've got to run. I'm meeting Vanessa Gomez at the hospital. She's agreed to let me interview her."

"I'll be honest, I'm nervous about you being so close to this serial killer case. It was one thing when you were just on the base where Sullivan might be also, but you're not one of his targets. Being actively involved in reporting on Sullivan might change that. I have to admit, it scares me. A lot."

"I'm careful, Nick. You know me."

"Yeah, I do."

She laughed. "Don't sound so morose." Turning serious, she said, "I promise, Nick, I'll be careful. No stupid moves on my part that put me in danger. Trust me, I've got too much to live for."

She hung up and headed for the hospital. It didn't take her long to find the cafeteria where Vanessa had agreed to meet. Heidi saw the woman sitting in the back, in a corner where she could watch the comings and goings of everyone in the place.

Heidi slid into the seat opposite her. "Hi."

"Hi."

"Thanks for agreeing to talk to me."

"Sure. I'm so sick of Boyd Sullivan and everything he's getting away with. If talking to you will help catch him faster, then I'm all for it."

"Okay, then just start at the beginning. I'll record your story, if that's all right."

"It's fine." Once Heidi had everything set up, she nodded. Vanessa drew in a deep breath. "Back in April, I received a rose in my mailbox. Along with a note saying, *I'm coming for you.* I was shocked. I simply had no idea why Boyd would target me. I only saw him a couple of times on base, and one of those times, I actually helped him out. He was kind. I was nice and professional and did him a favor."

"What kind of favor?"

Vanessa ran a hand over her hair. "Boyd got into a fight with someone. He was pretty beat up and came to me because he needed some stitches. He didn't want to go through official channels because he knew he'd be reprimanded." She shrugged. "At first, I was going to say no, but I was drawn to him. I felt sorry for him."

"You had a romantic thing going on?"

Vanessa recoiled. "What? No! Don't print that!"

Heidi held up a hand. "No, I won't, I promise. It's just that's what it kind of sounded like."

"Well, that's not it. When I say I was drawn to him, I just meant that Boyd reminded me so much of my brother, Aiden, that I simply couldn't refuse. I mean, if Aiden ever found himself in a similar situation, I would hope there would be someone there for him, you know?"

Interesting. "I understand. So, what was it about him that reminded you of your brother?"

"I'm not really sure I can put my finger on it. Maybe an intense restlessness or a boiling anger with no outlet or release."

"That would make sense. The anger part at least."

Vanessa frowned. "I guess. But one can be very angry without becoming a serial killer."

"Yeah. Too bad Boyd Sullivan didn't get that memo."

"Indeed. Now—"

An announcement over the PA system stopped her. She listened, then stood. "I'm sorry, I have to go. That's an emergency. If you have more questions, feel free to call me later and we can try to get together again when I'm not working."

With that, she was gone. "I do have more questions." But they could wait.

A hint of familiar cologne tingled her nose seconds before the kiss on the side of her neck made her smile. And forget all about stories and serial killers and busy nurses.

"Hey, you," Nick said. "Can I sweep you off your feet and take you to lunch?"

She turned to kiss him, a slow, leisurely melding of their lips that she wanted to go on forever. Except they had an audience. She pulled back, but couldn't resist one last quick peck. "You've already swept me off my feet, but you can certainly do it again."

"Come on out by the fountain. Annie and I have something we need to ask you."

"You can't ask me here?"

"Nope."

"All right, then."

He led her out a side door to the beautiful fountain surrounded by a three-foot brick wall. The fountain was set in the middle of a small grassy area that had a peaceful parklike feel to it. Annie settled into a shady spot and put her head between her paws. But she never took her eyes off Nick.

Heidi spotted a bouquet of flowers sitting on the wall and gasped. "Nick? Pink carnations?"

"Yes." He picked them up and pressed them into her arms.

She sniffed them and smiled. "Thank you. This is so sweet."

"That's not all."

"What else is there?"

"That thing I wanted to ask you."

"Ah…right. Okay."

"Heidi, you make me laugh. I can't believe how much you make me laugh." He cleared his throat. "I like that about you, Heidi."

"Well, thank you. I like a lot about you, too. In fact…" She paused. Did she dare say it? She drew in a deep breath. "I may even love some things about you."

He kissed her. Then drew back. "Stop doing that."

She blinked. "What?"

"Distracting me or I'll never get this said."

"Oh. Sorry."

He cleared his throat again. "Annie keeps looking at me."

"What does that have to do with anything?"

"A lot." He dropped to his knees in front of her and her heart stopped. Then pounded hard enough to echo in her ears.

"Nick?" she whispered.

"I have a confession to make—I'm an idiot."

"It happens to the best of us sometimes." She paused while he laughed. "I'm teasing," she said. "What are you talking about? You're not an idiot."

"I've been trying to think of the words for days now, but I can't find the exact right ones."

"For what?"

"You deserve better. A better place to be proposed to, a better, more romantic guy with the right words, a slow, drawn-out proposal with all the bells and whistles, but the truth is, Heidi, I'm impatient—one of my many flaws you'll learn about, I'm afraid—and I need to say this before I explode. I'm in love with you and I want to marry you. Am I crazy in hoping you feel the same way?"

Tears had started dripping down her cheeks by the time he reached the words, "I'm in love with you and I want to marry you." She sniffed. "You're not crazy," she whispered. "Not about this, anyway. This is a beautiful place. And I don't need bells and whistles, I just need you."

"Oh, good." His shoulders lost their military rigidness for a brief moment. "That's a relief." He dug into his pocket and pulled out a ring.

Heidi let out a gasp. "Nick?"

"It was my mother's," he said. "And her mother's before that. I'd be honored if you'd wear it. But if you don't like it or it's not your style, we'll go find something else."

She swallowed and took the ring from him. "It's gorgeous." The white gold setting held a teardrop diamond that was dainty and feminine. She loved it. Because of the history behind it but mostly because of the man who gave it to her. "I'd be proud and honored to wear it."

"Really?"

"Yes, Nick, really."

He kissed her, long and hard. Then set her away from him, but let his fingers trail down her cheek before he dropped his hand. "Want to go eat lunch and celebrate?"

She couldn't stop the grin. "I do."

"Just the words I can't wait to hear again in a church setting."

They rushed out to Nick's vehicle and Heidi

climbed in and Nick let Annie into her area.
Heidi glanced at her in the rearview mirror.

And thought the dog was smiling.

\* \* \* \* \*

*The hunt for the Red Rose Killer continues.
Look for the next exciting stories in the*
MILITARY K-9 UNIT *series.*

Dear Reader,

Thank you so much for coming along on Nick and Heidi's exciting adventure. Both characters had a lot to learn in this story and I think they were wise enough to take advantage of the opportunities to grow. Heidi had to curb her impatience when it came to working with a coworker who drove her crazy. In addition to that, she had to decide to be ethical and do her best on a story she wasn't super interested in doing. I was proud of her for doing that. ☺ I do hope you'll be sure to get the other books in the series. Don't forget, there are EIGHT books in this series, so make sure you have them all. Thank you again for reading. Be sure to check out my facebook page and join in the fun there. www.facebook.com/lynetteeason and my website, www.lynetteeason.com.

God Bless,
*Lynette Eason*

# Get 4 FREE REWARDS!

## We'll send you 2 FREE Books plus 2 FREE Mystery Gifts.

**Love Inspired®** books feature contemporary inspirational romances with Christian characters facing the challenges of life and love.

Counting on the Cowboy
Shannon Taylor Vannatter

Reunited by a Secret Child
Leigh Bale

**FREE** Value Over **$20**

---

# Get 4 FREE REWARDS!

## We'll send you 2 FREE Books plus 2 FREE Mystery Gifts.

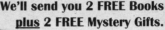

**Harlequin® Heartwarming™ Larger-Print** books feature traditional values of home, family, community and most of all—love.

FREE
Value Over
$20

# HOME on the RANCH

---

**YES!** Please send me the **Home on the Ranch Collection** in Larger Print. This collection begins with 3 FREE books and 2 FREE gifts in the first shipment. Along with my 3 free books, I'll also get the next 4 books from the Home on the Ranch Collection, in LARGER PRINT, which I may either return and owe nothing, or keep for the low price of $5.24 U.S./ $5.89 CDN each plus $2.99 for shipping and handling per shipment*. If I decide to continue, about once a month for 8 months I will get 6 or 7 more books, but will only need to pay for 4. That means 2 or 3 books in every shipment will be FREE! If I decide to keep the entire collection, I'll have paid for only 32 books because 19 books are FREE! I understand that accepting the 3 free books and gifts places me under no obligation to buy anything. I can always return a shipment and cancel at any time. My free books and gifts are mine to keep no matter what I decide.

268 HCN 3760 468 HCN 3760

| | | |
|---|---|---|
| Name | (PLEASE PRINT) | |
| Address | | Apt. # |
| City | State/Prov. | Zip/Postal Code |

Signature (if under 18, a parent or guardian must sign)

## Mail to the **Reader Service:**

**IN U.S.A.:** P.O. Box 1341, Buffalo, New York 14240-8531
**IN CANADA:** P.O. Box 603, Fort Erie, Ontario L2A 5X3

\* Terms and prices subject to change without notice. Prices do not include applicable taxes. Sales tax applicable in NY. Canadian residents will be charged applicable taxes. This offer is limited to one order per household. All orders subject to approval. Credit or debit balances in a customer's account(s) may be offset by any other outstanding balance owed by or to the customer. Please allow 3 to 4 weeks for delivery. Offer available while quantities last. Offer not available to Quebec residents.

**Your Privacy**—The Reader Service is committed to protecting your privacy. Our Privacy Policy is available online at www.ReaderService.com or upon request from the Reader Service.

We make a portion of our mailing list available to reputable third parties that offer products we believe may interest you. If you prefer that we not exchange your name with third parties, or if you wish to clarify or modify your communication preferences, please visit us at www.ReaderService.com/consumerschoice or write to us at Reader Service Preference Service, P.O. Box 9062, Buffalo, NY. 14240-9062. Include your complete name and address.

HRCBPA18R